SOUL SEX

The Alchemy of Gender & Sexuality

Thanks for shopping with us.
Kindest Regards, Customer Care

RETURNING GOODS

Please re-pack, in the original packaging if possible, and send back to us at the address below. **Caution!** Don't cover up the barcode (on original packaging) as it helps us to process your return.

We will email you when we have processed your return.

---✂--

PLEASE complete and include this section with your goods.

Your Name: ______________________________

Your Order Number ____________________________

Reason for return ______________________________

Select: Refund my order ☐ Replace my order ☐

(Please note, if we are unable to replace the item it will be refunded.)

Return to:

---✂--

RETURNS
Unit 22, Horcott Industrial Estate
Horcott Road
FAIRFORD
GL7 4BX

SOUL SEX

The Alchemy of Gender & Sexuality

A Guidebook for Fluidity in the 21st Century

Written and Illustrated by
Drake Bear Stephen

Wisdom Weaver Press
Clayton, CA

SOUL SEX

The Alchemy of Gender & Sexuality

A Guidebook for Fluidity in the 21st Century

Written by:	Drake Bear Stephen
Illustrated by:	Drake Bear Stephen
Cover Design by:	Drake Bear Stephen

Published by:	Wisdom Weaver Press PO Box 888 Clayton, CA 94517
ISBN #:	978-0-9862498-1-5

Library of Congress PCN#: 2015904369
Library of Congress Title: Soul sex

Printed and bound in the United States of America.
First printing, April 2015.

DEDICATED TO:

My family, friends, colleagues, teachers, doctors, therapists, and spirit guides who have supported me on my life journey no matter how many bends in the road I traveled through.

All the Two Spirits, living and passed on. May your way of life be resurrected in modern society.

All the individuals with non–traditional gender and sexual identities who have blazed the paths towards acceptance and human rights.

The generations of our descendants who will live in a world of fluid identity in peace and compassion.

TABLE OF CONTENTS

PROLOGUE:
SWITCHEROO
The True Story of a Boy Name Sue

GENDER BLENDERS

Gender Blenders put all the characteristics of masculinity and femininity together to create a unique blend of gender identity. Gender Blending is the blurring or blending of gender roles. Inside the blender is a combination of astrological symbols that represent Male (Mars), Female (Venus), Neuter (Mercury), and Asexual.

PRE–TRANSITION: 1952–1983

AS THE SOUL TURNS

Just one hour after midnight on May 3, 1952, I arrived on Earth in my new skin of a female body, having freshly forgotten everything that preceded my birth. Well, perhaps there was a dim recollection of looking down at my body while lying in my mother's womb, slightly shocked and sad, thinking "Oh crap, this is going to be quite something..." Because I knew then what a journey this life was going to be.

The 1950s was a time when people had specific roles and knew exactly where they were headed. It was the time of the Black and White Way. There weren't any Ifs, Ands, Buts, or Gray Areas allowed. This generation was thankful to own a piece of property or have butter on their bread instead of margarine as in the depression and war days. And of course, since they knew how bad it was, they wanted the best for their children, as long as their children also lived in the Black and White Way.

I grew up in a middle class, Midwestern, Caucasian neighborhood being the oldest of four children with two parents, an aerospace engineer who traveled a lot and a stay–at–home mom. Around the age of two, I began to suspect that things were not exactly right with me, as evidenced by my temper tantrums. By the time I was six, I knew I was not fitting in well with the Black and White Way. Not only did I not fit in but I felt like I was invisible.

Three years after I was born, my first brother arrived. Five years after his birth, twin brothers were born. I had desperately wanted a sister, perhaps to take the heat off me. In retrospect, I can see how lucky I really was because I had access to their toys. Every year at present–giving time, I wished for toy guns, toy cars, and bikes but sadly just received dolls. My mother arranged all my dolls on shelves and was happy they sat there unmolested by me. Instead I was out playing "war" and sports with my brothers and the neighborhood kids. I felt not only invisible but also unheard. I began to shrink further within myself. My favorite moments were spent inside books, living on the pages of some other land and some other life.

Puberty was when it became noticeable that I had derailed from the tracks of "normal" development. My mom was always telling me I was like a bull in a china shop. Later I figured out that is code for "you are too butch for that body". The little duck had grown into the ugly duckling.

I became the little engine that could. I tried to masquerade as a young woman. I tried to be attractive to boys. I tried and tried to live the life others told me to. Other people can sense things that one doesn't consciously recognize. And so I became a social wall flower.

My high school years coincided with the social movements of the late 1960s. I was deeply in tune with the human rights movements and the hippies' concept of freedom and free love. This was a major crack in the Black and White Way. The young people of the time were demonstrating that there were many Shades of Gray. Even so, I felt that I was on the Black side, as in the dark, of the Black and White Way because I did not know what a lesbian was until I was 17. And I did not know what a transsexual was until my mid–20s. This ignorance prolonged and intensified my confusion in trying to identify who I was.

DEVIATIONS FROM THE SCRIPT

After my high school graduation, the family relocated from Ohio to Southern California. By being uprooted from my high school friends, I was spun into a deeper place of isolation. In my twenties I became the Wild Child who was hell bent on self–destructive behavior. In retrospect it seems like I was trying to passively kill myself without taking direct responsibility of the process. I quit college, spent time in the Women's Army Corp, was investigated by the Air Force in a lesbian purge operation, wrecked motorcycles, experimented with guns, worked on a factory assembly line, got a tattoo, smoked, drank, partied at bars nightly, hung out with radical lesbian feminists at UCLA, and was arrested for assisting a friend of mine, who was dealing marijuana.

I jumped in and out of affairs with many different women. I experimented in romantic affairs with gay men, lesbian women, and a trans* woman. However, I felt I was not really clicking with any of them. The death of each affair pushed me a little closer to the edge of a steep cliff. I ended the decade by becoming a "cutter", one who uses razor blades on their own flesh. The physical pain of cutting the exterior reduces the focus on the much greater emotional pain on the interior. The sight of blood was a confirmation that I was still real even though I was invisible.

BEYOND THE BLUES

I have always been a slow bloomer. Many say that they know at a very young age that they are gay or transgender. I didn't have my first "same sex" attraction until I was a senior in high school. And I did not realize that I was trans* until my mid–twenties. One major reason is that I had no frame of reference about transsexuality. I had never heard of it and did not know it was a possibility. But one day I met a female–to–male trans* individual and then I knew I had found my identity. When it finally dawned on me I began to think obsessively about having a male body.

Even though my body was still fairly feminine, my energy was always very masculine. Being neither Black nor White drew lots of stares. Walking into mall stores, restaurants, and restrooms became a land mine of shame. Heads would turn to nakedly stare at me. I just wanted to be a turtle and withdraw into my hard shell. Even though I knew gender transition was an option, I was procrastinating because I was incredibly afraid that I would lose my friends, my family, and my job if I admitted who I really was.

In spite of my gender disorientation, I began to settle in during my early thirties. I had a long–term relationship with an Orthodox Jewish woman, went back to finish my Bachelor's degree, and was promoted into management at work.

IN TRANSITION: 1984-1986

SAME SOUL, SHAPESHIFTING BODY

By the time I was 33, I became so miserable, uncomfortable, and desperate I decided to try just one shot of testosterone to see what it would feel like. I had come to realize that it was transition or die. From the moment of my first injection, I never looked back. I mentally prepared myself for doing the rest of the transition process. Because I was kicked out of my house for being a lesbian, I was fully prepared to become an orphan and never talk to my family again. I was also ready to give up my job if I was fired. And I knew there was a great chance I would lose my girlfriend.

> **Observation Point**
>
> A common comment I get is "you are so courageous". My reply is that there is no courage involved — there is only the survival instinct — knowing that I would die if I did not become who I really was and knowing I had to find the strength within to live the life I wanted.

As it turned out, all these fears were just that, my fears. My family did find out about my transition, and were fine with it, even though I knew my parents would mourn the loss of their only daughter. Perhaps they thought it might "look more normal" for me to be a male or perhaps they had just mellowed by then. Whatever the reason, they did stand by me.

I was one lucky duck. I did not lose my job. In fact the district manager told me "we did not hire you because you are male or female. We hired you do to a specific job." Thanks to my co–workers I did not have any overly uncomfortable experiences on the job. In fact, after my transition, I busted through the glass ceiling, becoming much more successful in my rating, ranking, and salary treatment. Was it because I was no longer a female in a job traditionally held by males? Or was it because I felt so much better about myself that I was treated better? I'll never know the answer to that but I suspect it was probably a bit of both.

I did lose my girlfriend but I was the one that initiated the breakup. I was in my second puberty, a time of crazy emotional swings fueled by spiking sexual libido, and so I left her for other sexual adventures. Puberty is one of the toughest times in an individual's life. As if going through puberty is not difficult enough, adult transsexuals who transition get to experience it twice, once in each gender. I felt that my body took a wrong turn at my first puberty, but was put back on track during my second puberty.

The process of transition moved me from self–destruction to self–construction. In fact, I began a social gathering of a half–dozen FTM friends in transition. We got together to do "male" things as well as share our transition experiences. We called our group "Under Construction". Like many others, I faded away from the group as my transition finished however I believe that group may still be going on in Southern California.

Observation Point

I am fortunate that I had only a few awkward experiences but no really "bad" experiences during my transition. This is not always the case. Many trans* people are suffering the effects of prejudice, discrimination, and violence even today. I contribute the ease of my journey mostly to the fact that I was becoming congruent. My body was changing to match my identity.

The order and description of my transition consisted of:

Psychotherapy

I spent several years in therapy before beginning the physical journey of transitioning. At the time of my transition, psychotherapy was a requirement in order to get letters from therapists approving hormone and surgical treatment. Doctors would not treat you unless you had these letters. While today this practice has become optional, it is still required by many medical practitioners.

Hormone Therapy

Sex hormones are the magic gender changer. Testosterone is a power potion of liquid libido that I continue to take otherwise I would undergo the same hot sweats of menopausal women. I have injected testosterone for thirty–one years now and figure at the rate of one shot every two weeks, I have taken close to 800 injections. Hormones created a lot of physical changes to my body including: menstrual period cessation, deeper voice, increased sweating, clitoral enlargement, acne, coarser skin texture, redistribution of body weight, growth of muscle tissue, reduction of body fat, facial and body hair growth, increased sexual libido, and in my case, male pattern balding (although that took a number of years). The mark of manhood for me was not getting a penis but being able to grow a beard. It is the most prominent sign that says "I am a male".

Presentation

Shortly after beginning hormone therapy, I began wearing men's clothes full time, bound my breasts, cut my hair, and notified family, friends, and my company. I started working out and eating better. I quit smoking after my final surgery. The further I progressed with my body changes, the more my self–esteem and self–confidence increased.

I felt a bit like a multiple personality during transition. One moment I was publicly addressed as male, the next female. The biggest dilemma became whether to use the male or female restroom. It's a wonder more transsexuals are not hospitalized for burst bladders.

I never really thought much about how to act or present when I transitioned. There are a few details to learn, like male bathroom etiquette, but basically I just continued acting in the way I did before transition.

Mastectomy

Surgery is one small step for a lifetime, one huge step towards freedom. If your body happens to be a false foundation, such as in the case of a pre–transition transsexual, you are essentially walking around in a very fragile glass house. After surviving a lifetime stigma of masculine energy in a female body, the surgeon's scalpel seemed benign.

My mastectomy was performed by a Beverly Hills plastic surgeon in his private office. This surgery may have been the single, most powerful event in my life. I at last was becoming congruent, my perception of my body and my actual body were coming close to matching.

Hysterectomy and Oophorectomy

A year after my mastectomy, I had my hysterectomy and oophorectomy. My hysterectomy was performed in a hospital by a woman gynecologist. Another trans* buddy of mine was my roommate in the hospital because we had the same surgery on the same day. Our healing process was rapid and within four days we were walking around the mall.

Legal Changes

The last step of my transition was getting a court–approved name change and changing all my legal papers. At the time in California, it was a requirement to have undergone genital surgery before a gender change was legal. Unfortunately, my birth state of Ohio is one of five states that does not permit a gender change on the birth certificate. They do issue amendments so that I could apply for a passport in my new identity. But technically, I shall always remain a female due to Ohio law. I am not sure how this would affect my ability to marry in states that do not yet have legal marriage for gays or if it will affect the gender on my death certificate.

When all of my transition phases were complete I could successfully compete on "What's My Sex?" Will the real transsexual stand up? Today, no one would guess my original body just by looking at me. In fact, many times I have told someone that I am transsexual and they assumed I meant I wanted to transition from male to female.

Observation Point

Anatomy of a Name

The simplest question people can answer — and the one that is most difficult for a transsexual is — "What is your name?" A cis individual ("cis" means a non-transgender individual) usually answers that question easily because they have accepted their name as an identifier since birth. A trans* individual is never comfortable with their birth assigned name. The correct etiquette is to ask any individual their preferred name and pronoun. And then address them as they requested.

My female name was Susan. Instead of Black Eyed Susan, I was Black Sheep Susan. When I transitioned I picked Stephen to replace Susan. Stephen is the main character in the classic lesbian book, *The Well of Loneliness*[1] by Radcliffe Hall. I always believed that the main character, Stephen, may have been more trans* than lesbian, so I took this name to honor her.

Drake is my family name and I have always felt more connected to it than any other name. I eventually swapped the position of my names and adopted Bear as my middle name as a way to honor my power animal. Bear represents introspection, protection, healing, solitude, and inner knowledge. I see Bear as bigender, both as a masculine ferocious protector and as a feminine nurturing healer. Just like Bear, I need to hibernate in my cave on a regular basis to reflect, refresh, and rejuvenate.

I always hated the song "A Boy Named Sue"[2] by Johnny Cash when growing up because I felt like "A Boo Boo Named Sue". I thought this song was a personal persecution of my tomboy nature. Others did use it to taunt me. Today I perceive the Boy Named Sue as neither fully male or fully female but a combination of both. And I certainly don't feel like a "boo boo" any longer. Looking back now with humor at it all, I see that when I transitioned I actually committed "sue-icide".

> "One of the most amazing and exciting moments in the path of a transgender person's life is choosing, proclaiming, and christening a new name. This is an opportunity for many to name one's true self, one's core being, the person God created them to be... there is nothing quite like the experience of naming the person one has always been."
>
> *–Melanie Martinez & Angel Collie, MCC*

Even though the surgeries and shots were painful, my wallet hurt the worst, because none of the medical treatments were covered by insurance. Because I was charging my surgeries to my credit card and paying off the debts I had incurred from my college education, I was not keeping up with the Joneses well. I was buying a new body instead of a house, a trip to Europe, or a fancy car.

> **Observation Point**
>
> I transitioned at age 33. It sounds like I was fairly young. However, it will not be until my 66th birthday that I will have lived exactly half of my life in a female body and half in a male body.

POST–TRANSITION: 1987–PRESENT

SOUL SANCTUARIES

After my transition I receded into a reclusive life. I gave up my friends and relationships. I lived a life of a suburban hermit, going to work during the week, and heading to the mountains behind Los Angeles on the weekends or spending hours riding my bicycle. I felt perfectly content to live out my life like this. I did very well in my work even though I really didn't like my corporate job.

Then in my fiftieth year, a curious shift occurred, seemingly without a trigger. It was like I stepped through a spiritual portal.

I began exploring spiritual and metaphysical subjects, reading and studying. I stumbled on the concept of shamanism. I began to take classes in different healing modalities, eventually becoming certified in shamanic healing, energy medicine, hypnotherapy, and past life regression. Eventually I retired from my corporate job to focus on my personal business full time.

Through my spiritual work, I built a new network of friends and colleagues. I am simply not the same person I was before transition. I now am able to be visible, enjoy speaking on the radio, and in front of groups. I love teaching and sharing what my life experience has been and the gifts it has brought.

MEDICINE WALKER AND SPIRIT TALKER

A rose is a rose is a rose. But if a rose could talk and said it was not, would it still be a rose? What if it said it was a daffodil instead? I have learned in this lifetime that a rose can be exactly what it believes itself to be.

I have learned that I am a "tweener" and an odd duck. I am a person of many dichotomies; a self–disciplined person of habit that likes to control my environment, yet conformity, slavery, mediocrity, redundancy, and repetition bore me. I have always felt half and half about everything in my life. Half of me will see one point of view and the other half will see the opposite point of view. I even sleep half the night on my right side and the other half on my left side. I don't feel like I was born in the wrong body. I feel like I was born with fluid identities and that my soul chose this life as a trans* person for a specific purpose.

I guess I am living the *Reader's Digest* abridged version of fluid identity. I am a Four Spirit having lived as a straight female–bodied individual; as a lesbian female–bodied individual; as a straight male–bodied individual; and as a gay male–bodied individual in one lifetime. Perhaps my soul is homeless because it has wandered through so many different cultures, creeds, genders, sexualities, and spiritualties in so many lifetimes. I still feel like a kid in an identity shop, searching for the Holy Gale, that Wind of Life, on whose wings I can ride to peace.

In my current lifetime I have been a Scottish re–enactment soldier, an Army lineman, a Christian, a Jew, and a Pagan. I have changed all of the fundamental values given to an individual at birth: my name, gender, sexual orientation, and spiritual beliefs. I am a community of none, but a walker between the worlds. I am a community of one that can bridge multiple worlds.

In a female body I was the first to enter the Armed Forces lineman school and one of the first line foremen in the phone company. Yet I am quite often the only male body in healing, art, and intuition classes. In social settings, I am more comfortable conversing with females than hanging out with the males.

I cannot be visually distinguished from cis men but will never lose the consciousness I developed as a female. I still look nervously over my shoulder while walking alone in a dark parking lot. I avoid walking too close to a female who is walking alone so as not to scare her.

I am more comfortable cross–dressing as female in a male body than living as female in a female body. That is how strong gender identity is.

So why do I think I chose a trans* life this time? Here are some ideas:

1. I sense I have lived a lot more lives as male than female and now it's time to learn balance.
2. I had a past life as a submissive female. This life is about transcending that experience by learning independence and self–empowerment. My astrology chart shows life themes of independence vs. submission and empowerment vs. humbleness.
3. In my recent past life as a gay man in the German World War II death camps, I learned it was not safe to be a man in a sexual relationship with neither a man nor a woman that can be sexually abused by men. This has created ambivalence that is being resolved in this life.

4. Learning to be androgynous is part of a lesson being taught by my spiritual guides and a preparation of living full time in the spirit world, where souls have no gender.

One of the gifts of being a trans* individual is that I learned to question everything I was told. If I was told that I was a female and knew I wasn't then everything else I was told had to be tested as well. This has helped me broaden my perspectives and be self–referencing, sourcing directly from my Higher Self.

I have so much gratitude for the gifts I have received in this lifetime. I have no regrets and would not change any of it for anything. What I have done in this life has been done out of necessity for my survival and soul growth.

The Black and White Way is a binary system that only provides two choices. Isn't it time to retire that model and create an inclusive Shades of Gray Way? In order to live in the Shades of Gray way, individuals will need to own their unique identity. And to maintain a Shades of Gray society, all individuals will need to be compassionate. Being compassionate doesn't mean you need to walk a mile in my moccasins. It simply means walk a mile next to me. With respect.

Observation Point

There are four major forces that shape your physical body: genes, hormones, time, and what you think of yourself.

STANDING AT THE CROSSROADS OF GENDER DRIVE AND SEXUALITY STREET

This section is about the interconnectedness of my gender and sexual identities. I've done a lot of thinking about it over my lifetime especially during the writing of this book. In fact, writing this book has brought me an even deeper understanding of not only myself but of how multi–dimensional identity is.

My energy has always been very masculine in this lifetime, no matter what my body chemistry or physical attributes. However, my identity has been very fluid, evolving from one form to another. When I first identified as transsexual, I only considered two options (male and female). Now many years later I realize there are a lot of variations between the two extremes of male and female.

I can best describe myself if I break it down to separate energetic layers. The Physical Body is now transgender, socially presenting as male, but with female genitalia. My Energy Body feels very masculine. The consciousness of my mental and emotional bodies are very fluid, possessing both masculine and feminine energy.

During the writing of this book I changed how I label my own identity. I realized I did not completely transverse the gender spectrum completely from female to male but stopped at some point in the middle. I used to identify as FTM (female–to–male) but now I realize that language is not 100 percent accurate. Perhaps I am F2TG (female–to–transgender), or FT3G (female–to–third gender), or FTA (female–to–androgyne), or simply FTH (female–to–human). But then the "F" isn't truly accurate either, as I never started out as 100 percent female, did I? Perhaps the term "transdrogynous" might fit me?

Adding the sexual orientation dimension to the mix complicates things even more. Before my transition, I was mostly attracted to individuals that I thought were the opposite of me. After my transition, I find I am mostly attracted to individuals I most want to be like. I am more attracted to the extremes of gender such as manly men and feminine women than I am to individuals in the middle of the gender spectrum. Perhaps it is because they are too much like me.

I consider my own sexual identity to be quite complex and unique (and not representative of any group of individuals). My change in sexuality during my transition has always been a great mystery to me. When I started my transition, my expectation was that I would end up heterosexual because I was in a relationship with a woman at the time. However, the further along in my transition I was, the more attracted to men I became. Why did I love big–breasted women before my mastectomy but afterwards, I was no longer attracted to breasts at all? Why did the transition change my sexual desire for men? Here a few reasons I can think of:

1. After my transition, I was attracted to men that I most wanted to be like. So being with them sexually was a vicarious way to experience being them. After all, men have my desired genitalia that are in perfect working order.
2. Perhaps sexual orientation for some, like myself, is based on one's own body image and thus changes when the body image changes. For others, whose sexual orientation is based on another's body image, gender of sexual attraction would not change with body changes.
3. Post transition, I feel more comfortable living as a male so I am less threatened by other males. Being male–bodied allows me to not feel threatened by other men. Max Wolf Valerio, in his book *The Testosterone Files*, says that:

   "Many FTM transsexuals, who later identify as gay, may actually have been bisexual to begin with, but were unable to express their attraction to men until after their body had masculinized."[3]
4. Perhaps I am experiencing a thinner spiritual veil so that I can learn to embody Spirit, which has no gender or sexual identifications.

Because of my fluidity, I might say that I was a consecutive bisexual. In the latter part of my adult life, I have become a concurrent bisexual. Or perhaps, it might be more accurate to say I am an androphile, one who is sexually attracted to males, and a gynoromantic, one who is romantically attracted to females. Sometimes I wonder if I had been born as a cis male, would my sexual identity be different? Would I still be versatile? Would I be pansexual? I will never really know for sure because that is not the lesson of this lifetime.

Observation Point

Chameleosexual Pride Flag

I have always had the ability to shapeshift my sexual desires based on who my target of affection is at the time. The simplest way to explain this is to imagine that you are watching a movie with a man and a woman being romantically intimate. When the target of my love is a female, I identify with the man in the movie. But when my target of love is a male, I identify with the woman in the movie. In other words, when I am with a man, I want him to love me as he would a woman, not as another male partner. When I am with a female, I want her to love me as a man, not as another female partner.

I have yet to find another person on the planet that has expressed this phenomenon. It used to puzzle me until I wrote this book. It was then that I realized I should create a new sexual identity and its own pride flag to illustrate how I feel. So, I created the term "chameleosexual". I chose the term because a chameleon changes its characteristics to blend in with the environment. A chameleosexual, then, is an individual whose sexual self-perspective changes based on the gender of their sexual partner.

Immediately after my transition I went into a long period of celibacy that was concurrent with my years as a hermit. For more than ten years I dated no one. (I now look back on this time as a huge gift because this was the time that the AIDS epidemic began.)

LGBT*. Been there, done that (all of that). I have had sexual relationships with both males and females in both a female body and a male body. I have experienced the Groundhog Day of the

Closet, having come out four times; first as lesbian, then as transsexual, then as gay, and lastly as bisexual.

It might seem that this attempt at classification is compartmentalizing my identity. However, classification is necessary in order to express how we feel. I relate differently to others, depending on their identity. So even though I have been in my current gender role for many years, I will always feel like I am a conundrum, an enigma, a paradox.

Observation Point

There is a concept called "*tawantin*" in the Inka tradition, which means the "unity of four". The Q'ero, who are the direct descendants of the Inka, believe that every individual not only descends from a pair of humans but from a pair of nature beings, which are the male and female nature spirits from the geographic location of the individual's birth. Therefore each human carries four sources of spirit: DNA inheritance from the both the physical mother and father, and energetic inheritance from the both the nature mother (*paqarina*) and the nature father (*itu apu*).

I have been single precisely 88 percent of my adult life. For one, it is not easy trying to meet partners when one is a transgender individual. All potential mates I meet assume my body is biologically male. What do I do when I meet new people in a social situation such as a party? Wear a sign or name tag, perhaps saying "PIP" (pussy in pants)? I now know why the gay culture adopted the Hankie Code. It allowed an individual to make their identity and desires readily visible. In this way, time and misconceptions can be short–circuited. I used to worry about finding a soul mate.

I have been in love relationships with women during this lifetime but have not yet met a man willing to do so. Most gay men want a man who has male genitalia so I am automatically eliminated as a prospective partner. Straight, bisexual, or bicurious men see me as sexual entertainment. They have their emotional relationships with cis women.

Who does complement me if my male and female aspects are balanced? I have the best of all worlds. I can maintain the house, fulfilling the traditional female role, and I can maintain the yard and car, fulfilling the traditional male role.

My worries about being alone are mostly all gone now. I have come to a place of peace in the realization that I chose to spend most of this life alone in order to learn more about myself and my inner world. It certainly has been fascinating!

I have learned to appreciate what body parts I have and how to use them sexually. As much work as I have done about accepting my body, learning how to use it sexually, and seeing the gift of my life lived in so many points on the spectrum, I have always and still continue to grieve my missing cis male body. I may carry that grief to my grave. But who knows what body awaits me in my next life.

> "I'm living *la vida medea* – life in the middle. I have not crossed the bridge from 'female' on one side, over an immeasurable chasm, to become 'male' on the other side. Rather, I have *become* the bridge."
>
> –*Reid Vanderburgh*

To read more about my pre–transition and transition experiences, my poems are in the appendix of this book. They were all written many years ago but I keep them as a record of my transition times.

Observation Point

Unlike many cultural and racial minorities, my status in the trans* minority is not outwardly visible, which gives me the choice of disclosing my identity or keeping it private. I categorize people by whether they know my truth or don't. If they don't, I have to remember what not to say when relating anecdotes from the past. So, it's easier for me if I am fully "out". Every trans* individual has their own personal policy about disclosure but here is mine:

- I don't disclose immediately to random strangers I have just met (unless I am in the speaking or teaching role).
- I do disclose as soon as I know an ongoing relationship of any kind is forming.
- I would rather be known for my true self than be perceived as someone I am not.
- I would rather be hated for who I am than be loved for who I am not.
- I believe it is important to share my truth so that others can be exposed to an individual with non-conforming gender and sexual identity.

Recently I pulled out my old senior high school yearbook of 1970. I chuckled when I read my life goal, which was to be the first woman on Mars or find peace and happiness on Earth. I guess there is not much chance of fulfilling the first part but I know that I have accomplished the second part.

I have shared my real life story as an example of gender and sexual fluidity. You might think that my story would make a good script for a reality TV program. However, you would learn in subsequent episodes, that there an infinite variety of real life stories that others have experienced. All individuals together make up a common tapestry with each of their lives representing a unique and colorful thread. That is how the Black and White Way succumbs to the Way of the Rainbow, an array of beautiful, vibrant, living–out–loud colors.

In the following chapters we will examine all the independent threads of gender and sexuality to see how they weave together to create a beautiful textile. You will see how two–dimensional linear models that are limiting the human experience can be transformed into three–dimensional spherical models that are all inclusive. Transitioning our perception from a static form to a dynamic one enables us to stop thinking in black and white and start thinking in the colorful multi–shades of the spectrum.

Bumper Sticker Slogans

FTMs are self–maid men.

FTMs do it with prosthetics.

Sex Transformers are no robots to gender rules.

A transsexual's emancipation proclamation is a custom made body: Surgery is one small step for a lifetime, one huge step towards freedom.

THE CHANGING FACE OF TIME & GENDER

AGE 2

AGE 13

AGE 17

AGE 32

AGE 32

AGE 34

POST-TRANSITION

AGE 39

AGE 49

AGE 57

NOTES:

[1] Hall, Radcliffe. *The Well of Loneliness*. Anchor, 1990. Originally published in 1928.

[2] Silverstein, Shel. "A Boy Name Sue." Recorded by Johnny Cash on *The Essential Johnny Cash*. Do you need to state the year of the recording perhaps?

[3] Valerio, Max Wolf. *The Testosterone Files: My Hormonal and Social Transformation from Female to Male*. Seal Press, 2006.

[4] To read more about the experiences of female–to–males in their own voices, I highly recommend the following books:

Cooper, T. *Real Man Adventures*. McSweeney's, 2013.

Green, Jamison. *Becoming a Visible Man*. Vanderbilt University Press, 2004.

Kailey, Matt. *Just Add Hormones: An Insider's Guide to the Transsexual Experience*. Beacon Press, 2006.

Valerio, Max Wolf. *The Testosterone Files: My Hormonal and Social Transformation from Female to Male*. Seal Press, 2006.

Other female–to–male transition stories include:

Bono, Chaz. *Transitions: The Story of How I Became a Man*. Plume, 2012.

Cummings, Mark Angelo. *The Mirror Makes No Sense*. AuthorHouse, 2006.

Februari, Maxim. *The Making of a Man: Notes on Transsexuality*. Reaktion Books, 2015.

Hewitt, Paul with Jane Warren. *A Self–made Man: The Diary of a Man Born in a Woman's Body*. Trafalgar Square Publishing, 1997.

Jones, Aphrodite. *All She Wanted: The True Story of Brandon Teena*. Gallery Books, 2008. (About the subject of the movie *Boys Don't Cry*.)

Khosla, Dhillon. *Both Sides Now: One Man's Journey through Womanhood*. Tarcher, 2006.

Krieger, Nick. *Nina Here Nor There: My Journey Beyond Gender*. Beacon Press, 2011.

Martino, Mario with Harriett. *Emergence: A Transsexual Autobiography*. Crown Publishers, 1977. (This was the first published autobiography of a FTM.)

McBee, Thomas Page. *Man Alive*. City Lights Publishers, 2014.

Paris, Rico Adrian. *Transman – Bitesize*. AuthorHouse, 2005.

Raz Link, Aaron and Hilda Raz. *What Becomes You*. Bison Books, 2008.

Rees, Mark. *Dear Sir or Madam*. New York, 1996.

Sallans, Ryan K. *Second Son: Transitioning Toward My Destiny, Love and Life*. Scout Publishing LLC, 2013.

Thompson, Raymond, and Kitty Sewell. *What Took You So Long?: A Girl's Journey to Manhood*. Penguin Books Ltd, 1995.

Anthologies include:

Cotton, Trystan T. *Hung Jury: Testimonies of Genital Surgery by Transsexual Men*. Transgress Press, 2012.

Diamond, Morty. *From the Inside Out: Radical Gender Transformation, FTM and Beyond*. Manic D Press, 2004.

Keig, Zander and Mitch Kellaway, eds. *Manning Up: Transsexual Men on Finding Brotherhood, Family & Themselves*. CreateSpace Independent Publishing Platform, 2014.

Rohrer, Megan M. and Zander Keig. *Letters for My Brothers: Transitional Wisdom in Retrospect*. Lulu.com, 2014.

CHAPTER 1: INTRODUCTION

Welcome to the Art and Soul of Gender and Sexuality

OMNIGENDER

The symbols for Mars (Male) and Venus (Female) are combined with a third arm that represents non-binary trans* people. The strike through the circle in this version represents those individuals that don't identify as male or female. The inverted triangle was a symbol the Nazis made camp prisoners wear during World War II. Different colors represented different groups. Homosexuals had to wear the pink triangle. Today the inverted triangle has been reclaimed for use as a symbol for pride.

(Inner Symbol: Designer Unknown)

INTRODUCTION

The soul, when not incarnated, is a being of light and energy. It has no gender and no sexual orientation. Therefore, gender and sexual identity are constructs of human incarnation. This means that the states of gender and sexual identity are created for the purpose of a soul's learning. The question, then, is why do we choose specific gender and sexual identities while we are incarnated?

Gender is the lens through which everyone in the physical world perceives an individual. It is the most observable quality about an individual. We usually "read" others' gender from surface clues present on the Physical Body but an individual also has a gender energy that is not always as recognizable even though it is always present. In this book you will discover how to "read" gender, not only on a physical level but on the energetic level as well.

First let me deconstruct the title of this book, *Soul Sex: The Alchemy of Sex and Gender*, because the title really is a summary of the contents of the book.

- ***Soul*** here implies spirituality. We humans are spirits that have souls whether we are incarnated on the physical plane or not. This book examines all aspects of gender and sexual identity, especially spiritual impacts, which are very often overlooked or omitted by the scientific, medical, and psychological community.
- ***Sex*** is a multi–meaning word. It implies the biological classification of the male or female body but it can also mean the act of having sexual relations.
- ***Alchemy*** is the process of changing from one state to another. It is a fluid process. This book will discuss how gender and sexual identities are also fluid and changeable. Identity is a point on a wide spectrum and not a choice between one or two options.

- ***Gender and Sexuality*** are two of the most basic but powerful aspects of our personal identity. They comprise the bedrock upon which we build our self–concept and the lens through which we view the outer world. Everyone has gender and sexual identity. Many have automatically accepted theirs while others have questioned theirs since birth.

  Originally I was going to write only about gender identity but it became clear to me early on that gender and sexuality are inseparable. Even though they are independent identities, one is the warp and the other the weft of threads that create the tapestry of human identity. Much of the prejudice held against individuals with alternative sexual orientations is really gender bias. In other words, these individuals are commonly viewed as not acting "appropriately" in their birth assigned sex roles.

In addition, this book will discuss how assuming a gender and sexual identity is not about putting on one outfit and wearing it for a lifetime. As outfits become outdated or outgrown, they are discarded.

WHO THIS BOOK IS FOR

It is my highest hope that this book will help individuals with any gender and sexual identity to develop more self–empowerment and self–love.

- This book is for you if you have ever questioned your gender and sexual identity.
- This book is for you if you have *never* questioned your gender and sexual identity.
- This book is for you if you know someone who has a non–conforming gender or sexual identity.
- This book is for you if you would like to broaden your perspective on gender and sexual identity.

This is a book for the lay individual, written in down–to–earth language. This book is not intended to be an intellectual or scholarly undertaking. My ideas are not supported by clinical studies. This book is dualistic in that it presents both factual and philosophical perspectives. I present the entire breadth of perspectives that relate to gender and sexuality instead of drilling down in any one perspective.

It is not my goal to convince you, the reader, of anything that is presented. I am just planting the seeds of awareness for you to explore further. I am offering a buffet, from soup to nuts, of perspectives on gender, sexuality, and identity. I invite you to sample each of the dishes as food for thought.

The perspectives I share in this book are based on my own personal research and experiences. It is my intent that this book remain non–political and non–dogmatic. I am not a spokesperson for any community of trans*, gender–nonconforming, or diverse sexual identity individuals. These communities have a host of micro–communities that maintain their own unique beliefs and culture.

In writing this book, I took the advice of Bruce Lee's following words:

"Research your own experience.
Absorb what is useful.
Discard what is useless.
Add what is uniquely your own."

NAVIGATING THE BOOK

In the first part of the book, I present the different theories of how gender and sexual identities are created. I begin with the densest layer of reality, which is the physical world, and progress to the more ethereal and esoteric phenomenon of the spiritual world.

I was a psychology major in college in the 1980s. I was always the one in class with a raised hand, asking, "But what about reincarnation? Wouldn't our past lives have a tremendous effect on who we are today?" There was always a pregnant silence as if a stinker was released and then the teacher would try to sweep the question under the rug. It seems that since there is no "scientific proof" that reincarnation exists, it cannot be included in the study of Western medicine and psychology.

Well, color me stubborn, but I was just not going to give up on this idea so I developed a list of the influences that create who we are at any moment in time. These influences are energies that are dynamic (always changing), multi–dimensional, and powerful as they blend to create who we are at any given moment in time. To know who we are we must view ourselves holistically. And this means owning the parts that are obvious but also exploring the parts that may not be readily seen. I view the creation of identity as the result of a perfect storm where the forces of biology, sociology, psychology, and spirituality come together to form a vortex of energy that becomes the journey a soul travels throughout a lifetime.

You might think that you began when you were born. But a lot happened before that moment.

- First your parents came together to create you which is how you inherited your genes from your ancestors.
- Then you were exposed to your mother's hormones and emotions for nine months in the womb, while on the spiritual plane your guides were helping you plan the last minute details of your upcoming life.
- As you were born, the astrological energies of the universe imprinted you. A portion of your Energy Body descended to overlay your Physical Body.
- Then as you grew, your family and social culture began to program you.

All of these forces influenced you long before you were old enough to develop the consciousness of your personal identity. Divided into three aspects, the influences on how we are created include:

PHYSICAL ASPECTS

Physical Properties – Our biological properties include every aspect of what we look like and how our bodies function.

Hormones – Hormones are a biological property of the body but I list them separately because they have a huge influence on us. The hormones present as we developed in the womb helped create our gender and sexual identity as well as other characteristics.

DNA and Genetics – Our chromosomes determine who we are and they also provide a map that we have inherited from our biological ancestors.

Energetic Frequency – Although energy is usually more felt than seen, everything, including our bodies, is made of energy. Our energy vibrates at a dynamic frequency. How we are attracted to or repulsed by others depends a lot on how compatible the frequency of our energy is with the frequencies of others.

MENTAL and EMOTIONAL ASPECTS

Nurturing and Family – When we are born we depend on our family unit for survival. How we are nurtured and who we see as role models greatly influences who we are.

Culture and Society – On a broader scale, our culture, its values and characteristics, are imprinted on us as we grow.

Personality – Each person has a unique personality and temperament. Personality characteristics are created from a combination of many factors. Whether personality is inherent or learned, I add it to the list of influences because it is so unique and distinctive in each individual.

SPIRITUAL ASPECTS

Astrological Influences – Not only does the astrological position of the planets and other forces of the heavens heavily influence who we are at birth, but the effects of our ever–changing position in the universe continues to influence our lives.

Past Lives and Parallel Lives – This current life is a sum of all the experiences and lessons we have encountered in past lives. If our soul is living parallel lives, there may be some bleed over that affects our current life.

Karma, Contracts, and Vows – This current life is a result of all the karma we have accumulated. This life was created to add lessons for our learning experiences. In addition, we may still be feeling the effects of past life contracts and vows that were made.

Pre–Life Selection – Most souls confer with their spirit guides to choose the parameters of their life before being born. There is always free will available while incarnated but many of the circumstances and some of the details of our lives were pre–arranged by us before we arrived. Gender and sexual identity is a part of that pre–life selection.

Soul Purpose – We all have a specific soul purpose and unique life purposes. The course of our life journey will try to support our purposes (even if we are not consciously aware of it).

The following figure summarizes the energetic forces that shape who we are:

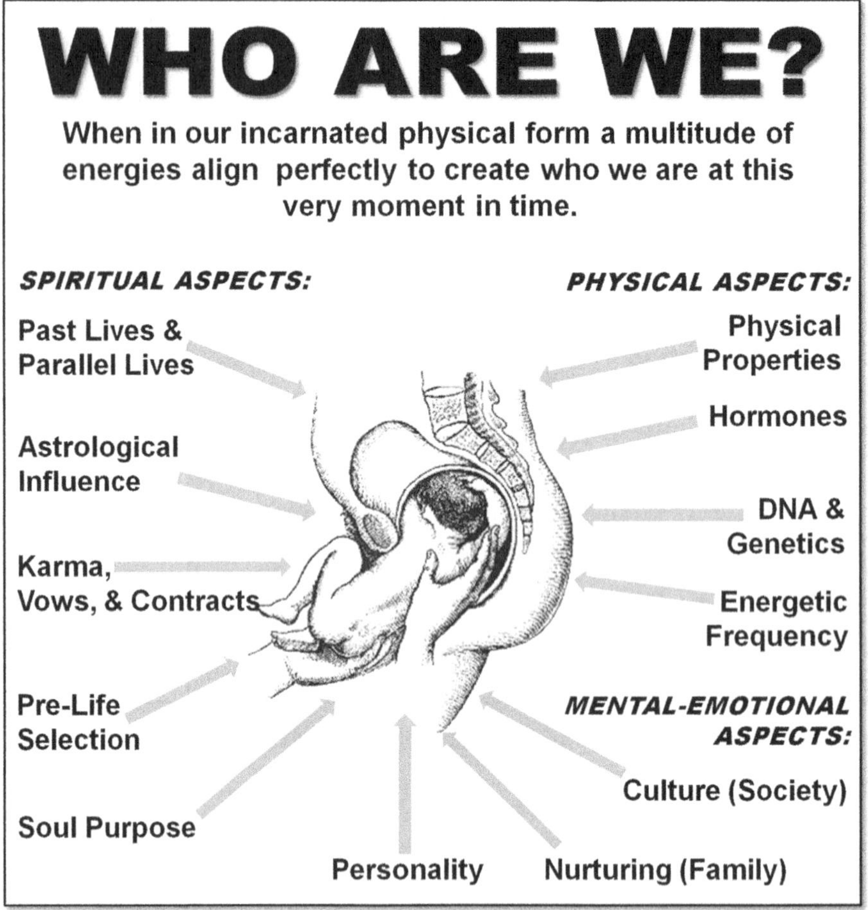

In the second part of the book, I present a deeper inspection of identity that includes models of gender and sexual identity, the comparison of the Energy Body to the Physical Body, and how gender changes in the course of one lifetime or over the course of multiple lifetimes. Biological (or physical) sex, gender identity and expression, and sexual orientation are all independent aspects that make up an individual's identity. They are like pieces of a pie, each slice contributing to the whole. I conclude with a chapter on Two Spirit and third gender cultures, a chapter on self–empowerment, and a summary of support services that I offer.

In the seventh episode of the third season of *Star Trek,* Gene Roddenberry presented the Vulcan Philosophy that states: "Infinite diversity in infinite combinations (IDIC)". This book presents the IDIC of gender and sexual identity. It discusses and illustrates how gender and sexual identity lie on an infinite spectra of diversity and because of their fluidity, can change over time providing infinite combinations of possibilities.

I am not advocating that everyone become androgynous or gender fluid. I am advocating that we all accept individuals, no matter what their gender and sexual identities. Let us allow diversity to thrive. Because in so doing, not only are we living in lovingkindness but we are living out our spiritual characteristics while incarnated on Earth.

DEFINING LANGUAGE

In order to create common points from which to communicate, I will present some definitions of terms that will be used frequently throughout the book. Many individuals do not like to be categorized or labeled in any way. I agree that labels may "box one in" but an individual's self–identity is critical. We must know who we are. It is labels that translate our identity to language. I will be using labels and language for convenience, a short cut to convey concepts and facts. The spirit world is a place in which souls can be fluid, boundary free, label–less, and uncategorized. However the purpose of incarnating on Earth is to experience dualities, polarities, and various points on a spectrum. From these experiences a soul learns balance.

I strive to avoid the use of the terms that are negative or derogatory when describing diversity. Such terms include: aberrant, abnormal, atypical, deviant, disorder, irregular, malformation, nonstandard, normal, odd, opposite sex, pathology, same sex, strange, typical, wrong, usual, and unusual. These terms may create judgment, separation, stigma, shame, exclusion, marginalization, and ostracism of individuals with diverse and non–conforming identities.

Pronoun usage gets tricky because language is based on binary gender models. My desire is to be inclusive of multiple points on a gender spectrum. There are multiple proposals for pronoun usage that I will cover in more detail in Chapter 6. Some authors alternate between the feminine and masculine pronouns, which perpetuates the binary model. Some authors use invented pronouns, but I fear this will seem very unfamiliar to readers. So for now, please note I will use grammar incorrectly in the following instances:

1. I use the plural form “they” to represent the singular forms of “he” and “she”.
2. I use the plural form “their”, “theirs”, “their self”, “them”, and “themselves” to represent the singular forms of “his”, “hers”, “himself”, and “herself”.
3. I occasionally use an abbreviated form “s/he” for the pronoun of “he” and “she”.

Please refer to the glossary in the back of the book for a complete list of terms and their definitions that are used frequently in describing gender and sexual identities.

CHAPTER 2:

BIOLOGY OF GENDER AND SEXUAL IDENTITY

The Forces of Nature

PAGAN UNION OF MALE & FEMALE

A symbol of Androgyny is created from the union of the God and Goddess. The God is represented by the symbol of the Horned God: a half moon pointing up. The Horned God is Associated with nature, sexuality, and hunting. The Goddess is represented by the symbol of the Triple Moon: a circle representing the full moon in the middle, a half moon on the left (waxing moon of new beginnings), and a half moon on the right (waning moon of endings). The Triple Moon can also symbolize the Maiden, the Mother, and the Crone.

(Designed by Drake from Classic Symbolism)

BIOLOGICAL THEORIES OF SEX DETERMINATION

In this chapter biological theories of sex determination are presented to show that varieties in sex and gender occur naturally and more often than we are aware of. A hierarchy was created to assist Western medical professionals in the classification of different degrees of sexual characteristics. It starts at the simplest level and progresses towards increasingly complicated levels produced over the course of a human life. They are:

- Chromosomes
- Gonads
- Hormones
- Genitalia (Primary Sexual Characteristics)
- Secondary Sexual Characteristics
- Brain Structure
- Gender Identity (psychological)
- Gender Role (sociological)
- Erotic Preference

THE NATURE THEORY

In this section we will look at what is commonly called the Nature Theory. The Nature Theory indicates that humans are products of heredity. The traits that individuals possess are a product of the genes that make up the Physical Body. Those who support the Nature Theory are called nativists and believe humans are a product of evolution and the result of genetic code.

First, let's see exactly how the sexes are typically created. The path of biological sex creation follows these steps:

1. **Sex Determination** – Chromosomes are established he sperm fertilizes the egg.
2. **Sex Differentiation** – Gonads are created, internal ducts are created, genitalia are created, and the brain and

hypothalamus differentiate. Secondary sex characteristics are created in puberty.

Here is a description of how differentiation occurs during fetal development:

Conception: The sperm adds either an X (female) or a Y (male) chromosome to the X in the ovum. During the first 7 weeks after conception the genitalia and reproductive organs of a male and female embryo are identical.

7–11 Weeks – The embryo begins to differentiate, with the female as the default path for a developing fetus. The Y chromosome triggers masculinization through androgen hormones to form a male. The absence of the Y chromosome, plus estrogen and other hormones, create the female.

12 Weeks – The female reproduction organs are formed. Ovaries contain over six million eggs. This number will be reduced to about four hundred by puberty. The male foreskin has developed.

20 Weeks – External genitalia changes are complete. Ultrasound may indicate the sex of the baby however there is still a 50 percent possibility of presuming the wrong sex.

28 Weeks – The male's testicles descend from the abdomen into the scrotum.

Observation Point

If you are a male or have intimate access to a male body, look under the testicles to see a scar-like line running the longitudinal length. This was the opening to the vagina the first two months after conception. In the third month, male hormones, triggered by genetic instructions, close and seal the vagina of a male-bodied fetus.

By birth, the reproductive organs and genitalia of the male and female are homologous, in other words, they have corresponding structures. The figure below lists the corresponding genitalia.

FEMALE	MALE
Ovaries	Testis
Vagina	Vagina Masculina
Uterus	Prostatic Utricle
Fallopian Tubes	Appendix Testis
Canals & Ducts of Gartner	Seminal Vesicles, Vas Deferens, & Epididymides
Bladder	Bladder
Urethra	Prostatic Urethra
Vestibule	Penile Urethra
Labia Minora	Shaft of the Penis
Labia Majora	Scrotal Sac
Clitoris	Penis
Clitoral Hood	Penal Foreskin
Bartholin's Glands (Vestibular Glands)	Cowper's Glands (Bulbourethral Glands)
Prostate Gland (Urethral Glands)	Prostate Gland (Urethral Glands)

The next two figures illustrate the internal and external evolution of the fetus from a common structure to differentiated structures of male and female. Note that an intersex individual will have partial or complete characteristics of both the male and the female structure.

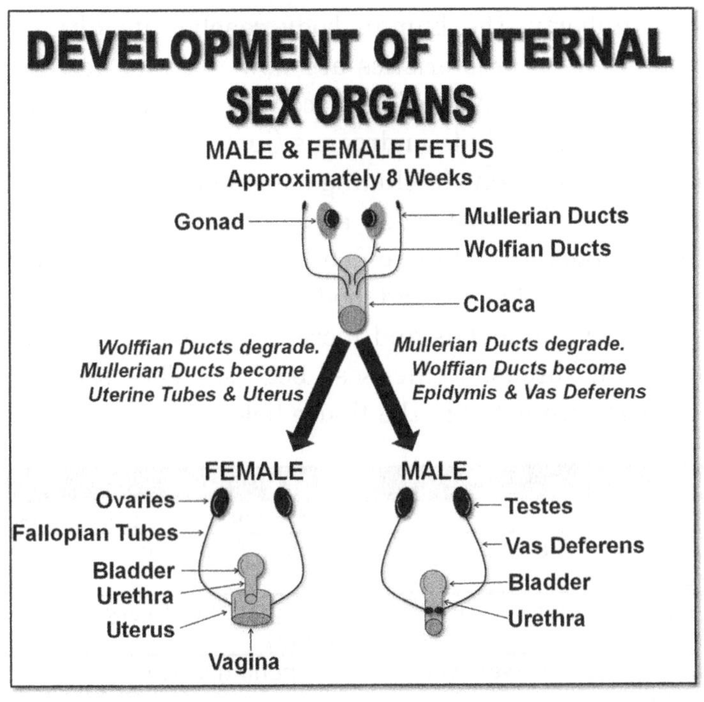
DEVELOPMENT OF INTERNAL SEX ORGANS
MALE & FEMALE FETUS
Approximately 8 Weeks
Gonad
Mullerian Ducts
Wolfian Ducts
Cloaca
Wolffian Ducts degrade. Mullerian Ducts become Uterine Tubes & Uterus
Mullerian Ducts degrade. Wolffian Ducts become Epidymis & Vas Deferens
FEMALE
MALE
Ovaries
Fallopian Tubes
Bladder
Urethra
Uterus
Vagina
Testes
Vas Deferens
Bladder
Urethra

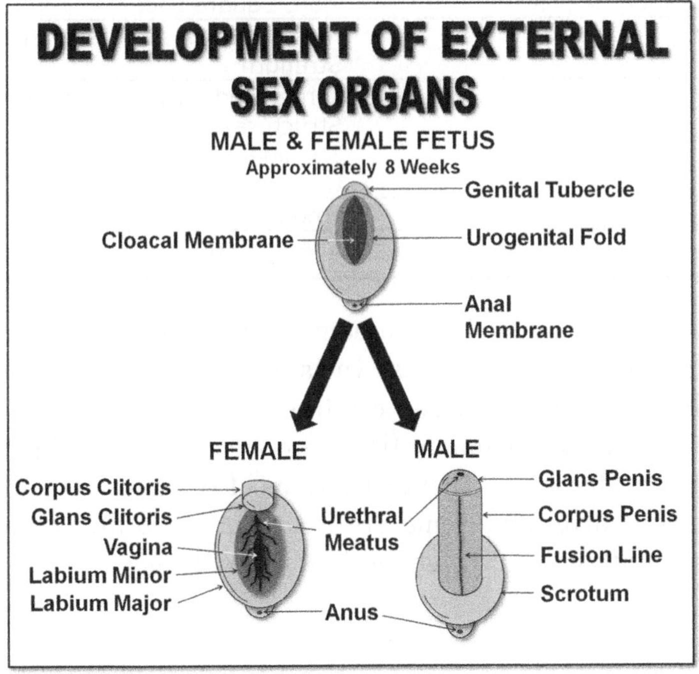
DEVELOPMENT OF EXTERNAL SEX ORGANS
MALE & FEMALE FETUS
Approximately 8 Weeks
Genital Tubercle
Cloacal Membrane
Urogenital Fold
Anal Membrane
FEMALE
MALE
Corpus Clitoris
Glans Clitoris
Vagina
Labium Minor
Labium Major
Urethral Meatus
Anus
Glans Penis
Corpus Penis
Fusion Line
Scrotum

During puberty, the human body reaches its ultimate form. The primary sex characteristics are now fully formed. Hormones stimulate the development of the secondary sexual characteristics. The sex hormones include androgens (including testosterone) in a male body and estrogens (including estradiol, estriol, and estrone), small amounts of testosterone, and anti–androgens in a female body. In the male, testosterone increases the size of muscles, vocal cords, and bones. Facial and body hair grows. In the female, estrogen widens the pelvis and increases body fat in hips, thighs, buttocks, and breasts. Menses begins. The secondary sex characteristics are listed in the figure below:

FEMALE	MALE
Body Hair Growth	Body Hair and Facial Hair Growth
Enlargement of Breasts and Erection of Nipples	Balding (for some)
Increased Subcutaneous Fat	Enlargement of Larynx (Adam's Apple)
Widening of Hips, Lower Waist-to-hip Ratio	Deepening Voice
Mensuration Begins	More Square Face
Rounder Face	Increased Muscle Mass and Strength
	Larger Body, Heavier Bone Structure, Broadening of Shoulders & Chest, Higher Waist-to-hip Ratio
	Lower Body Fat
	Coarser Skin

Not all babies develop the same. There are more than forty biological conditions that cause variations in sex determination or sex differentiation. These conditions are commonly called disorders of sex development (DSD) by Western medical personnel however I prefer to call them variations of sex development or sex development diversity. Some are extremely rare and some occur much more often than the general public realizes.

INTERSEX CONDITIONS

"Intersex" is a modern term for the now obsolete term "hermaphrodite". Intersex is a variation in sex characteristics that does not allow a distinct identification of biological sex. In other words, sex determination is ambiguous due to:

- Genitalia that cannot be classified as male or female.
- An incomplete development of internal reproductive organs.
- Variations of the sex chromosomes.

The Intersex Society of North America states that in approximately one in 1500 to 2000 births, a sex differentiation specialist has to be called in to consult on ambiguous sexual organs. They estimate that sexual ambiguity to some degree occurs as often as one in 100 births[1]. A list of rates of occurrence of various intersex conditions is available at www.isna.org/faq/frequency.

I wonder, then, if intersex conditions occur this frequently, why are they still being "swept under the carpet", not socialized or discussed, and intersex individuals still suffer incredible stigmatization? Certainly we, as a society, now have the opportunity and potential to broaden our perspectives about gender and sexuality, as never before, and begin accepting that there are many natural variations in both gender and sex.

Some intersex conditions may not surface until puberty or adulthood. Individuals may then choose to undergo surgical procedures to align their physical sex characteristics with their gender identity.

Sometimes, intersex conditions are not even detectable without genetic testing. Jamison Green, in his book *Becoming a Visible Man*,[2] states that the textbook, *Smith's General Urology*, reports that one in 20,000 men have two X chromosomes rather than one X and one Y. These men will not even know until they find that they are infertile.

Options to manage intersex traits include surgery and psychosocial support. Typically, surgery is performed shortly after birth, before the baby's gender identity is known. Western medical doctors have routinely performed surgery on infants with ambiguous outer genitalia or strongly recommended surgical correction to parents. Sadly, the gender identity later in the life cycle may not match the Physical Body altered by surgery. Many who disagree with this approach say that surgical treatment is socially motivated and therefore ethically questionable. In addition, 20–50 percent of surgical cases result in a loss of sexual sensation later in life. Other harmful consequences may include loss of fertility, chronic pain, severe emotional confusion and/or devastation.

Anne Fausto–Sterling, professor of Biology and Gender Studies at Brown University and a leading expert in biology and gender development, advocates replacing a binary sex model for a new model that includes intersex conditions. In other words, why are we limiting biological sex to only two options when more than that occur naturally?

The Prader Scale was created as a scoring system to evaluate the range of variations between female and male genitalia. At one end, "0", the genitalia are unvirilized female. At the opposite end, "5", are the genitalia of a completely virilized female.

Anne Fausto–Sterling, in her book *Sexing the Body*[3], describes a Phall–o–meter that assesses the size of a baby's genitals. It playfully points out that Western medical authorities have determined "acceptable" ranges for female clitorises and male phalluses. If a baby's genitalia are found to be outside of these parameters, corrective surgery is performed or highly recommended. A phallo-meter can be view at this link: http://thesocietypages.org/socimages/2008/09/04/the-phall-o-meter/.

The Story of Cheryl Chase

Cheryl Chase was born with mixed male/female sex organs in 1956. For the first 18 months she was raised as a boy but when ovaries and a uterus were discovered, a clitoridectomy was performed to remove her "oversized" clitoris. From then on, she was raised as a girl, albeit one with very limited ability to experience orgasm. She is now an intersex activist and the founder of the Intersex Society of North America. She advocates that sex organ surgery should only be done on individuals who are able to give informed consent. She agrees that children should be assigned a gender at birth but that they should be fully supported if a gender transition is desired later on.

I am completely incapable of understanding how performing surgical mutilation of infants' genitalia is helping them to avoid a lifetime of suffering. And why is it that a doctor is able to enforce *his/her* standard of what is acceptable genitalia? It is not the bodies of intersex individuals that need to be altered. It is the perception of the rest of us that must change to accept differences. We must strive to understand that which we have not experienced personally. Who is to judge that being born with male and female genitalia isn't actually the best of both worlds? Our inability to accept differences in others has the power to destroy lives. Furthermore, karma being what it is, individuals that persecute others because of differences will be experiencing the other end of that persecution in a future life.

If you are interested in reading more stories of intersex individuals, I have listed some good books in the footnotes at the end of this chapter.[4]

BIOLOGICAL ROOTS OF GENDER AND SEXUAL IDENTITY

To date there has been no clearly identified biological cause of gender identity variance or alternative sexual identity. However, there are studies that have shown that biological influences are very probable. Transsexualism can be considered to be a neuro–

developmental condition. Scientists hypothesize that a combination of genetic, hormonal, and social factors determine sexual identity.

Scientific studies that have been done in the areas listed below have validated that there are measurable biological distinctions between transgender and cisgender individuals as well as between individuals with heterosexual identities and individuals with homosexual identities.

1. Genetics
2. Brain structure
3. Brain function
4. Alcohol, stress, and hormone exposure on fetus development
5. Number of siblings and order of birth
6. Pheromones

The Brain Organization Theory states that brains can be gendered by the same hormones that develop the internal sexual organs and external genitalia of the fetus. These hormones cause changes in the brain that lead to gender identity as adults.[5]

From these studies, we can draw the conclusion that the developing fetus responds to many different influences while in the womb. Some of these influences can affect gender and sexual identity.

If you are interested in more detailed information presented by expert authors, I highly recommend Anne Fausto–Sterling's book *Sexing the Body: Gender Politics and the Construction of Sexuality*[3], Joan Roughgarden's book *Evolution's Rainbow: Diversity, Gender, and Sexuality in Nature and People,*[6] and Rebecca M. Jordan–Young's book, *Brain Storm: The Flaws in the Science of Sex Differences*.[7]

Transgender and Multi-gender Animals

Joan Roughgarden, in her book *Evolution's Rainbow*[6], defines multi-gender species as having more than two genders (male and female). Gender classification is based on physical characteristics, mating habits, lifestyle, and length of life.

Species with One Female and Two Male Genders:
Red Deer
Plainfin Midshipman Fish
Coho Salmon

Species with One Female and Three Male Genders:
Bluegill Sunfish
Spotted European Wrasse
Cichlid
Tree Lizard

Species with Two Female and Two Male Genders:
White-throated Sparrow

Species with Two Female and Three Male Genders:
Side-blotched Lizard

Hermaphroditism and Intersex in Animals and Plants

Hermaphroditism occurs naturally in the plant and animal kingdoms, most often in invertebrates and fish. There are two classifications of hermaphroditism: simultaneous (the organism has both genders at once) and sequential (the organism changes gender). Sequential hermaphroditism can further be divided into three categories: protandry (the organism transitions from male to female), protogyny (organism transitions from female to male), and bi-directional. True hermaphroditism in mammals is rare, however, intersex conditions occur when an organism has a mixture of both male and female sex organs.

Sequential Hermaphroditism

Anemone Fish
Angel Fish
Anthias
Bees
Clownfish
Cushion Sea Stars
Flatworms
Gobies
Groupers
Guppies
Limpets
Mollusks
Moray Eels
Oysters
Parrotfish
Rana Rugosa Frogs
Ray Finned Fish
Sea Bass
Sheephead Fish
Shrimps
Some Jellyfish
Snooks
Swordtails
Worms

Simultaneous Hermaphroditism

Angler Fish
Barnacles
Bryozoans
Earthworms
Flukes
Hamlets
Most Plants
Slipper Shells
Slugs
Snails
Worms

Intersex

Bears
Bowhead & Fin Whales
Deer
Kangaroos
Kangaroo Rats
Moose
Spider Monkeys
Spotted Hyenas
Striped Dolphins
Vanuatu Pigs

Bisexuality and Homosexuality in Animals

Over 1500 animal species practice bisexuality or homosexuality, including over 100 mammal species. Some animals live a completely homosexual life. This occurs about 4–5 percent of the time among birds that are monogamous.

Examples:

Apes
Baboons
Bats
Bears
Bed Bugs
Bison
Black Headed Gulls
Black Swans
Blue Herons
Cattle Egrets
Cheetahs
Chimpanzees
Deer
Dolphins
Dragonflies
Elephants
Eurasian Oystercatchers
Fox
Fruit Flies
Gazelles
Geese
Giraffes
Gorillas
Gulls
Hedgehogs
Ibises
Insects
Kangaroos
Killer Whales
Koalas
Lions
Lizards
Mallards
Manatees
Monkeys
Moose
Mountain Goats
Musk Oxen
Parakeets
Penguins
Pigeons
Polecats
Pronghorns
Pukekos (bird)
Razorbills
Seals
Sheep
Spiders
Spotted Hyenas
Squirrels
Swans
Terns
Tree Swallows
Vultures
Walruses
Wolves
Zebras

NOTES:

[1] Intersex Society of North America "*How Common is Intersex?*" 1993–2008. http://www.isna.org/faq/frequency

[2] Green, Jamison. *Becoming a Visible Man.* Vanderbilt University Press, 2004.

[3] Fausto–Sterling, Anne. *Sexing the Body: Gender Politics and the Construction of Sexuality.* Basic Books, 2000.

[4] Recommended books about intersex individuals:

Colapinto, John. *As Nature Made Him: The Boy Who Was Raised as a Girl.* Harper Perennial, 2006.

Eugenides, Jeffrey. *Middlesex: A Novel.* Author Picador, 2007.

Foucault, Michel. *Herculin Barbin: Being the Recently Discovered Memoirs of a 19th–century Hermaphrodite.* Vintage, 1980.

Winter, Katherine. *Annabel.* Grove Press, Black Cat, 2011.

[5] Valla, Jeffrey and Stephen J. Ceci. "Can Sex Differences in Science Be Tied to the Long Reach of Prenatal Hormones? Brain Organization Theory, Digit Ratio (2D/4D), and Sex Differences in Preferences and Cognition." *Perspectives on Psychological Science.* Mar 6(2), 2011. http://www.ncbi.nlm.nih.gov/pmc/articles/PMC3230041/

[6] Roughgarden, Joan. *Evolution's Rainbow: Diversity, Gender, and Sexuality in Nature and People.* University of California Press, 2013.

[7] Jordan–Young, Rebecca M. *Brain Storm: The Flaws in the Science of Sex Differences.* Harvard University Press, 2011.

CHAPTER 3:
SOCIOLOGY AND PSYCHOLOGY OF GENDER AND SEXUAL IDENTITY

The Forces of Nurture

PANGENDER

The five-sided pentagon stands for the numbers "2" (the Male) plus "3" (the Female) which adds up to "5" (the Androgyne). Inside the pentagon are Male (Mars astrological symbol), Female (Venus astrological symbol), and Neuter (Mercury astrological symbol). All are enclosed by a circle which symbolizes circular living and the throwing away of linear thinking.

(Designed by Drake)

PSYCHOLOGICAL AND SOCIOLOGICAL THEORIES OF GENDER DETERMINATION

THE NURTURE THEORY

The Nurture Theory indicates that humans are more likely products of environmental factors than of heredity. Nurture refers to all environmental influences that occur after conception. The traits that individuals possess are a product of their upbringing. B.F. Skinner is the father of behavioral psychology which theorizes that human behavior can be conditioned the same as animal behavior can be. Supporting the nurture theory is the fact that identical twins, if reared apart, are not exactly alike.

Those that support the Nurture Theory are called empiricists and believe that the mind at birth is a *tabula rasa* (a blank slate), which is filled with learning experiences as an individual grows.

The psychological and sociological influences on an individual's development and identity are: rearing style and family influence, cultural influence, geographical influence, and personal experiences.

Rearing Style and Family Influence

Rearing style as a cause of non–conforming gender identity includes the theories that mothers are too overbearing, fathers are absent, parents desire a child of the opposite sex, parents don't provide a good role model, or individuals are victims of trauma or sexual abuse.

Gender identity develops in the first few years of life. Individuals may be biologically predisposed to a specific identity but upbringing is the catalyst that launches it.

Unsuccessful attempts to raise some individuals who were sexually reassigned at birth show that environment does not, by itself, determine an individual's gender identity. Individuals born male but raised as female, or vice versa, often have the same gender dysphoria as transsexual individuals. Dysphoria is a psychological term that means a generalized feeling of anxiety, discontent, and/or physical discomfort.

Cultural Influence

Cultural systems are comprised of language, religion, and ethnic traditions. Although gender and sexual identity develop independent of cultural and social influence, these influences can greatly affect an individual's expression of identity. In reverse, when taboos are lifted, exploration of alternative identities increases.

Sexual patterns to some extent can be a product of society's expectations. Anthropologists observed that uncompetitive cultures (such as those that do not reward the best hunters) have virtually no homosexuality. There is also a correlation between a culture's view of women and the acceptance of gay men. In cultures that honor women as equals, homosexuality is much more accepted. In cultures that consider women's status as lower than that of men, homosexuality is looked down upon.

Ken Zucker, a psychologist and sexologist and head of the gender identity clinic at Toronto's Centre for Addiction and Mental Health, believes that transsexuality is a result of people treating an individual as if they were the "opposite" of their birth assigned sex based on some physical characteristics. For example, treating boys with girlish features as girls and treating girls with boyish features as boys. However, this theory doesn't take into account some of these boys and girls don't identify as transgender or gay and that some transgender individuals do not display any characteristics of the "opposite" gender of their assigned sex at birth until they are ready to disclose their gender identity status.[1]

Many sociologists agree that gender is learned and that the interpretation of gender roles is based on society's expectations. Maria do Mar Pereira, the deputy director for the University of Warwick's Centre for the Study of Women and Gender, conducted a study of 14–year old children in Lisbon. She observed these children modifying their behavior in harmful ways in order to adhere to preconceived notions of gender norms. She concluded that making children conform to rigid gender roles can be detrimental to their physical and mental health. It can produce anxiety, insecurity, stress, and low self–esteem. She says:

> *"Usually we think of gender as natural and biological, but it's not. We actually construct it in ways that have problematic and largely unacknowledged health risks."*[2]

For more information, read her book called *Fazendo Género no Recreio (Doing Gender in the Playground).*

Personal Experiences

Most individuals with non–conforming gender identities report that they have had feelings of gender identity for as long as they are able to remember. Young children can be aware of their gender identity as early as 1.5 to 2 years of age. Their gender stereotypes are set in place by 4.5 years of age.

Daryl Bem, social psychologist and professor emeritus at Cornell University, has an Exotic Becomes Erotic Theory that states that children will become sexually attracted to the gender which they see as different (the exotic aspect). Some children are attracted to activities that are enjoyed by other children of the same gender. Other children prefer activities that are typical of another gender. The feeling of difference is what evokes a psychological arousal, which later becomes a sexual arousal, when a child is near members of the gender which it considers as being different. Gender identity is then based on which gender the child considers to be the same and which is opposite.[3]

Differences in male and female viewing preference can be seen the first day of life. Toy preference based on gender can be seen at three to eight months. As children grow, they are attracted to toys which have been labelled for their gender or toys that they have seen other members of their gender playing with (socialization process). Some cultures, such as some Native American tribes, present a choice to a baby or child between a stereotypical masculine item (such as a bow) and a stereotypical feminine item (such as a basket). Whichever item the child chooses determines the gender identity of the child. The child is then treated according to their gender identity not biological sex.

William Holmes (1998) reported in *The Journal of the American Medical Association* that sexually abused adolescents, particularly those abused by males, were up to seven times more likely to identify as gay or bisexual.[4] Tomeo and Templer (2001) found that 46 percent of the gay men in contrast to 7 percent of the straight men reported gay molestation. Twenty two percent of lesbian women in contrast to 1 percent of straight women reported gay molestation.[5]

GENDER DEVELOPMENT MODELS

Social construction theories state that individuals develop gender identity through observation and imitation. Below are examples of some social constructive theories of gender development.

Kohlberg's Cognitive Developmental Theory of Gender Identity

Lawrence Kohlberg, a psychologist, created the Cognitive Developmental Theory of Gender Identity, in 1966. It states that children learn gender in three stages: gender labeling and basic gender identity (age two to three), gender stability (age four to five), and gender constancy/consistency (age six to seven).[6]

Bem's Gender Schema Theory

Sandra Bem, a psychologist at Cornell University, developed a Gender Schema Theory in 1981. Schema comes from the Greek word "*skhēma*", which means shape or plan. In psychology, a schema is a cognitive framework that helps organize and interpret information. The Gender Schema Theory states gender characteristics are transmuted by way of schemata. Children develop male and female gender schemas from observing parents, teachers, and others around them. Their schemas then influence how they experience and interact in the world.[7]

Bandura's Social Learning Theory of Gender Development

Albert Bandura, a psychologist, developed a Social Learning Theory of Gender Development in 1999. His theory states that there are three basic processes in gender development: children model others' gender–related behavior, children experience consequences for their gender–related characteristics, and children are directly taught about gender roles. In other words, children develop their gender identity by being reinforced for gender–typed behavior and being punished for cross–gender–typed behavior.[8]

Veale's Identity Defense Model of Gender Variance

Jaimie Veale, a transgender psychologist, created an Identity–defense Model of Gender Variance in 2010. The model explains how gender–variance is manifested in individuals and takes into account the additional factors of sexual orientation and cross–gender eroticism. The model consists of two stages in development of gender–variant identity: 1) biological factors and early childhood influences determine to what degree gender–variant identity develops, and 2) additional personality and environmental factors determine whether defense mechanisms are used to repress gender–variance. The degree to which the defense mechanisms are used determine whether an individual identifies as transsexual, transgender, cross–dresser, or drag artist.[9]

Diamond's Biased–interaction Theory of Gender Development

Biopsychosocial theories of gender development state that gender identity is created by many factors, including biology, psychological experiences, and social interactions. One such theory was created by Milton Diamond, professor and director of the Pacific Center for Sex and Society at the University of Hawaii, in 2006. His theory, Biased–interaction Theory of Gender Development, states that early biological factors (such as genetics and/or fetal hormones) predispose an individual's preferences and aversions. Gender identity is subsequently formed by the individual's comparison of others based on them being alike or different.[10]

For more in depth reading on theories of gender development, refer to Blakemore, Berenbaum, and Liben's book, *Gender Development.*[11]

> "As long as we live within a heterosexist system that decrees that there are only two genders and therefore only one sexual orientation–the attraction between these two opposites–we're going to lose out... If [gender is] socially constructed, then why can't there be more than two?"
>
> –*Will Roscoe*

A Question of Nature or Nurture?
An Account of David Reimer

David Reimer was born an identical twin boy in 1965. While still an infant, his penis was accidentally destroyed in a surgical procedure. After a consultation with psychologist John Money, considered an "expert" in gender identity, the family agreed to reassign David to be raised as a female named Brenda. To accomplish this, Brenda underwent surgical, hormonal, and psychological treatments. Money's theory was that nurture, not nature, is what determines gender identity and sexual orientation. So Brenda became his experiment to prove his theory.

Brenda had ongoing annual visits with Money. Until Brenda was 11, Money reported that her reassignment was successful and evidence that gender identity is primarily learned. However, Money wasn't reporting the truth. Later it was revealed that David had felt that he was not a girl beginning at age 2 and displayed pronounced masculine behavior. At age 15, he was finally told the truth and decided to transition back to male, which involved multiple operations to remove breasts and create a penis and testicles as well as regular testosterone injections.

This "experiment" in gender identity destroyed an entire family. The mother attempted suicide, the father became an alcoholic, David's twin suffered depression and eventually died of an overdose of anti-depressants two years before David committed suicide by shooting himself with a sawed off shotgun at the age of 38.

David went public with his story to help discourage similar medical practices that are performed routinely on intersex babies. In addition, John Colapinto wrote about Reimer's story in his book *As Nature Made Him: The Boy Who Was Raised as a Girl.*[12]

So, it seems that what forms gender identity is far deeper than nurture. Nature has a big part in the formation and I believe, our soul's spiritual journey plays an even bigger part. However, sadly, the spiritual component is something that never gets addressed in our Western culture.

STATUS OF NON–CONFORMING GENDER AND SEXUAL IDENTITY IN THE COMMUNITY

Psychotherapy to "convert or cure" transsexuality is generally ineffective. The American Medical Association Committee on Human Sexuality (1972) stated that therapists have a zero success rate in "curing Gender Identity Disorder" or by changing the transgender individual's perceived gender to match their birth–assigned sex.[13] Aversion therapy, conversion therapy, psychotropic medications, hormone treatments consistent with the individual's assigned sex at birth, electroconvulsive therapy, and hypnosis are ineffective. The same is true when trying to change an individual's sexual orientation.[14]

Gender identity diversity and intersex conditions are still classified as a "medical or psychological disorders" in two classification systems listed below. Homosexuality as a psychological disorder was removed from DSM–II in 1973.

The *International Classification of Diseases* (ICD) [15] sponsored by the UN's World Health Organization. The latest edition, *ICD–10 (1990)*, lists the following gender "disorders":

F64.0 Transsexualism
F64.1 Dual–role transvestism
F64.2 Gender identity disorder of childhood
F64.8 Other gender identity disorders
F64.9 Gender identity disorder, unspecified
Q50–Q56 Congenital malformations of genital organs (intersex)

The *Diagnostic and Statistical Manual of Mental Disorders* (DSM) [16] sponsored by the American Psychiatric Association. The latest edition, *DSM–V (2013)*, lists the following gender "disorders":

302.6 Gender Dysphoria in children
302.85 Gender Dysphoria in adolescents and adults

Many people, including me, support declassification of gender identity disorders altogether because this diagnosis pathologizes non–conforming gender variances, reinforces the binary model of gender, and stigmatizes gender–nonconforming individuals.

The anxiety, depression, and suicide rate of gender non–conforming individuals suggests that gender identity is not a choice and is not changeable. In addition the pressure to conform by families, society, and medical professionals marginalizes, stigmatizes, and ostracizes individuals that don't fit the traditional binary gender mold.

The following statistics on individuals with non–conforming gender identity individuals are shocking. I believe that as long as individuals with alternative gender and sexual identities are not accepted by the majority in a social culture, these levels of sad statistics will continue.

Victims of Violence

- The Human Rights Council (HRC) estimates that 1 of every 1,000 homicides in the US is an anti–transgender hate crime.[17]
- Trans* individuals are 1,000 times more likely to be murdered than cis individuals.[18]
- One quarter of the trans* population are victims of assault.[18]
- One half of the trans* population are victims of rape.[18]

Suicide

- 50 percent of trans* individuals attempt suicide by the age of 20.[19]

Homelessness

- 19 percent of trans* individuals have experienced homelessness.[20]
- 40 percent of all homeless youth are transgender.[21]

Medical Care

- 19 percent of trans* individuals have been refused medical care because of their gender identity.[22]
- 28 percent of trans* individuals reported being verbally harassed in a medical setting.[22]

Employment

- 26 percent of trans* individuals have been fired because of their gender identity.[23]
- 97 percent of trans* individuals have been harassed while on the job.[23]

Education

- 59 percent of gender non–conforming students experienced verbal harrassment because of their gender expression.[24]
- 80 percent of trans* students felt unsafe at school because of their gender expression.[24]

Legal

- 41 percent of trans* individuals cannot change their gender on their IDs.[20]
- 30 percent of trans* women have been incarcerated.[24]

Social

- 57 percent of trans* individuals have experienced rejection by their families.[20]
- 26 percent trans* individuals have used alcohol and drugs to cope with the impacts of discrimination.[22]
- 94 percent of trans* individuals report an improvement in their quality of life due to transitioning.[24]

There is progress towards freedom of gender expression in some countries. In 2002, the British government stated that transsexualism is not a mental illness. In 2009, the French government declared that transsexual gender identity is no longer classified as a psychiatric condition. In 2010, the commissioner for human rights for the Council of Europe opposed the mental disorder classification of transgender individuals and removed the requirement for surgical sterilization to change legal status of gender.

In Germany, India, Pakistan, Bangladesh, and Nepal, third gender status has been legalized for passports and legal status. Australia and New Zealand issue Gender "X" passports. Gender "X" is an alternative classification for individuals who identify as non–gender, bi–gender, or intersex. There is currently a motion in the UK to issue Gender "X" passports as well. In 2013, Germany was the first country to allow parents to leave the gender box on birth certificates blank. The aim of this law is to prevent "normalization" surgeries being performed on intersex children.

Observation Point

I don't know the origin of using "Gender X" to represent genders other than male and female. It seems more logical to call this category "Gender Z" since the chromosomes that determine female and male sex are labeled as "X" and "Y".

As of the writing of this book, engaging in homosexual acts is a crime or capital offense in 77 countries. However, over twenty countries have now legalized same–sex marriage. In the United States, President Obama signed an executive order in 2014 that ends discrimination against LGBT* individuals in the federal work force. In addition, Medicare and federal insurance policies now cover payment for genital reassignment surgery. California has become the first state to allow transgender students to choose which restrooms and locker rooms to use and which sport teams to join based on their gender identity. It is now illegal to use the defense called "gay panic" and "trans* panic" in cases of hate crimes against LGBT* individuals in California. Gay and trans* panic occurs when a defendant claims that they acted in a state of violent temporary insanity because the victim was LGB or T.

In 2006, a group of international human rights experts met in Yogyakarta, Indonesia to outline a set of principles for gender identity and sexual orientation. The result, the *Yogyakarta Principles on the Application of International Human Rights Law in Relation to Sexual Orientation and Gender Identity*, is a universal guide to human rights containing 29 principles. It states that:

> *"Persons of diverse sexual orientation and gender identities shall enjoy legal capacity in all aspects of life. Each person's self–defined sexual orientation and gender identity is integral to their personality and is one of the most basic aspects of self–determination, dignity and freedom." (Principle 3)* [25]

> *"A person's sexual orientation and gender identity are not, in and of themselves, medical conditions and are not to be treated, cured or suppressed [as such]." (Principle 18)* [25]

Sex Role Reversal in Animals

In sex-role reversal in animals the male will look after the young and some females will defend the territory. Seahorses are the most interesting example because the males become pregnant and carry the babies.

Examples:

- African Cichlid Fish
- Black-Chinned Tilapia
- Butterflies
- Buttonquail (bird)
- Coucals (bird)
- Frogs & Toads
- Green Acouchi (rodent)
- Jacana (bird)
- Pipefish
- Seahorses
- Spotted Sandpiper
- Ten-spined Stickleback
- Wilson's Phalarope
- Zebra Finch

NOTES:

[1] Conway, Lynn. "Drop the Barbie: Ken Zucker's Reparatist Treatment of Gender–variant Children." Last modified April 5, 2007. http://ai.eecs.umich.edu/people/conway/TS/News/Drop%20the%20Barbie.htm

[2] Culp–Ressler, Tara. "Forcing Kids to Stick to Gender Roles Can Actually Be Harmful to Their Health." Last updated August, 2014. http://thinkprogress.org/health/2014/08/07/3468380/gender-roles-health-risks/ http://www2.warwick.ac.uk/fac/soc/sociology/staff/academicstaff/mariadomarpereira/

[3] Bem, Daryl J. "Exotic Becomes Erotic: A Developmental Theory of Sexual Orientation." *Psychological Review*, 1996, Vol. 103, No. 2. http://dbem.ws/Exotic%20Becomes%20Erotic.pdf

[4] Holmes, William C. "Sexual Abuse of Boys". *The Journal of the American Medical Association,* 280, December, 1998.

[5] Tomeo, M.E. and D.L. Templer. "Comparative Data of Childhood Adolescence Molestation in Heterosexual and Homosexual Persons". *Archives of Sexual Behavior,* 30 (5) 2001.

[6] Maccody, E. E. ed. *The Development of Sex Differences.* Kohlberg, L. "A Cognitive–developmental analysis of Children's Sex–role Concepts and Attitudes." Stanford University Press, 1966.

Craddock, Burton. "Kohlberg's Cognitive–Developmental Theory." 2002. http://human-development.tripod.com/sexrole/kohlberg.htm

[7] Bem, Sandra L. "Gender Schema Theory: A Cognitive Account of Sex Typing". *Psychological Review, 88,* 1981.

Bem, Sandra L "Gender Schema Theory and Its Implications for Child Development: Raising Gender–aschematic Children in a Gender–schematic Society". *Signs, 8,* 1983.

[8] Bandura, Albert and Kay Bussey. "Social Cognitive Theory of Gender Development and Differentiation." *Psychological Review*, 106, 1999. http://www.uky.edu/~eushe2/Bandura/Bandura1999PR.pdf

Bandura, A. "Social Cognitive Theory: An Agentic Perspective." *Annual Review of Psychology,* 52, 2001.

[9] Veale, J. F., Lomax, T. C., and Clarke, D. E. "The Identity–defense Model of Gender–variance Development." *International Journal of Transgenderism*, 12, 2010. http://www.academia.edu/202152/The_Identity-Defence_Model_of_Gender-Variance_Development

[10] Diamond, Milton. "Biased–interaction Theory of Psychosexual Development: How Does One Know if One is Male or Female?" *Sex Roles,* 55, 2006.

de Vries, Annelou, Baudewijntje P. C. Kreukels, Thomas D. Steensma, and Jenifer K. McGuire. "Gender Identity Development: A Biopsychosocial Perspective." 2013. http://link.springer.com/chapter/10.1007/978-1-4614-7441-8_3

[11] Blakemore, Judith Owen, Sheri Berenbaum, and Lynn Liben. *Gender Development*. Psychology Press, 2009.

[12] Colapinto, John. *As Nature Made Him: The Boy Who Was Raised as a Girl.* Harper Perennial, 2006.

[13] The American Medical Association Committee on Human Sexuality. "Human Sexuality" Chicago, 1972.

[14] Herek, Gregory. Attempts To Change Sexual Orientation" http://psychology.ucdavis.edu/faculty_sites/rainbow/html/facts_changing.html

[15] World Health Organization. *The ICD–10 Classification of Mental and Behavioural Disorders: Clinical Descriptions and Diagnostic Guidelines.* World Health Organization, 1992. ICD–10 can also be accessed on line at http://apps.who.int/classifications/icd10/browse/2010/en

[16] American Psychiatric Association. *Diagnostic and Statistical Manual of Mental Disorders, 5th Edition: DSM–5.* American Psychiatric Publishing, 2013. DSM–V can also be accessed on line at http://www.dsm5.org/Pages/Default.aspx

[17] Marzullo, Michelle A. and Alyn J. Libman. *"Hate Crimes and Violence against LGBT People."* Last modified May 2009. http://www.hrc.org/resources/entry/hate-crimes-and-violence-against-lgbt-people

[18] *Transadvocate.com.* http://www.transadvocate.com/about-2/graphics

[19] *Tglynnsplace.com.* "Transgender Suicide." Last updated February 22, 2012. http://tglynnsplace.com/suicide.htm

[20] *Transequality.org.* http://transequality.org/Resources/index.html

[21] Florida International University Division of Student Affairs.

[22] Grant, Jaime M., Lisa A. Mottet, Justin Tanis, Jody L. Herman, Jack Harrison, and Mara Keisling. "National Transgender Discrimination Survey Report on Health and Health Care." Last modified October 2010.

[23] 2008–2009 National Transgender Discrimination Survey by the Task Force and the National Center for Transgender Equality.

[24] Trans Student Equality Resources. "Infographics." http://transstudent.org/graphics

[25] *Yogyakartaprinciples.org.* "The YogyaKarta Principles." Last modified March 2007. www.yogyakartaprinciples.org/principles_en.htm

CHAPTER 4:
SPIRITUALITY OF GENDER AND SEXUAL IDENTITY
The Forces of the Spirit World

ALCHEMICAL UNION OF MALE & FEMALE

This image of the divine Male and divine Female, conjoined as one being, represents non-duality. This is the alchemical symbol for the union of Male and Female. The Logos (soul) deconstructs into male and female on the physical plane. The 6-pointed star represents the reconstruction of Male and Female into an Androgyne.

SPIRITUAL THEORIES OF GENDER AND SEXUAL IDENTITY DETERMINATION

In the two previous chapters we have examined the physical/biological and the psychological/sociological influences on the creation of gender and sexual identities. In this chapter we will look at a third aspect which is comprised of the influences of spirit. The spiritual aspect is largely overlooked in Western medicine and psychology. It is a subject typically left to religious institutions. In Western culture there is a distinct separation of the body, mind, and soul. However, an individual's body, mind, and soul cannot be separated from one another. All three parts are required in order for the individual to live. I will present different aspects of spiritual influences from a neutral position that strives to be non–denominational, non–judgmental, and non–dogmatic.

VIEWPOINTS OF MAJOR RELIGIOUS FAITHS

First, I will examine various viewpoints on alternative gender and sexual identities that the major religious faiths of the world have. Most traditional religious organizations have a long history of ostracizing and persecuting individuals with alternative gender and sexual identities. Fundamental and orthodox organizations usually give LGBT* individuals one of two options: 1) repent and convert to heterosexuality or 2) repress and live a chaste life. These mainstream religious faiths often preach compassion and inclusion but practice oppression and exclusion. However, some faiths, especially the more progressive or liberal branches, have begun to accept individuals with alternative gender and sexual identities.

Below is a summary of various religious faiths and their perspective on individuals with alternative gender and sexual identities. These perspectives are a generalized view of the faith as a whole. The individual congregations of each faith may vary greatly. In addition, most faiths have outreach organizations that support the LGBT* community. For the latest information on faith perspectives concerning LGBT* individuals, go to: www.hrc.org/resources/category/religion-faith.

Beliefs amongst religious faiths that are in support of alternative gender and sexual identities range from:

- Welcoming and supporting LGBT* individuals.
- Performing and blessing LGBT* marriages.
- Ordaining LGBT* individuals.
- Providing gender–neutral language in religious ceremonies.

Beliefs amongst religious faiths that do not support alternative gender and sexual identities range from:

- Discouraging homosexual activity.
- Loving the sinner but hating homosexual actions.
- Forbidding same–sex sexual or sex/gender reassignment practices.
- Actively opposing social acceptance of LGBT* individuals.
- Proscribing imprisonment or execution of LGBT* individuals.
- Classifying gender based on biological sex not an individual's self–perception or identity.

Below is a general overview of the beliefs for the world's major religious faiths. They usually fall into one of three categories:

- **Inclusive** – Welcome and support LGBT* individuals. Perform LGBT* marriages. Allow LGBT* individuals to serve as clergy.
- **Inclusive with Conditions** – Welcome LGBT* individuals as long as they abide by the conditions outlined, usually involving celibacy.
- **Exclusive** – Condemn LGBT* individuals. Condemnation may range from ostracism, imprisonment, punishment, to death.

Because of the lack of acceptance by many traditional religious faiths, many LGBT* individuals turn to alternative spiritual paths, such as shamanism and Goddess religions. Pagan faiths, such as Wicca and Voudou, are generally very inclusive of LGBT* individuals.

The Abrahamic religions are Judaism, Christianity, and Islam. They generally consider sodomy to be a sin based on Bible passages in Leviticus:

> *"Thou shalt not lie with mankind, as with womankind: it is abomination." –Leviticus 18:22 (Bible KJV, Public Domain)*

> *"If a man also lie with mankind, as he lieth with a woman, both of them have committed an abomination: they shall surely be put to death; their blood shall be upon them." – Leviticus 18:22 (Bible KJV, Public Domain)*

However, each denomination varies in their general policy on LGBT* individuals. According to most interpretations of the Bible, God created only two sexes, separate and distinct. Most Christian fundamentalists believe that non–conforming gender and sexual identities are chosen and therefore can be changed through prayer, therapy and/or being "saved". However, there is one Bible verse that seems to support transsexuality:

> *"For there are some eunuchs, which were so born from their mother's womb: and there are some eunuchs, which were made eunuchs of men: and there be eunuchs, which have made themselves eunuchs for the kingdom of heaven's sake. He that is able to receive it, let him receive it." –Matthew 19:12 (Bible KJV, Public Domain)*

The following Abrahamic faiths have become relatively inclusive:

- **Episcopal**
- **Lutheran**
- **Metropolitan Community Church**
- **Conservative, Reform, and Reconstructionist Judaism**

- **Religious Science**
- **Religious Society of Friends (Quaker)**
- **Unitarian Universalist Association**
- **United Church of Christ**
- **Unity**

The following Abrahamic faiths are exclusive:

- **Church of God in Christ**
- **Church of the Nazarene**
- **Methodist** (However they do ordain trans* individuals.)
- **Orthodox Judaism**
- **Pentecostal**
- **Seventh Day Adventist**
- **Baptist**
- **Islam** – Islamic law equates same–sex intercourse to fornication between unmarried heterosexual couples, which is punishable by death. Some Islamic countries enforce this law, others punish through imprisonment, and yet others have legalized same–sex intercourse. Sex/gender reassignment surgery is acceptable under Islamic law. Iran has the highest rate of execution for homosexuality but also the highest rate of sex/gender reassignment operations than any other nation in the world except for Thailand. The Iranian government provides up to half the cost for a sex/gender change.

The following Abrahamic faiths seem to be moving from exclusive to a more inclusive policy:

- **Church of the Latter Day Saints** (Mormon) – Policy has been changed from excommunicating LGB individuals to allowing church participation as long as they are celibate.
- **Church of Scientology –** Policy is now changing to encourage congregants to not judge individuals' private lives.

- **Presbyterian** – LGBT* individuals are still banned from ordination however LGBT* holy union ceremonies are blessed but not marriages.
- **Roman Catholic Church** – LGB individuals are welcome as long as they are celibate. Recently, Pope Francis has begun calling for a change in policy saying gay people should not be marginalized. Only birth assigned sex is valid in marriage and ordination.

The Eastern religions include:

- **Baha'i** – All unmarried individuals must abstain from sex and marriage can only be between one man and one woman. Transgender individuals are permitted to marry after undergoing sex/gender reassignment surgery.
- **Buddhism** – Sexual orientation is not directly referred to in the Buddhist sacred texts or teachings however sexual activity might be considered misconduct under the third of the Five Buddhist Precepts, which states that sexual misconduct that is harmful to self or others should be avoided. How is the definition of sexual misconduct interpreted? Some believe that it includes alternative sexual orientation.
  - *Liberal Buddhists* – Support all sexual orientations and consider marriage as a personal statement.
  - *Thai Buddhists* – Homosexuality and transsexuality is a karmic consequence of previous heterosexual misconduct.
  - *Tibetan Buddhists* – The Dalai Lama believes that sexual misconduct includes any sex that is not penis–vagina intercourse for the purpose of procreation. However, he also supports human rights for all, regardless of sexual orientation.
  - *Zen Buddhists* – There is no distinction between same–sex and opposite–sex relationships.

  The Buddhist term for LGBT*I individuals is "*pandaka*". Intersex individuals are called "*ubhatovyanjañaka*".

- **Confucianism** – Has little focus on sexuality.
- **Hinduism** – Hinduism is a conundrum. While Hindu sacred texts do not promote nor condemn homosexuality, LGBT* issues remain taboo subjects. The *Kama Sutra* portrays many homosexual as well as heterosexual activities. But in the 1800s, British colonial rulers made homosexuality illegal. In 2009, homosexuality was decriminalized in India. Hinduism has many deities that change gender or are gender ambiguous. Hindu texts state that some individuals are born with mixed male and female natures. Indian third gender individuals and androgynous deities are discussed in Chapter 10.
- **Sikhism** – Supports homosexuality. Since the soul is considered genderless, LBGT marriage may be acceptable.
- **Taoism** – Does not have a single official position however some Taoist schools consider homosexuality as a form of sexual misconduct.
- **Zoroastrianism** – Orthodox members consider male homosexuality as a form of demon worship. Reform members believe that homosexuality is not prohibited by the religious texts.

Fluid Spiritual Identity

Fluidity is not just applicable to gender and sexuality. Any personal identity can be fluid. My spiritual identity is fluid. I was brought up Protestant, but in high school announced to my mother that I was leaving the church. She said, "Oh, you'll be back." She turned out to be partially right. Even though I did not return to Christianity, I did turn to other forms of spirituality.

Just prior to my gender transition, in my late 20s, I converted to Judaism. I was living with an Orthodox girlfriend at the time and loved the Jewish theology and ceremony. After my gender transition I began studying shamanism. It was then that I felt I had finally "come home" spiritually. I converted to paganism, where I feel connected to Spirit at all times. My daily life is now rich with intent, gratitude, ceremony, and purpose.

THE HERMETIC VIEWPOINT

The term "hermetic" is derived from the name of the Greek god, Hermes. "Hermeticism" is a religious and philosophical tradition based upon the writings of Hermes Trismegistus, who was a wise pagan prophet. His writings, such as *The Emerald Tablet of Hermes*[1], greatly influenced Western esoteric traditions.

In *The Kybalion: A Study of the Hermetic Philosophy of Ancient Egypt and Greece*, the authors known as "The Three Initiates" discuss the seven Hermetic principles. Of these the following two are related to gender and sexuality:

The 4th Principle: Polarity

> "*Everything is Dual; everything has poles; everything has its pair of opposites; like and unlike are the same; opposites are identical in nature, but different in degree; extremes meet; all truths are but half-truths; all paradoxes may be reconciled.*"[2]

This principle positively supports the spectra of gender and sexual identities. All points on the spectra are not separate and different but actually different degrees or variations of the same entity. We become holistic and balanced by experiencing all points on the spectra. If we judge, deny, or ostracize others at specific points on the spectra, we are in fact, condemning a part of our own self that may have already existed or will exist in the future, on these same points.

The 7th Principle: Gender

> "*Gender is in everything; everything has its Masculine and Feminine Principles; Gender manifests on all planes.*"[2]

Sex is a material manifestation of gender on the physical plane. Gender is a consciousness that can reside beyond the physical plane. The word "gender" is derived from Latin and means "to beget; to procreate; to generate; to create; to produce." This principle can be interpreted to mean the principle of gender is invoked whenever anything is created on any plane.

THE ALCHEMIST VIEWPOINT

Alchemy is a medieval chemical philosophy that incorporates two basic goals:

1. The transmutation of base metals into gold.
2. The discovery of the elixir of longevity.

But the magical power of transmutation in alchemy is also a metaphor for the transformation of consciousness where emotional debris (lead) is transformed into self–realization (gold).

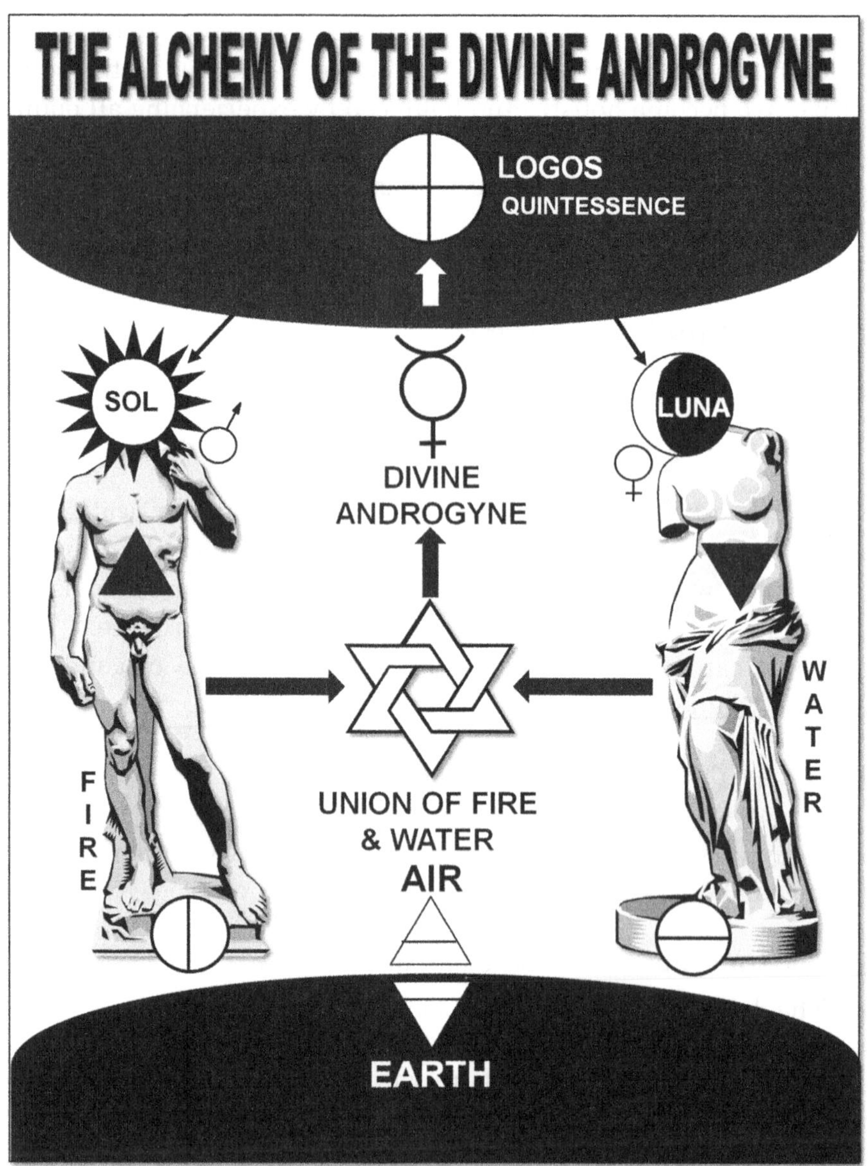

Alchemy also has a concept of the Divine Androgyne. The above diagram portrays the cycle of life which is similar to the cycle of reincarnation shown in Chapter 9. The Logos (Fifth Dimension) deconstructs into Male and Female on Earth (Third Dimension). Through the union in a Sacred Marriage, Male and Female are reconstructed as the birth of the Divine Androgyne who then ascends in Consciousness, returning to the Logos in the

Fifth Dimension. There are at least two ways to create this "Sacred Marriage". One is through the regular marriage or partnership of a male-energied individual and a female-energied individual. Another way is through personal gender identity that is equally balanced with male and female energy.

So Source/Creator, through the process of involution, emanates to the physical world by populating it with humans that are pieces of Its soul–consciousness. It is then the humans' mission, in a process of evolution, to make their way back to the Source/Creator. Ascension requires the uniting of the male and female into an androgynous being.

> "Alchemy is a bridge between Earth and Heaven, matter and spirit, the solid and the fluid, the visible and the invisible, bringing the horizontal and the vertical together."
>
> *–J. Ramsay*
>
> To the above quote I would add that alchemy is also a bridge between the male and female.

MORE ABOUT THE ANDROGYNE

An Androgyne possesses feminine and masculine traits equally and simultaneously, or neither. It is a combination of the ancient Greek words "andro" for "man" and "gyne" for "woman".

In *The Complete Idiot's Guide to Alchemy,* Dennis William Hauck describes the sacred marriage as:

> *"A union is achieved through coitus or the sexual union of Sol and Luna. Their lovemaking symbolizes the mystical union of opposites. The bride represents the soul or incarnate self, and the bridegroom represents the spirit or disincarnate self. The product of this sacred marriage, the child of Sol and Luna, is a new archetype known as the Divine Child or Divine Androgyne. This is the same*

archetype as the alchemical hermaphrodite or Rebis (the double thing)."[3]

This alchemical concept appears in many different cultures and religious teachings. The *Apocrypha,* a collection of writings which were published in the original King James Bible but subsequently removed, says:

> *"For the Lord Himself, having been asked by someone when His kingdom should come, said, 'When the two shall be one, and the outside as the inside, and the male with the female.'"*[4]

The *Vedanta,* an ancient Indian sacred text, says:

> *"Brahman fell asunder into man and wife, and that in the striving of these sundered poles for reunion, worlds were put forth. When the two again become one, the male with the female, there ensues the night of Brahm, ending the cycle of manifestation."*[5]

The Androgyne is a symbol of holistic perfection and plays a part in the creation myths of numerous cultures.

In her book, *Androgyny*[6], June Singer says that the *kundalini* experience brings to consciousness the idea of unity within one's self, a unity of energy and matter, the feminine and the masculine, the physical and the spiritual.

In acupuncture, the rebalancing of the *yin* (female) and the *yang* (male) is what restores health. Balanced interplay between an individual's male and female components as a necessity to well–being has been a consistent, almost universal theme throughout history.

In *The Healing Mind,* Dr. Irving Oyle says:

> *"Ease, as opposed to disease, may be seen as a state of harmonious equilibrium between the two equipotent, autonomous, cerebral hemispheres, one of which is conscious (sun, yang, male), and one of which is*

subconscious (moon, yin, female). If contact is established between the two hemispheres (the alchemical mystical marriage), healing energy (the panacea) is released."[7]

Carl Jung, a psychiatrist and philosopher, referred to the inner man within a woman's psyche as the *animus* and the inner woman inside a man's psyche as the *anima*. This manifests in the physical world as the two sides of the human brain: the brain's right hemisphere, which controls the left side of the body, is considered masculine and the brain's left hemisphere, which controls the right side of the body, is considered feminine.

In *Great Dialogues of Plato*[8], W.H.D. Rouse translates from Plato the following story that I have paraphrased: Originally there were three sexes; male, female, and both (androgynes). The shape of each was round with four arms, four legs, two sets of genitalia, and one head with two faces and four ears. The male was born of the sun, the female of the earth, and the androgyne of the moon. Zeus wanted to make them weaker so he sliced them through the middle, resulting in two beings each with two legs. The halves began dying, though, from missing their other half. If one of the halves died, the remaining half would then hunt for another half. Zeus moved their genitalia to the front so that if a man–half met a woman–half, they might reproduce the race. All those who were originally androgynous seek their other halves through a heterosexual relationship. All those who were originally female remain attracted to women. All those originally male remain attracted to men. In other words, souls are seeking their other half.

In *I Am All over That*[9], Shirley MacLaine, describes her memories of being a Lemurian in a past incarnation with both male and female genitalia and both female and male energetic vibrations. Some of them, including her, decided to divide the female and male vibrations so as to see them more objectively. During the division, her soul entered the female side of her separated body and her soul mate entered the male side. From then on she has been looking for her other half.

In *Contemporary Spirituality for an Evolving World,* Nicolya

Christi describes how a Soul, when first coming to Earth, was a single androgynous being. The connection to Creator/Source was lost as the descent from spirit into matter progressed. In its place, Ego was born and the androgyne split into two halves, one male and one female. Since then, the purpose of reincarnation is for souls to reunite with their twins. She says:

> *"The balance of male and female energies within the individual is a prerequisite, alongside one's capacity for self–actualization, to magnetize a lasting union, and in rare cases reunion with the lost twin from the days of the androgynous Self."*[10]

She believes that after having lived in patriarchal and matriarchal societies we are moving into an epoch of neither male nor female domination. She states:

> *"Instead, male and female will be together, side by side as equals to inspire, co–create, and collaborate for the highest good of humanity."*[10]

THE KABBALISTIC VIEWPOINT

The study of Kabbalah supports the principle that masculine and feminine energy exists in everything and evolution of the soul involves balancing the two energies. In *The Experience of Kabbalah*[11], Michael Laitman discusses the gender of the soul. He says that the higher up the evolutionary ladder an entity exists, the more sex is divided. All souls originated from an androgynous First Man but divided into masculine and feminine souls when they separated. An individual alternates between the masculine soul and the feminine soul as they climb the spiritual ladder.

Kabbalists teach that Source/Creator is neither male nor female but only humans seek this balance in a world of duality. Similar to other creation stories, in Judaism, the first human, Adam Kadmon, was androgynous, created as a single two–faced body but was split into two, divided by male and female. A female was created from Adam's side (not his rib) when Adam was split in half. This separated soul is united through marriage and the physical joining through making love, especially on the Sabbath, as a way to honor and merge with Source/Creator. So, symbolically, just as in alchemy, the masculine and feminine energies unite to give birth to the next levels of the spiritual worlds on the Tree of Life.

"So God created man in his image, in the image of God created he him; male and female [God] created them both."

–Genesis 1:27 (Bible KJV, Public Domain)

"As they set out from their place above, each soul is male and female as one. Only as they descend to this world do they part, each to its own side. And then it is the One Above who unites them again. This is His exclusive domain, for He alone knows which soul belongs to which and how they must reunite."

–Rabbi Shimon bar Yochai, Zohar, Book I, 85b

CHANNELED ENTITY VIEWPOINTS

Channeling is a process of an individual receiving and relaying information from an outside entity while in an altered state of consciousness. Channeled entities can include spirits, ancestors, angels, ascended masters, and other–dimensional beings. The following passages are from very well–known entities via their channelers. These entities are considered to be higher–dimensional beings. Below I present some of the teachings about gender and sexuality that these higher spiritual beings have passed to incarnated souls on Earth.

Seth Channeled by Jane Roberts

Seth is an entity who was channeled by Jane Roberts. In *The Nature of the Psyche*, Seth says:

"Physically speaking, you would have no males or females unless first you had individuals. You are each individuals first of all, then after this, you are individuals of a specific sex, biologically speaking. You have categorized human abilities so that it seems that you are men or women... primarily, and persons secondarily. Your personhood exists first, however. Your individuality gives meaning to your sex, and not the other way around. Except for the fact that males could not bear children, the abilities of the sexes were interchangeable."[12]

In *Seth Speaks*, Seth says that:

"Both sexes must be taken on, and the various characteristics developed. This does not mean that an equal number of male and female lives must be lived. Some find it far easier to develop as one sex or the other, and will need more opportunities for experience as the sex with which they experience difficulty."[13]

Seth continues, saying:

"The inner ego is the source of all gender and sexual orientation, a bank from which sexual affiliations are drawn. Since physical manifestation often includes hundreds of simultaneous lifetimes there are many permutations of gender, including male, female, and in between. As such, sexual orientation for each outer ego includes the potential for heterosexual, bisexual, homosexual, and other choices. This means that all outer egos are inherently bisexual by design to some degree."[13]

Seth also says that:

"If a personality believes that it is doing a poor job in a male life, it may activate the anima's qualities, taking on the characteristics of a past female existence in which it handled itself well. Reversing the picture, the same can

happen to a woman. On the other hand, if the personality finds that it has so over–identified with its present sex that its individuality is deeply threatened, then it may also bring to the fore the opposite picture, going so far as to identify again with a past personality of the opposite sex.” 13

Kryon Channeled by Lee Carroll

Kryon is an entity channeled by Lee Carroll. Kyron says that just as society's views on interracial marriage have changed over the past 30 years, so will the view of homosexuality change within the next two generations. In *Kryon Book VI*, Kyron says:

“Your sexual attributes are simply chemistry and setups within your DNA. They are given by agreement as gifts for you to experience in this life. Look on them in this fashion, and be comfortable with that fact that you are a perfect spiritual creation under Source/Creator, loved beyond measure, just like all humans.”[14]

Kyron continues with:

“Sexual energy is so related to so many other things that create lessons, drama, and turmoil. But the more it is discovered within a spiritual framework instead of a solely biological one, the more those around will change what they have perceived it to be.”[15]

In another passage he says:

“Old souls, let me tell you something. If you are old enough you have been everything. You have been both genders. All of you have been between genders, and that means that all of you have had gender switches.”

Kyron goes on to say that after dozens of lifetimes as one gender it will be time to switch. This switch will take approximately three lifetimes of gender confusion while adjusting. He says it is actually not confusion but:

> *"...absolutely normal, yet society often will see it as abnormal."*[16]

Michael Channeled by Joya Pope and Shepherd Hoodwin

Michael is a group soul, a collective consciousness of 1050 essences. In *The World According to Michael,* Joya Pope relays what Michael says:

> *"An individual takes on a particular ratio of male to female energy for the cycle of lifetimes. The ratio has nothing to do with male or female bodies, though it may have to do with a preference for being one sex over the other. Female–energied people are often more comfortable in female bodies and may tend to take on many more lifetimes as a woman until the balancing act of the Old Soul period begins. Similarly, male–energied people are often easier in male bodies. Most people display a degree of balance of male to female energy."*[17]

In *The Journey of Your Soul,* Shepherd Hoodwin relays what Michael says about gender identity:

> *"Souls choose a body that gives them the best of the particular opportunities for which they are looking. ...Male and female energies are not separate, they are two ends of the same stick, opposite ways in which energy can move. A person's male/female energy ratio describes their tendencies of function rather than a static state."*[18]

Michael on sexual identity:

> *"The type of body we are used to and our male/female energy ratio can affect our sexuality as well. Souls high in male energy (over 70 percent) are more likely to emphasize*

> *heterosexuality in male lifetimes and be homosexual in female lifetimes. Souls high in female energy (over 65 percent) are more likely to emphasize heterosexuality in female lifetimes and be homosexual in male lifetimes, although less emphatically so, because the feminine is receptive; therefore, it can receive a soul of either gender who has high male energy. This does not suggest that women with high male energy and men with high female energy are likely to be gay. ...Couples often have complementary male/female energy ratios. Older souls can be bisexual because they remember many lifetimes as both male and female and therefore are not strongly identified with their current body, since the soul has no gender. Every soul will have at least one gay lifetime, since it is part of the curriculum of the physical plane.*"[18]

The Pleiadians Channeled by Barbara Marciniak

In *Path of Empowerment*, Barbara Marciniak relays wisdom from the Pleiadians, who are a collective energy from the Pleiades. The wisdom from the Pleiadians is:

> *"You are composed of layers of energy connected to a spiritual self that journeys into and out of many different realities. When you come to Earth, you adapt to a set of agreements, specifically accepting a body with a gender genital identity as a vehicle for experiencing physical reality. Your spiritual self naturally conforms to any particular time frame through the celestial imprint your body receives at birth, as well as to the mass belief system of your particular culture and the genetic belief system of your family and local community. Even though you have a prominent gender, you have both male and female vibrations within you: the left side of your body is feminine and ruled by the right brain, and the right side is masculine, ruled by the left brain. According to your biology, your genitals decree the identity you are learning*

how to become, although the degree of male or female energy will vary. There are no mistakes in biology, and no mistakes in who you are and the identity you have chosen. Each and every life you live is significantly interwoven with layers of purpose and plans that are connected in a much larger vista of reality. You have been both man and woman on your multidimensional journey through the human form, and even though you may not consciously recall your various identities, your personal timeline records are stored in various layers of the subconscious and unconscious minds. Sometimes bleed through talents and abilities will create more masculine–like qualities in a woman, and feminine characteristics in a man. Self–acceptance is not only an important key to understanding your identity; it is the sign of an awakening mind."[19]

The Hierarchy of Ascended Masters Channeled by Joshua David Stone

In *Ascension and Romantic Relationships*, Joshua David Stone has asked The Hierarchy, a group of ascended masters, their opinions on gay relationships. He says:

"The masters have said that they are in total support of gay marriages. The Hierarchy views us as souls in incarnation. They view each incarnation as an opportunity for growth, wherein the soul extensions and their monads come into a greater balance and unity with their own divine nature. This is done more commonly through the mating of soul extensions of opposite gender in order to balance the male/female polarities within each person and within the group body of the couple. However, this is not always the case, as sometimes two souls come into incarnation with a more fully balanced male/female polarity already operative within them."[20]

He continues:

> *"From the soul's perspective there is absolutely no judgment of gay or lesbian relationships. They are not sins as some traditional religious teachings would have you believe. All that matters is 'To thine own self be true.' As for homosexual marriages, the Hierarchy is very much in favor of our forming group bodies that are committed in love to one another. The Hierarchy finds that official ceremonies can be of enormous value because they anchor on the physical realm what has been created between the two upon the etheric, astral and mental realms. They feel that all couples, gay or straight, should have the freedom to decide their own paths."*[20]

WALK–INS

Adult onset of gender confusion could be a result of a cross–gender walk–in. Walk–ins are souls that enter into a Physical Body that is already an adult. In order to walk–in, the current soul must agree to walk–out. This agreement was made by the two souls prior to birth. The incoming soul agrees to take on the remaining life issues and karma of the exiting soul. It is not known how often walk–in experiences occur but I estimate that it is a relatively rare occurrence.

When a new soul replaces another in the same Physical Body, some of the programming from the original soul will always remain. The replacement process may take some time as the incoming and outgoing souls alternate in the body. Or the replacement process may happen instantaneously, which can happen if there is a traumatic incident such as an accident. Some walk–in experiences happen during near–death experiences. And some walk–ins are temporary situations because the original soul exits to complete a mission in another dimension, but eventually returns.

If an individual has just undergone a walk–in experience, they may feel the following:

- Speech problems
- Loss of coordination and memory
- Sudden interest in the spiritual realm
- Sudden strong sense of mission
- Sudden change in relationships with family and friends
- Sudden change in tastes, career, hobbies, and self–identity

In *Welcome to Planet Earth*, Hannah Beaconsfield, describes examples of how the walk–in phenomenon might benefit the soul. A female vehicle whose life theme is victimhood and powerlessness might walk–out allowing a masculine spirit to bring in a balance of assertiveness and empowerment. Conversely a male vehicle may have a life theme of developing intuitive skills. He might walk–out and allow a feminine spirit to come in bringing a deep level of sensitivity and empathy. She says:

> *"Cross–gender walking–in is not very common, but in some cases, it is useful. When the characteristics of the walk–out are already well integrated, the stepping in of a spirit that resonates the energy of the opposite gender is a natural progression in development. This has the effect of fulfilling a project that has been considered by the original occupant as his or her path of growth and expansion."*[21]

As a cross–gender walk–in steps in, the change in gender identity may take a period of time to integrate. Hannah Beaconsfield states that:

> *"The cross–gender spirit replacements who are going through adjustment might translate their conflicts into fears about proper behavior or projects to undertake. Or the period of adjustment might play out as confusions in sexual preference that were not present before."*[21]

STARSEEDS

An individual with non–conforming gender and sexual identities may be influenced by their past experiences as an entity on another planet, in another universe, or in another dimension.

A starseed is a soul that has lived on other planets or in other universes before incarnating on Earth. All of us are starseeds if we were to trace our soul's journey back towards its origination. However, some starseeds have come to Earth much more recently. Those that have fresh memories of their home planet, may feel quite alone and separate on Earth. Many starseeds have originated from more advanced civilizations and have volunteered for specific missions on Earth to be in service assisting others or to study Earthlings and report back home with their findings.

A starseed may have come from a planet where gender and sexual identity is far different than here on Earth. They may have inhabited hermaphroditic bodies or sexual attraction and union may have occurred telepathically. The memories of alternative identities and characteristics may be residing in the subconscious of a starseed individual newly born in an Earth body. These starseeds may have brought their gifts of non–conforming gender and sexual identities to share with the souls incarnated on Earth.

A starseed individual may have the following characteristics:

- They may feel lonely, isolated, and different than others. They may experience despair or depression often connected to the desire to return "home". They may question the ways of Earth and may feel like the black sheep of their Earth family. They may be perceived by others as different or aloof.
- They may have been advanced or gifted as a child. They may have a higher than average IQ and read avidly, drinking in knowledge.
- They may have had an imaginary childhood friend that spoke to them.

- They may have a sense of purpose or mission to fulfil, even though the details may be elusive. They may have a longing for something deeper in life.
- They may be receiving some form of communication from a higher source or off–planet entity.
- They may have an aversion to bright lighting, extreme hot or cold, pain, loud noises, violence, fighting, war, sexual joking, racial joking, foul language, mundane employment, repetitive tasks, and dead–end jobs. They may have a low tolerance for alcohol, medicines, drugs, and extreme male or female dominant religions.
- They may be artistic, sensitive, and possess higher consciousness. They may have noticeable gifts in the areas of healing, helping, channeling, and psychic sensitivities.
- They may have a deep interest in spirituality. They may experience paranormal and psychic experiences, prophetic dreams, visions, astral projection, encounters with star guides, UFOs, and mystical experiences.
- They may be fascinated with the stars, outer space, science fiction, and feel as though their home is out "there".
- They may have a deep connection with animals. They may be very empathic and may be able to read people, seeing beyond their facades.

A hybrid soul is a term for individuals with mixed incarnation origins. These souls have developed from genetically different–than–human forms before incarnating as humans on Earth. A hybrid soul has memories of incarnating in other planet worlds before coming to Earth.

In *Destiny of Souls*[22] and *Journey of Souls*[23], Michael Newton says that sometimes his hybrid soul clients confuse their early incarnations in other physical worlds with being on Earth. In this way, I believe it is possible that they can bring characteristics of non–conforming gender and sexual identities that were learned in other dimensions to their experiences of Earth incarnations.

TIME TRAVELERS

Time travelers, also known as chrononauts, are our souls 1,000 to 3,000 years in the future, returning to the present to assist ourselves in our spiritual growth. Some people believe crop circles are created by our future selves, who are returning to the present to relay important messages to us. Time travelers have mastered hyperspace travel between dimensions, and can move through walls and solid objects. They exist in the fifth dimension where they can observe us while remaining invisible. These time travelers could be coming back to aid us in the understanding of identity fluidity by modeling for us as they have already lived it in future lives.

PARALLEL LIVES

In *Destiny of Souls*[22] and *Journey of Souls*[23], Michael Newton explains how souls who come to Earth leave a portion of their energy (the soul or Higher Self) in the spirit world. The percentage of energy left in the fifth dimension can vary and is a decision the soul makes before incarnating. Any portion of the energy can replicate the whole identity. This is similar to the properties of holograms that will be discussed again in Chapter 6.

In this way it is possible for the soul to split during incarnation and live parallel lives. This is a huge energy drain, therefore it is not undertaken very often and is only undertaken by more advanced souls. The reason a soul would want to attempt this is to accelerate learning.

Bleed through occurs when some consciousness from one dimension is perceived from another dimension. In other words, if a soul were living parallel lives, it might be possible for some thoughts to flow through the veil. So theoretically, if a soul chose to have concurrent lives, one as a male and one as a female, some confusion could occur if feelings or thoughts were flowing between the parallel lives.

SPIRIT ATTACHMENTS

Spirit attachment is when an entity without a Physical Body attaches to another individual. The attaching entity gets permission from the host individual although it most likely is subconsciously given by the host. In this way, the individual is not consciously aware of the attachment but the relationship is symbiotic because both beings are benefiting in some way. Often these types of spirit attachments are loved ones or strangers that have not yet gone to the Light (Fifth Dimension). They are usually lost, scared, or confused.

Spirit possession is when an entity takes control of an individual's Physical Body. The entity feeds off the host's energy and tries to fulfil their personal agenda through the host's body. Individuals who abuse their body through risky or destructive actions, drink heavily or take recreational drugs, and frequent places where disembodied entities tend to congregate (such as bars, cemeteries, hospitals, or accident scenes), are especially vulnerable to spirit attachment and possession.

There are many types of spirit entities. Some of them have positive intention and support individuals (such as angels, allies, ancestors, power animals, and spirit guides). These will never try to exert their will on another individual because they know it is ethically wrong. They support an individual without having to attach to the body. Some spirits are neutral (such as devas, nature spirits, fairies, and elementals). Others have negative intentions (such as some ghosts, poltergeists, or disembodied "lost" and "fallen" spirits). They form a destructive relationship by using a soul's body as a host.

Spirit attachments can cause all types of symptoms, specifically feeding off of and draining the host's energy. If you have been to Western medical practitioners and they have ruled out physical dis–ease, then you may have at least one entity "on board". Here is a list of symptoms that might be a result of spirit attachment:

- New phobias or aversions
- New allergies, food cravings, or taste preferences
- New attitudes or prejudices
- Sudden onset of physical problems with no obvious cause
- Sudden weight gain especially after surgery or a traumatic event
- Sudden changes in behavior such as increased anger, depression and thoughts of suicide
- Sudden cravings for alcohol, cigarettes, drugs, etc. especially after surgery or a traumatic event
- Feelings of depersonalization or dissociation (not feeling like oneself)
- Low energy level
- Night terrors and nightmares
- Multiple personalities
- Hearing inner voices (usually negative)
- Unexplained or unusual negative emotions or thoughts
- A feeling of being watched or not being alone
- Use of the pronoun "we" when talking about "I"

In *Remarkable Healings,* Shakuntala Modi discusses earthbound spirit possession. She says that homosexuality may be induced in an individual by:

> *"An entity of the opposite sex [causing] confusion in their [the subject's] sexual identity especially when the possession occurred before puberty. A female spirit in a man may desire sex with a man, and this desire and attraction may in turn become the desire of the male host toward another male. The host may think he is a homosexual, when in fact he is only acting on the spirit's desire."*[24]

She says transsexualism may be:

"A possession by an entity of the opposite sex, who is unhappy being stuck in a wrong body, [and] may push the host to have a sex–change operation."[24]

And she says transvestitism may be:

"An entity of the opposite sex [that] can force the host to wear clothes of the opposite sex."[24]

Unfortunately, most of us were not educated about entities as we were growing up. Most people try to avoid the subject because of its unpleasantness and the fear that the unknown generates. However, the best way to deal with entities is to be completely informed and then to face them. They only have power over you if you give them permission to.

Awareness is the best defense! Being aware of and actively protecting yourself through intention is the best way to stay entity free. Each of us has control over our own personal space consisting of the physical and energetic bodies. When we are not feeling completely empowered we become susceptible to entities.

If you suspect you have an entity, it is recommended that you contact a professional who is trained in spirit attachment and removals. Professionals typically experienced in entity extractions are shamans and shamanic practitioners. Some hypnotherapists and psychotherapists are trained in spirit releasement therapy (SRT).

I am not advocating that individuals with alternative gender and sexual identities have any more occurrences of spirit attachments than any other individuals. Most individuals will know if their gender and sexual identity is their own because it has been there since early childhood. If, however, an individual has a sudden onset of change in gender or sexual identity and it is associated with other feelings of not "being one's self", then get a professional consultation about spirit attachments.

It is important that once you have all spirit attachments removed that you stay entity free. In order to do that, some personal work may be required. Entities are attracted to the energy vibrations that they themselves vibrate at. The higher your personal energy vibration the less likely you will be to attract lower–level entities. Having a positive attitude and a loving heart is the best way to raise your vibration. Negative emotions lower your vibration, and positive vibrations raise your vibration.

In *Transcending the Levels of Consciousness: The Stairway to Enlightenment* [25], David Hawkins ranked the vibration level of qualities of mind on a scale of 1 to 1000. He used muscle testing[26] to develop this scale. The critical point of consciousness is at 200. An individual who harbors emotions that score below 200, such as shame, guilt, grief, fear, and anger, has a very low vibration. Emotions that score above 200, such as courage, acceptance, joy, peace, and love, will not only raise an individual's energetic vibration but contribute to raising the collective energetic vibration of Earth. Not only does how we feel affect our personal space but it affects the rest of the planet and most likely the entire universe as well.

In most of the scenarios above, it is the speed of onset that may be the distinguishing factor between an authentic identity and an outside influence. If an individual begins in very early childhood to form an identity that grows or is consistent over a life time, that is a good indication that the identity is authentic and true. If, however, all of a sudden, seemingly out of the clear blue, someone seems to shift their identity and not be feeling their consistent self, then I would consider spirit attachment or a walk–ins situation as a possible cause.

SOUL AGES

One of the distinct differences between a younger soul and an older soul is how they perceive their life theme. A younger soul usually finds fault outside of them. They require rules and regulations that are set by society and religious organizations. Older souls find no fault or blame but realize that everything they experience is for their personal growth. They realize that everything they perceive in the world is a reflection of how they feel about themselves. They do not rely on rules and regulations on the Earth plane because they are self–sourcing. They calibrate from their Higher Selves and from the universal concepts of the spiritual world.

A predominant characteristic of older souls is that they come onto the Earth plane with a sense of knowing. My message to old souls is, don't let others talk you out of or shame you away from what you know just because you feel you are in a minority position. Go with your gut instinct because it is the truth for you.

As mentioned previously "Michael" [27] is a causal plane entity composed of 1,050 individuals. Individuals incarnated on Earth channel teachings from them. One of their teachings is a model of seven soul stages. The first five stages, which are called the "Infant Soul", the "Baby Soul", the "Young Soul", the "Mature Soul", and the "Old Soul", are souls who are still incarnating on Earth. "Transcendental Souls" and "Infinite Souls" are beyond the human soul stages but may occasionally take human bodies in order to be in service of completing a specific mission as a teacher or guide. A new soul must progress through the stages just as we progress through the grades in school. Each soul stage has specific issues the soul focuses on. In addition, there are seven levels within each soul stage, each level requiring between one to ten lifetimes to complete. The seven levels within each stage of consciousness are: initial adjustment to new consciousness, building new foundations, exploring new consciousness, integrating and enjoying new consciousness, expressing new consciousness with full visibility, harmonizing new consciousness with others including burning off karma, and showing mastery of new consciousness.

Learning about the different soul stages and levels was of great value to me because it helped me better understood why individuals think and act the way they do. I realize that no soul is any better than, smarter than, or higher than another. Each soul is on its unique path with its own unique timing. Experiencing different flavors of gender and sexual identity are some of those lessons of learning encountered along the way.

> "The Earth value system still operates on the illusion that if someone is right, then someone who thinks or acts differently must be wrong. There is really no 'yes' or 'no'; there is only 'yes' and 'yes'. As you operate from a base of self-love, you cannot do or be anything that is not aligned with your growth, your spiritual expansion, or your reason for coming to assist this world. Self-love is the first and most important step on the spiritual path. Unconditional love is built on self-love."
>
> *–Hannah Beaconsfield*

SEX AND GENDER IN DREAMS

I am not aware of any studies relating to dreams of individuals with diverse gender and sexual identities. I do think it would be very interesting to know what genders individuals dream they are in and what genders they dream they have sex with. I suspect that many individuals dream that they are both male and female and that they have dreams of having sex with both males and females.

Unless an individual is lucid dreaming, the conscious mind doesn't control dream themes. Therefore remembering and analyzing dreams may provide clues to gender and sexual identity. We dream approximately one–sixth of our life. Dreams can relay important messages to us during sleep. They may also be metaphoric messages from our spirit guides. Recurring dreams carry important and powerful messages.

The first step in analyzing a dream is to determine which type of dream it is. There are different types of dreams:

- ***Personal***: Scenarios that help process conscious or unconscious issues such as identifying problems, revealing true feelings, relieving pressures, providing insights, and experimenting with different solutions.
- ***Recall***: Memories that come from past life experiences.

- ***Nightmares***: Usually related to deep fears.
- ***Symbolic***: Messages from the unconscious that are shown through metaphors or mythic and cultural symbols.
- ***Spiritual***: Precognitive, voices, visions, wisdom from spiritual sources such as the Higher Self and guides.
- ***Visitations***: The easiest way for spirits and souls that have passed over the veil to contact us is to appear in dreams.
- ***Out–of–Body***: Astral projection, visiting other dimensions while sleeping.
- ***Lucid***: Being fully conscious of dreaming while the dream is happening.

The second step in analyzing a dream is to sort out the images and symbols by determining if they are to be taken literal or symbolically. Dream dictionaries are fun and helpful but each symbol will have its own unique meaning to every individual. Many dream experts advise not to rely on dream dictionaries but instead to intuit what your own personal meaning is. Often, the people in your dream represent qualities, not the literal, actual people represented. Also another way to analyze a dream is to see you as each person in the dream.

SEX IN DREAMS

Sexual dreams can come in different forms and perhaps give individual clues to their sexual identity. Some dreams are quite erotic and graphic. They may seem like fantasy fulfillment because these dreams may help to satisfy a natural sexual appetite. Sexual dreams that involve influences or inhibitions of sexual activity may represent an issue of intimacy occurring in an individual's daily life. Sexual dreams that focus on past relationships are ways to process them and how they relate to an individual's current life.

Most of the time, sex dreams aren't literal but are symbolic of something else. They may represent a desire to balance masculine and feminine energy, a desire to be more creative or more spiritual, a desire to merge several aspects of the self, a desire to love a part of self that has been judged or rejected, a desire to heal old sexual trauma and abuse, or a desire to become whole through a union of opposites. Mostly, though, they are messages about an individual's sexual life, portraying conscious and unconscious desires and fears. Sometimes sexual dreams may also be influenced by other individuals' thoughts and hopes.

In *Dreams for Dummies*, Penney Peirce says that:

> *"Dreams are usually speaking to issues of working with energy flows and new character traits within [an individual's] own makeup."*[28]

Conversely a dream can be about other items that are a metaphor for sexual subjects. For example some objects that could be sexual metaphors include pointed objects inserted into openings, rabbits, snakes, or bananas.

The act of intercourse with a particular individual in a dream can symbolize a blending or merger of masculine or feminine qualities within the Self. It may also be showing the Self how to accept and love itself.

In *The Dream Dictionary from A to Z*, Theresa Cheung says that:

> *"If you are gay and dream of making love to a person of the same sex, this will have much the same interpretation as dreams concerning heterosexual sex and partnerships. If you are gay and have dreams of heterosexual sex, your unconscious may be highlighting unconscious attractions or emphasizing the closeness of your emotional bonds with friends of the opposite sex."*[29]

If a woman dreams of a satisfying sexual experience with a male it might represent a harmonious union with the masculine aspects of her character, and her power to be competitive and challenging in the world. An unsatisfactory sexual experience might mean the opposite. If a woman dreams about multiple male lovers it may represent different aspects of her. If a woman dreams about a female lover it may represent something she deeply craves, needs, hopes for, or avoids.

If a man dreams about a female lover it may represent his relationship with the feminine aspects of his personality. Sex with more than one female may point to a conflict in desires. The younger the woman in the dream, the more vulnerable his emotions might be. If a man dreams of a satisfying sexual experience with a female it might represent a harmonious union between masculine and feminine aspects of his personality. If a man dreams about a male lover it may represent something he deeply craves, needs, hopes for, or avoids.

If a heterosexual dreams about having sex with same–sex individuals it may mean one of the following:

- They might have a repressed attraction to same–sex individuals.
- They may have a need to explore same–sex activities in a safe environment without socially–conditioned objections.
- The dream may be highlighting the intimate nature of same–sex friendships or a desire to meet someone similar to them.
- The dream may be highlighting a feeling of closeness to friends that is greater than to a romantic partner.
- The dream may be an unconscious message to be more open–minded and less homophobic.

GENDER IN DREAMS

In *Seth Speaks*[13], Seth, an entity channeled by Jane Roberts, says that the *anima* is all the memories of a male's past lives as female. When a male dreams he is a female, he is receiving information on his characteristics as a female in past lives. The reverse is also true, that a female's *animus* is the memories of her past lives as a male. These memories can come to her when she dreams she is a man.

In *The Mystical Magical Marvelous World of Dreams*[30], Wilda Tanner says that individuals are mostly taught to express and suppress masculine and feminine qualities based on the sex of the body. Dreams can show imbalances and aid in integrating them towards a balanced state.

A male that dreams he is a female isn't necessarily becoming female–identified. It usually means he needs to consciously integrate the feminine qualities that he possesses. Likewise, a female dreaming that she is a male might be integrating the masculine qualities she needs. Role–playing the opposite gender helps an individual develop their *anima* or *animus*.

In *The Dream Dictionary from A to Z*, Theresa Cheung says that when there is conflict between the masculine and feminine, it can sometimes show in dreams as bisexuality or transvestism. She says:

> *"Dreaming of a person who is both masculine and feminine either suggests bisexuality or the perfect balance in one person of the masculine and feminine qualities. If you have a gender–shifting dream in which you believe that you are a member of the opposite sex, this generally is a dream about changes in perspective or exploring different aspects of yourself."*[29]

Observation Point

Dreaming can be a dipstick with which to measure one's true gender and sexual identity because there is no conscious control over the dream themes. They are free to bubble up from the unconscious.

My dreams seem to be firmly rooted in waking reality. I have dreamed of being in a cis female body and a transmasculine body but I have never dreamed I was in a cis male body.

My sexual dreams alternate between sex with cis males and sex with cis females. Only once have I had a dream where I had sex with both (consecutively, not simultaneously). Usually I get all the way to the actual act of intercourse and the dream ends. Rarely is the sexual act consummated.

My interpretation is that I am doing a lot of work on balancing masculine and feminine energies not only in waking hours but in sleep time as well. Both my *anima* and *animus* are being fed through my dreamtime.

CONCLUSION

Through the study of quantum physics, we are beginning to accept the idea that spiritual concepts can not only be true but can be proven true. Quantum physicists have now established that:

1. Consciousness exists in a matrix outside of the Physical Body.
2. Energy in motion can take an unlimited number of paths. The most probable path will be the one that consciousness focuses on the most.
3. It is our personal observation (intention) focused on an energetic event (attention) that creates reality (manifestation).

The bottom line is that ALL THINGS ARE POSSIBLE in the world of energy. And our entire universe and all its multi–dimensions, known or unknown, consists of energy.

When applying this logic to gender and sexual identity, it just doesn't make sense that reality is limited to only two states of gender, male and female, or that there is only one natural state of sexual orientation, that of a man with a woman. The energetic universe provides so many alternatives, degrees, shades, variations, and spectra for us to experience that to limit our choices is absurd.

> "Absence of evidence is not evidence of absence."
>
> *–Shirley MacLaine*

NOTES:

[1] Trismegistus, Hermes. *The Emerald Tablet of Hermes.* Merchant Books, 2013.

[2] The Three Initiates. *The Kybalion: A Study of the Hermetic Philosophy of Ancient Egypt and Greece.* CreateSpace Independent Publishing Platform, 2013.

[3] Hauck, Dennis William. *The Complete Idiot's Guide to Alchemy.* Alpha, 2008.

[4] Baker Publishing Group, compiler. *The Apocrypha.* Press Syndicate of the University of Cambridge, 1983.

[5] Thibaut, George. *The Vedanta.*

[6] Singer, June. *Androgyny: Toward a New Theory of Sexuality.* Anchor Press/Doubleday, 1976.

[7] Oyle, Irving. *The Healing Mind: You Can Cure Yourself without Drugs.* Celestial Arts, 1974.

[8] Plato. W.H.D. Rouse, translator. *Great Dialogues of Plato.* Signet Classics, 2008.

[9] MacLaine, Shirley. *I Am All over That: and Other Confessions*. Atria Books, 2012.

[10] Christi, Nicolya. *Contemporary Spirituality for an Evolving World: A Handbook for Conscious Evolution.* Bear & Company, 2013.

[11] Laitman, Rav Michael. *The Experience of Kabbalah.* Bnei Baruch, Laitman Kabbalah, 2005.

[12] Roberts, Jane. *The Nature of the Psyche: It's Human Expression A Seth Book.* Amber–Allen Publishing, 1996.

[13] Roberts, Jane and Robert F. Butts. *Seth Speaks: The Eternal Validity of the Soul.* Amber–Allen Publ., 1994.

[14] Carroll, Lee. *Partnering with God: Practical Information for the New Millennium. Kryon: Book VI.* Kryon Writings, 2002.

[15] Carroll, Lee. "Free Transcripts from Lee Carroll." Last modified July, 2014. http://www.kryon.com/k_25.html

[16] Carroll, Lee. "The Akashic Circle." Last modified October, 2011. http://spiritlibrary.com/kryon/the-akashic-circle

[17] Pope, Joya. *The World According to Michael: An Old Soul's Guide to the Universe.* Emerald Wave, 1992.

[18] Hoodwin, Shepherd. *The Journey of Your Soul: A Channel Explores the Michael Teachings.* North Atlantic Books, 2013.

[19] Marciniak, Barbara. *Path of Empowerment: New Pleiadian Wisdom for a World in Chaos.* New World Library, 2004.

[20] Stone, Joshua David. *Ascension and Romantic Relationships.* Light Technology Publishing, 2000.

[21] Beaconsfield, Hannah. *Welcome to Planet Earth: A Guide for Walk–Ins, Starseeds, and Lightworkers of All Varieties.* Light Technology Publications, 2011.

[22] Newton, Michael. *Destiny of Souls: New Case Studies of Life between Lives.* Llewellyn Publications, 2000.

[23] Newton, Michael. *Journey of Souls: Case Studies of Life between Lives.* Llewellyn Publications, 1994.

[24] Modi, Shakuntala. *Remarkable Healings: A Psychiatrist Discovers Unsuspected Roots of Mental and Physical Illness.* Hampton Roads Publishing, 1998.

[25] Hawkins, David R. *Transcending the Levels of Consciousness: The Stairway to Enlightenment.* Veritas Publishing, 2006.

[26] Muscle Testing, also called kinesiology, is based on traditional Chinese medicine's concept of internal energy. It is a noninvasive way of evaluating the body's responses when slight pressure to a large muscle is applied. For more information, refer to John Thie's excellent book, *Touch for Health.* DeVorss & Company, 2005.

[27] Stevens, Jose and Simon Warwick–Smith. *The Michael Handbook: A Channeled System for Self–Understanding.* Warwick Press, 1990. Also see http://personalityspirituality.net/articles/the-michael-teachings/reincarnation-the-35-steps and http://www.michaelteachings.com/welcome.html

[28] Peirce, Penney. *Dreams for Dummies.* For Dummies, 2001.

[29] Cheung, Theresa. *The Dream Dictionary from A to Z.* Harper Element, 2006.

[30] Tanner, Wilda B. *The Mystical Magical Marvelous World of Dreams.* Wild Comet Publishing LLC, 2004.

CHAPTER 5:
THE ENERGY BODY AND THE PHYSICAL BODY

The Layers of Body Consciousness

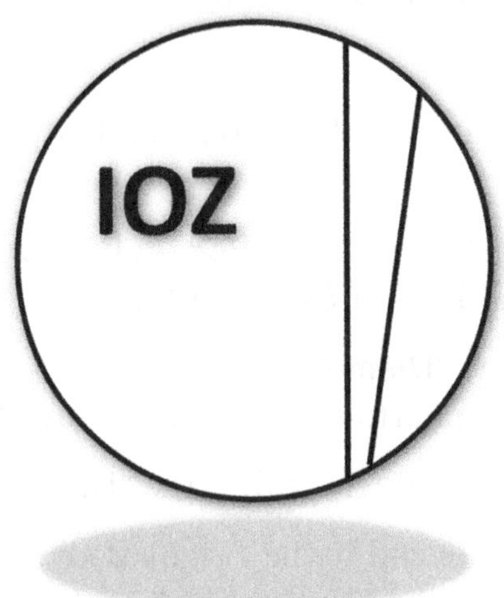

INTERNATIONAL ORGANIZATION OF ZEROPHILIACS

IOZ is a fictional but intriguing concept from the movie *Zerophilia*. It is about individuals that are born with an additional chromosome, the "Z" chromosome. These individuals change sex whenever they are sexually aroused to orgasm with an individual of the opposite sex or with another zerophiliac.

(Zerophilia, 2005: Written by Martin Curland)

INTRODUCTION TO ENERGY BODIES

The Physical Body is the form that a soul takes while incarnated in the third dimension (i.e. on Earth). The Physical Body consists of energy so dense that it can be felt and seen. However, the soul consists of more energetic layers than just the Physical Body.

According to spiritual, esoteric, occult, and mystical teachings, souls have a Physical Body and an Energy Body, commonly called a Subtle Body. The origin of Subtle Body teachings was principally from Indian yogic tradition, where the Subtle Body is described as sheaths that cover the immortal soul.

The Energy Body is known by various names in different spiritual traditions:

- Christians call it the “Resurrection Body” or the “Glorified Body”.
- Sufis call it the “most Sacred Body” (*Wujud Al–aqdas*) and the “Supra–celestial Body” (*Jism Asli Haqiqi*).
- Taoists call it the “Diamond Body”. Those who have attained it are called “the Immortals” and "the Cloudwalkers."
- Yogic schools and Tantrics call it the “Divine Body.
- Tibetan Buddhists call it the “Light Body” or “Rainbow Body” (*Jalü or Jalus*). In the *Tibetan Book of the Dead* it is called the “Shining Body”.
- Kriya Yogis call it the “Body of Bliss”.
- Hermetics call it the “Immortal Body” (*Soma Athanaton*).
- In the alchemical tradition, it is called the “Golden Body.”
- In the Mithraic liturgy it is called the “Perfect Body."
- In Gnosticism it is called the “Radiant Body.”
- In the Vedanta it is called the “Superconductive Body.”
- The ancient Egyptians called it the “Luminous Body or Being” (*Akh*) or the “*Karast*”.

- Alberto Villoldo, a scientist and shaman, calls it the "Luminous Energy Field" (LEF). He says the LEF dwells outside of time having existed since before the beginning of time and endures throughout infinity. It manifests in time by creating new physical bodies lifetime after lifetime. The LEF contains imprints of a soul's memories, traumas, and wounds from former lifetimes.
- Clairvoyants see it as an aura or cloud of colored lights surrounding the Physical Body.

Our Energy Body is a luminous body. It is a vehicle that is used for traveling through other dimensions. The Energy Body is a vehicle of consciousness that exists as frequency levels on the subtle planes and as a yogic body that consists of *ch'i* or pranic energy (aura), energy vortexes (chakras), and energy channels (*nadis* or meridians). Astral projection and death are two ways to separate the Energy Body from the Physical Body.

In *Seth Speaks*, Seth, an entity channeled by Jane Roberts, explains how the Energy Body molds the Physical Body during incarnation. He says:

> *"Each inner self, adopting a new body, imposes upon it and upon its entire genetic makeup, memory of the past physical forms in which it has been involved. The physical pattern of the present body, therefore, is a genetic memory of the self's past physical forms. There are invisible layers within the body. These are invisible layers, 'shadow,' latent layers that represent previous physical images that have belonged to the personality."*[1]

The Energy Body can be differentiated into multiple layers. The number and names of the layers vary according to different spiritual models and theories. I have simplified the layers into six levels:

1. ***Physical Body*** (aka The Gross Body, The Biological Body, The Dense Body, The Material Body)

2. ***Etheric Body*** (aka The Life Force Body, The Auric Energy Fields)
3. ***Astral Body*** (aka The Psychic Body)
4. ***Emotional Body***
5. ***Mental Body*** (aka The Mind)
6. ***Causal Body*** (aka The Higher Self, The Soul, The Spiritual Body, The Divine Body, Nirvana, The Celestial Body, The Cosmic Body)

There is a seventh layer but its characteristics are beyond our comprehension as still–incarnating souls and so it not listed here.

The Energy Body is depicted in the graphic diagram below as having different layers that reside on various dimensions of consciousness. There is a portion of the Energy Body, called the Higher Self, which never descends to the Physical Body, but remains resident on the spiritual planes. The Higher Self retains all of a soul's consciousness and memories.

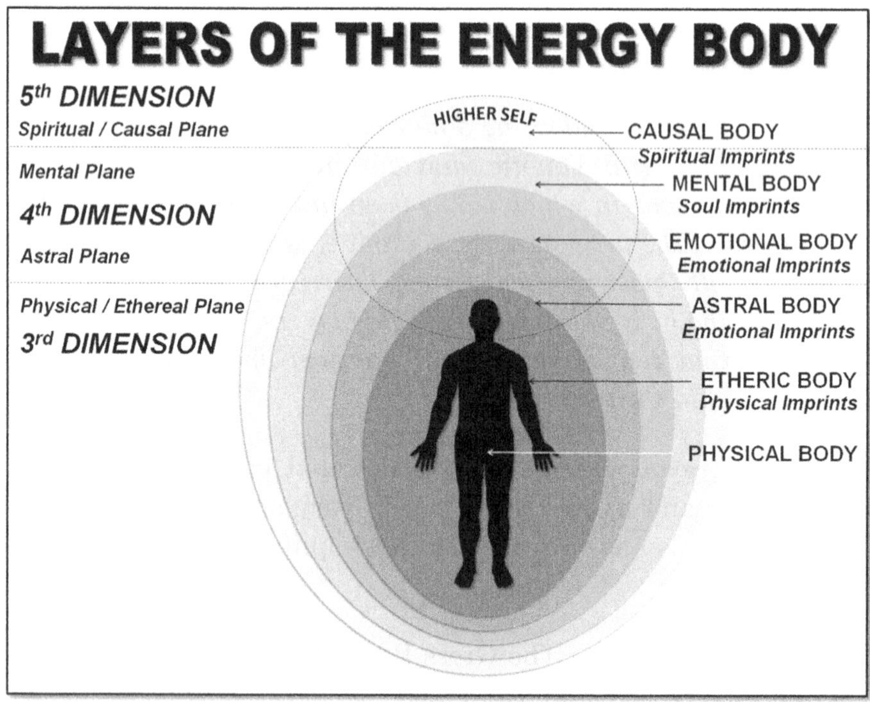

However, for the purposes of this book, it is not necessary to distinguish the different layers of the Subtle Body. The term Energy Body or EB will be used to refer to the Subtle Body and the term Physical Body or PB will be used to refer to the Physical Body.

Our consciousness resides on multiple levels. Consciousness is resident in the Physical Body, stored in the DNA of every cell of the body. Consciousness is also resident in the Energy Body, stored on non–physical levels of existence and it is a part of universal consciousness.

The following table summarizes the basic differences between the Energy Body and the Physical Body:

ENERGY BODY (EB)	PHYSICAL BODY (PB)
Is Formless	Has Form
Exists in Timelessness	Exists in Linear Time
Composed of energy as Light	Composed of energy as Dense Matter
Maintains a connected Oneness identity	Maintains a separate Ego identity
A product of past lives and karmic activity	A product of ancestors and genetic material
Memories are stored in the Akashic records	Memories are stored in the genes and passed through heredity
Has high energy, low density	Has low energy, high density
Stores trauma from past lifetimes	Stores trauma from the current incarnation
Does not age and does not die	Ages and dies
Is immortal and is kept over many lifetimes	Is mortal and kept only for the current incarnation
Taken with you when you die	Left on Earth when you die
Can be seen by the mind's (third) eye. Can be seen by the physical eye but more often is felt.	Can be seen by the physical eye and experienced through the other four senses.
Eternal. Is carried in between lives and through multiple lives	Temporary. Only lasts one lifetime
Exists on the higher planes of existence (i.e. the spiritual world)	Exists on the Physical Plane (i.e. the third dimension)

MISMATCHES OF THE ENERGY BODY AND THE PHYSICAL BODY

The reason it is important to understand how the Energy Body and the Physical Body are related is that in some cases where the Energy Body does not match the Physical Body it can have a significant impact on an individual. The Energy Body is usually described as a round, egg–shaped, or asymmetrical energy field. Often this energetic field is referred to as the aura. Although usually invisible to most people, it has pronounced characteristics. Sometimes these characteristics are congruent with the Physical Body and sometimes they are incongruent. Some major instances where the Energy Body does not match the Physical Body include:

1. *Individuals whose Energy Body weight does not match their Physical Body weight.* An example is someone diagnosed as anorexic. The mirror indicates the Physical Body is of an acceptable weight, but when seen in the mirror it is perceived as a "fat" body. In reverse, many overweight people are surprised when their body cannot fit between two objects because their perception is that it does.
2. *Individuals that feel "young at heart" while living in an older Physical Body.* Have you ever looked in a mirror and been shocked at how old you look because when you look out on the world from behind your eyes, you see the world from a much younger perspective? Many individuals in contact with souls on the spiritual plane see that they look to be about thirty years of age. Even though the Energy Body exists outside of Time, perhaps it does so in a state similar to a Physical Body of thirty years of age.
3. *Individuals that feel they are part human, part animal.* Mythology is full of examples of therianthropes such as centaurs, minotaurs, mermaids, fauns, sphinxes, and satyrs. Anyone might feel as if they are part mineral, plant, or animal as well as human. There is even a subculture of individuals that identify as anthropomorphic animal characters with

human personalities and characteristics, known as "Furries", "Yiffies", "Anthros" or "Morphs".

4. *Individuals that feel they are of a different culture or race than the Physical Body displays.* Many people have a very strong identification with different cultures, skin color, and physical shapes rather than the ones they were physically born with. An example of this may have been Michael Jackson. He underwent many cosmetic procedures to alter his Physical Body of darker skin to match the image of his Energy Body of lighter skin and refined facial features.

5. *Individuals that have Physical Body disabilities.* An example is someone that has had a limb amputated. The feelings and sensations of the limb still exist. In fact, a Kirlian photograph[2] of a leaf that has been cut in half still shows the complete, intact energy fields of the whole leaf.

6. *Individuals that feel they have a different gender than the Physical Body.* Sex is assigned at birth based on a Physical Body's sexual organs and genitalia. However, it is the Energy Body that defines gender identity. Many individuals have a Physical Body that matches their Energy Body. However, there are many others that do not have a Physical Body that matches their Energy Body. These individuals identify as transsexual, transgender, or gender fluid.

   The identity of the Energy Body seems much stronger than the identity of the Physical Body thus it is easier to alter the Physical Body to match the Energy Body. After all, we have owned our Energy Bodies for many lifetimes but this Physical Body for only one lifetime.

Individuals that have incongruent bodies have been ostracized, persecuted, bullied, and discriminated against simply because they are "different". If we were to recognize and value others' Energy Bodies as much as we do their Physical Bodies, wouldn't our perceptions about incongruency shift? We would be able to accept individual differences much easier. Remember that old proverb, "don't judge a book by its cover"? In this instance, it certainly rings true. And if you can't quite figure out what the Energy Body is, simply respectively ask the individual.

> **Observation Point**
>
> An interesting study was conducted by Vilayanur Subramanian Ramachandran, a neuroscientist, in 2008. He found that 60% of cis males who had their penis removed experienced a phantom penis while only 30% of male-to-female transsexuals experienced a phantom penis after genital reassignment surgery. In addition, over 60% of female-to-male transsexuals experienced a phantom penis as early as childhood.
>
> He hypothesizes that the feeling of phantom penises is a result of "a mismatch between the brain's hardwired gender-specific body image and the external somatic gender."[3] I call it the ability to feel the imprints of the Energy Body even when the Physical Body does not match.

The most common instances where the Energy Body does not match the Physical Body are illustrated below.

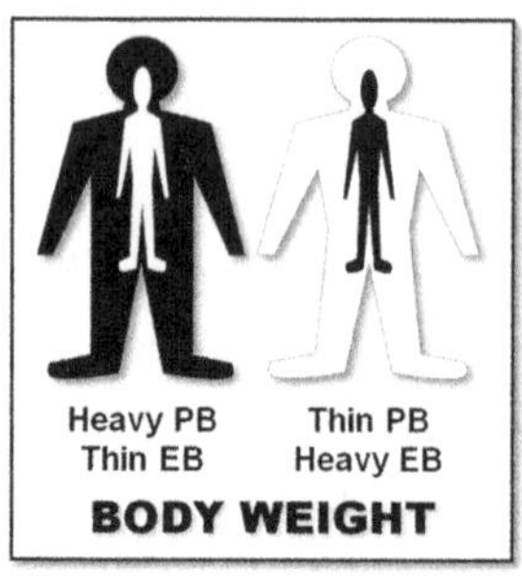

BODY WEIGHT

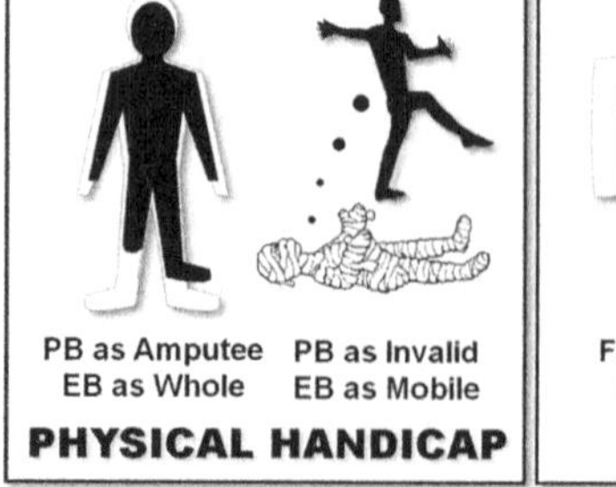

PHYSICAL HANDICAP

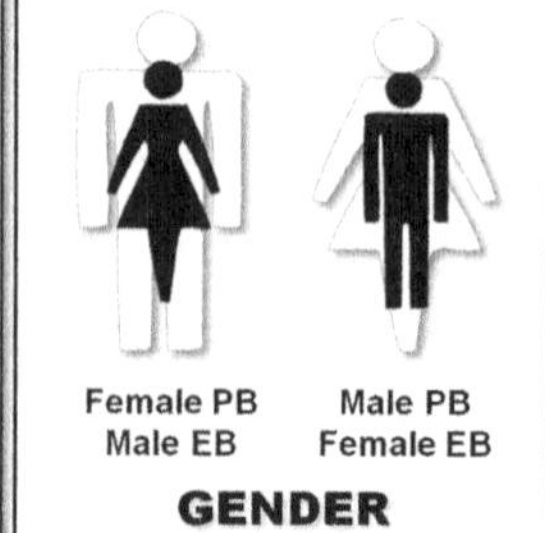

GENDER

Observation Point

I will share with you three examples from my own life experiences that illustrate the incongruence between the Energy Body and the Physical Body. In the first example, before my Physical Body transition to male physical characteristics, I was stared at constantly. If I walked into a room of strangers all conversations would stop. When I was in the Army (in a female body) I was repeatedly accused of being in the wrong restroom. This was a result of my masculine Energy Body that was incongruent with my female Physical Body.

The second example is related to how I answer a question I am asked quite often: "how do you know whether you are male or female?" My answer is because I can feel it. I vividly remember one of many times while still in my female Physical Body during my mid–20s, I was sitting by a fountain on the UCLA campus and was able to feel my masculine beard stubble even though my face was as smooth as a baby's butt. Energetically, that beard did exist!

The third example is the mutilation of my Barbie doll. As a pre–teen, I took a razor blade and cut Barbie's plastic breasts off. For many years I thought I had done it because I was acting out of anger and frustration at being incongruent in my Physical Body, however, now I wonder if I was simply altering Barbie's Physical Body to match the Energy Body I imagined she had.

BRIDGING THE ENERGY BODY TO THE PHYSICAL BODY

People tend to ostracize, stigmatize, and shame individuals who are different. Many times the difference is a result of the Energy Body not matching the Physical Body. If an individual takes on the judgments of others, those judgments can lodge in the Energy Body as body stories. Body stories are energy blocks or blocked energy imprints that eventually migrate into the Physical Body and manifest in the form of dis–ease.

We must stop looking only at the shell of a person, which is the Physical Body, and begin to honor what we each feel, which is the Energy Body. The more the Energy Body is acknowledged by others, the more at peace an individual will feel.

The Energy Body is like a hologram that houses our true Nature. Trying to change it might be futile. Instead, I propose building a bridge between the Energy Body and the Physical Body. A bridge brings awareness from one side to the other. Once a bridge is created between the identities of the two bodies, both bodies become validated. The Energy Body can expand because it is acknowledged and the Physical Body becomes healthier because energy is flowing freely. The more solid the bridge, the easier it becomes to cross back and forth and integrate the two sides.

There are two grand advantages to being aware of your Energy Body:

1. Western medicine only focuses on treating the Physical Body. If you are educated about your Energy Body, you can implement ways to maintain a healthy one. For instance, you can learn about ways to create a healthy Energy Body for yourself or go to practitioners who are experienced in energy medicine techniques. Energy Body tune–ups should include aura repair, chakra restoration, grounding cord check, and an energy fill up. Deeper energy work may be indicated and could include energy extraction, power restoration, and soul retrieval work.

2. Acknowledging the existence of the Energy Body will broaden your perception. Many indigenous people look to Condor and Eagle as teachers showing us not only how to fly high enough to see the big picture but how to fly wingtip to wingtip with Spirit. This is a metaphor for knowing that the Physical Body is a very small part of our soul. Our existence extends all the way into the spiritual world and is forever eternal. When we tap into the consciousness of our Higher Self, we are able to see a much bigger picture, because the view is from the spiritual plane.

Here are some steps to building a bridge between the Energy Body and the Physical Body:

1. *Awaken* – Awareness can be a simple introduction such as saying "Hello, I see and feel you" to both Bodies.
   - Visualize what your Energy Body looks like. Find and cut out pictures from magazines that represent your Energy Body images. Paste them on a vision board.
2. *Acknowledge* – Create an environment of unconditional love and acceptance. Try some of these activities:
   - Perform positive affirmations daily.
   - Banish negative thoughts and self–talk whenever it begins.
   - Do guided meditations, mantras, and individual meditations.
   - Seek out and surround yourself with non–judgmental people who practice unconditional love and acceptance.
   - Throw a tea party for all your Bodies to celebrate their uniqueness and the gifts that they are.
3. *Align* – Your Physical Body gets fed every day. But how do you feed your Energy Body daily? Find out what makes your Energy Body happy and nourish it regularly. Energetic alignment methods can include:
   - Grounding meditations and exercises. Grounding on a daily basis puts you into your Physical Body. To learn how, find a teacher or refer to these books listed in the footnotes at the end of the chapter.[4]
   - Develop astral travel and lucid dreaming skills.
   - Go on shamanic journeys. Shamans are very good at understanding transformation and metamorphosis, living between the worlds, and bridging different realities.
   - Receive massages, Reiki, and other body therapies.

- Receive energy healings such as aura–chakra cleansings, shamanic healings, and various other forms of energy medicine and therapies.
- Do shapeshift exercises: Examples are ecstatic dancing, creating masks and costumes that celebrate your Energy Body, tattooing the Physical Body with Energy Body characteristics, changing the Physical Body through cosmetics, clothes, hair style, surgery, or any other physical means.

A great way to develop a daily practice is to purchase and use Donna Eden's *Energy Medicine Kit*[5]. This kit provides a daily energy medicine practice of various exercises, which include movements, pressure point massages, and breath work. They are documented in a book, demonstrated on a DVD, recorded on an audio CD, and illustrated on energy medicine cards.

SUMMARY: A DOZEN ENERGY BODY PRINCIPLES

1. *The Energy Body merges with the Physical Body at birth and leaves the Physical Body at death.* The Energy Body remains connected to the Physical Body during incarnation through energetic systems such as the aura, chakras, and meridians. When the Energy Body leaves, the Physical Body sleeps or dies. If the Energy Body leaves the Physical Body temporarily, it is called Astral Projection. If the Energy Body leaves the Physical Body permanently it is called Death. A psychopomp's job is to help the Energetic Body leave the Physical Body at death and seal the Physical Body chakras so the Energetic Body does not return.
2. *The Energy Body has many layers.* The inner most layer is the closest to the Physical Body and the outer most layer extends into the fifth dimension (spiritual plane). This layer is the Higher Self that never incarnates into a Physical Body. The Higher Self retains memory of all lifetimes and all time between lives.

3. *The Physical Body is made of slow, dense energy so it can be seen by the physical eye.* The Energy Body is made of faster, higher vibrating energy and can be seen by some through the third eye. Some basic energy systems of the Energy Body include the chakra system, the aura, and the meridians.

4. *When the Energy Body overlays the Physical Body at birth it only brings a portion of the soul's energy.* Some energy always remains in the outer layer, i.e. in the fifth dimension.

5. *The Energy Body is the vehicle that carries our consciousness from one lifetime to another and holds our consciousness in between lives.* It also carries imprints of past life Physical Bodies including physical characteristics and traumatic injuries. The Energy Body can also house imprints of impending dis–eases. If the cause of the dis–ease is not identified and healed, the dis–ease will descend into the Physical Body.

6. *The Energy Body receives and sends energy.* This is a form of communication that is in addition to the standard forms of communication that most of us are familiar with and use every day, such as verbal and body language. The Energy Body "gives off vibes" and these vibrations are received by the universe. The Law of Manifestation states that what vibration you give out is what you will attract back to you.

7. *The Energy Body can "feel" the same as the Physical Body can.* Have you ever felt angry or frustrated when someone has cut you off in traffic or in line at the market? Even though they have not touched your Physical Body, you are reacting to the sudden intrusion of their energy touching your Energy Body. People can send energy "whacks" to you simply by giving you the "evil eye" or thinking nasty thoughts about you.

8. *The Energy Body may not match the Physical Body.* For instance, individuals may have a different gender identity (energetic level) than biological sex (physical level). Some Energy Bodies may be larger than Physical Bodies (anorexia)

or may be smaller than Physical Bodies (obesity). The Energy Body can even retain feelings when a physical limb is lost through amputation or feel body parts that aren't physically present.

9. *Western medicine practitioners usually treat only the Physical Body.* To receive Energy Body treatments, an individual must visit Western medical personnel that practice integrative medicine, alternative health providers, shamanic energy medicine practitioners, or Eastern medicine practitioners.
10. *The more the Energy Body can be integrated with the Physical Body, the more whole and healthy a person will feel.* Acknowledging the Energy Body is a big step towards integrating it with the Physical Body.
11. *Healers that are trained in energy medicine techniques can provide clearing, healing, and maintenance for the Energy Body.* They also can provide a daily Energy Body tune–up regime for an individual to follow.
12. *The Energy Body is the one thing you will never shed and it will be with you always.* It is ageless and eternal. Treat your Energy Body well so that you perpetually maintain its health!

> "People seem to think with their eyeballs, not seeing doesn't allow for believing."
>
> *–E. Tristan Booth*
>
> However, just because the energy body is not physically seen by most, doesn't mean it is not there.

NOTES:

[1] Roberts, Jane and Robert F. Butts. *Seth Speaks: The Eternal Validity of the Soul.* Amber–Allen Publ., 1994.

[2] Kirlian photography, a high voltage contact print photography, which involves a special type of camera, captures coronal discharge. Kirlian, the inventor, believed that images created by Kirlian photography depict an energy field or aura that surrounds living things.

[3] Ramachandran, Vilayanur Subramanian. "Phantom Penises in Transsexuals". *Journal of Consciousness Studies,* 15 (1) 2008.

[4] Recommended Books on Grounding, Protecting, and Clearing:

Friedlander, John and Gloria Hemsher. *Basic Psychic Development: A User's Guide to Auras, Chakras & Clairvoyance.* Weiser Books, 2012.

Linn, Denise. *Sacred Space: Clearing and Enhancing the Energy of Your Home.* Wellspring/Ballantine, 1995.

[5] Eden, Donna. *Energy Medicine Kit.* Sounds True Incorporated, 2005.

CHAPTER 6:
GENDER IDENTITY
The Consciousness of Gender

UNISEX RESTROOMS

Individuals with any gender identity may use a unisex toilet or restroom. Unisex restrooms benefit families that have small children as well as disabled and elderly individuals that need assistance. In addition, trans* and gender fluid individuals may use a unisex restroom without fear of harassment or embarrassment.

GENDER 101

Whereas biological sex relates to the physical form, gender identity relates to the energetic form. Gender identity is a psychological quality that can only be reported by the individual.

Gender identity and sexual identity reside in our consciousness which resides outside the Physical Body. Consciousness resides within the soul of our Higher Selves on the spiritual plane. While on the spiritual plane, the soul is pure energy and perfectly balanced with all qualities of masculinity and femininity. Therefore it can be considered genderless.

The figure below draws a comparison between the Physical Body identity spectra and the Energy Body's identity spectra. It also illustrates that the Physical Body resides in the third dimension and gender and sexual identity resides in our consciousness, which is in the fifth dimension.

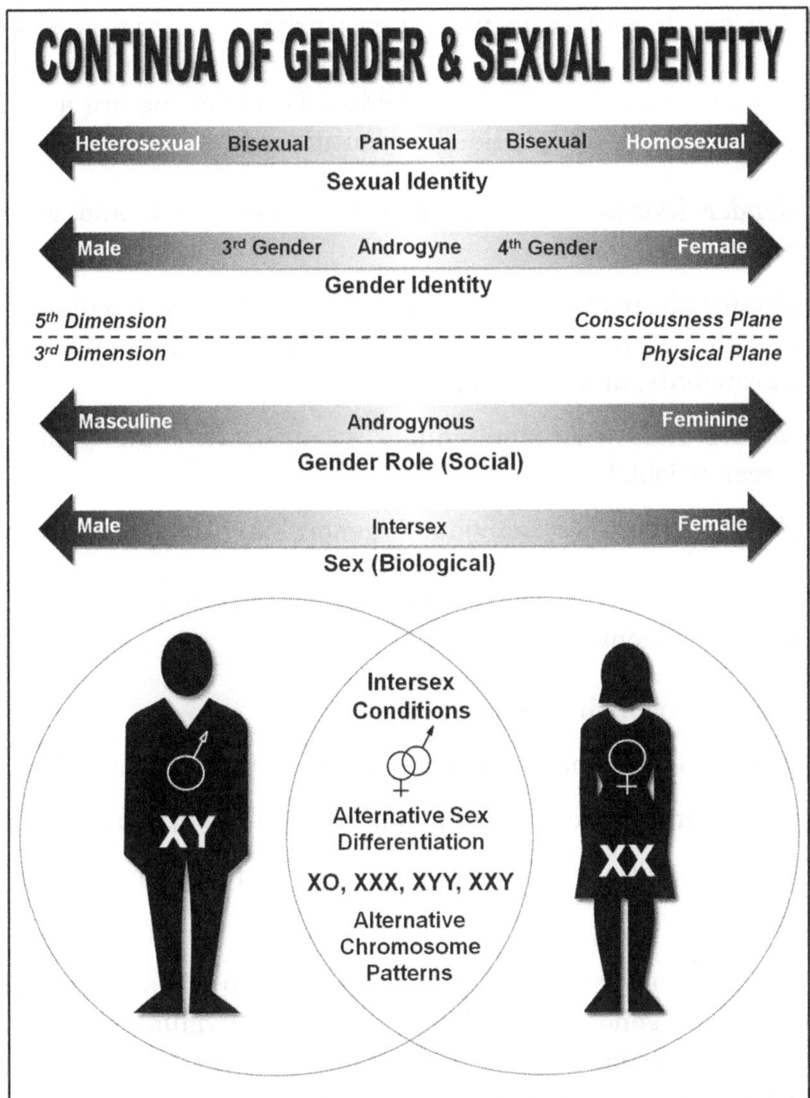

The following figure defines gender by what it is and what it is not:

GENDER IS	GENDER IS NOT
A spectrum	Just male & female
A range of expression	Defined by body parts
A personal identity	Determined by chromosomes

Gender identity is an individual's private experience of who they are. Gender expressions, gender roles, and gender scripts are public expressions of who an individual is. Following are a list of components that make up gender identity:

1. ***Gender Identity*** – An individual's sense of self and gender belief system.
2. ***Gender Expression*** – An individual's communication of gender to others. It includes clothes, hair style, mannerisms, adornments, and way of speaking.
3. ***Gender Role*** – An individual's social status, family status, career or job(s).
4. ***Gender Script*** – An individual's general and sexual behavior.

Any individual assessing their gender identity will ask the following questions:

- What is my birth assigned sex?
- Who am I and what is my personal expression of gender?
- What is my gender role and public expression of gender?
- How does my physical being match my emotional and mental being?

For a cisgender individual, the biological body matches gender identity and gender role. For a trans* individual there is a mismatch between the biological body and the gender identity and gender role.

Even though it seems we live in a bigender world, with only two options of male and female, there are really many more options available. Following is a list of gender identities. I tried to make the list as inclusive as I could. Many identities may seem very similar to others, but each one is a bit unique in definition to the individual that claims it as a label. These gender terms are defined in the glossary at the back of the book.

Gender Identity Options

Agender
Ambigender
Androgyne
Bigender
Boi/Boy
Cisgender
Crossdresser
Demiboy
Demigirl
Eunuch
Female/Woman/Cis Woman
Female to Male (FTM/F2M)
Femme
Gender Diverse
Gender Fluid
Gender Free
Gender Neutral
Gender Nonconforming
Gender Queer
Gender Questioning
Gender Variant
Genderqueer
Hermaphrodite (obsolete)
Human Gender
Intergender
Intersex
Male/Man/Cis Man
Male to Female (MTF/M2F)
Metagender
Metrosexual
Multigender
Neutrois (Null)
Non–binary
Non–gender
Neuter
Omnigender
Other
Pangender
Polygender
PoMogendered
Postgenderist
Queen
Third Gender
Tomboy
Trans*
Trans–androgynous
Transsexual
Transfeminine
Transgender
Transgenderist
Transman
Transmasculine
Transsexual
Transvestite
Transwoman
Trigender
Twink
Two–Spirit

Today we are living in a bigender society but it is becoming increasingly difficult to accommodate all the individuals that live outside of the bigender polarities of male and female. Some problems inherent to the bi–gender system are:

1. ***Restrooms*** – Most facilities only provide Male or Female. How should the individuals that fall in between the two polarities be accommodated?

2. ***Language*** – English and many other languages only accommodate male and female pronouns. How should the individuals that fall in between the two polarities be addressed?

3. ***Health Charts*** – Standards and measurements are only provided for males and females. Which chart do trans* individuals and others that fall in between the two polarities refer to?

4. ***Civil Laws and Rights*** – Laws for marriage, parenting, immigration, military service, birth and death certificates, wills and trusts, and many other social institutions only provide for straight males and females. Are all other individuals with diverse gender and sexual identities excluded from these because they are "outside" the bigender box?

5. ***Etiquette*** – People are trained from childhood to treat others based on their gender and age. That is how we know who opens the door for whom, etc. If we create a social system that is all inclusive, all the rules of etiquette will have to be redefined. The rules of etiquette for humans need to become universal rules for the individuals regardless of their status.

GENDER CHARACTERISTICS

Gender characteristics can be viewed in two different ways:

1. ***Dualistic*** – Everything in the universe has an opposite. A dualistic system categorizes characteristics into opposite polarities. The basic premise is that a characteristic cannot be experienced or defined without having an opposite characteristic to compare it to. How do we know how until we have experienced cold? How do we know sweet until we have tasted bitter?

2. ***Monistic*** – Everything in the universe is connected and related therefore all is one. There is no distinction between masculine and feminine characteristics. All characteristics are simply human characteristics.

Even though monism is the foundation that supports fluid identities, dualism shows us how to learn from the extremes of difference. Dualism is a prominent system on Earth that labels specific categories of identity for simplicity.

It is my theory that as a young soul begins its journey of lifetimes on Earth, it lives at the extreme opposite ends of a spectrum. But as the soul progresses, gradually becoming wiser through experience, each consecutive lifetime moves a little more toward living in the middle. Thus the polar qualities become balanced.

How the Law of Polarities Creates Balance

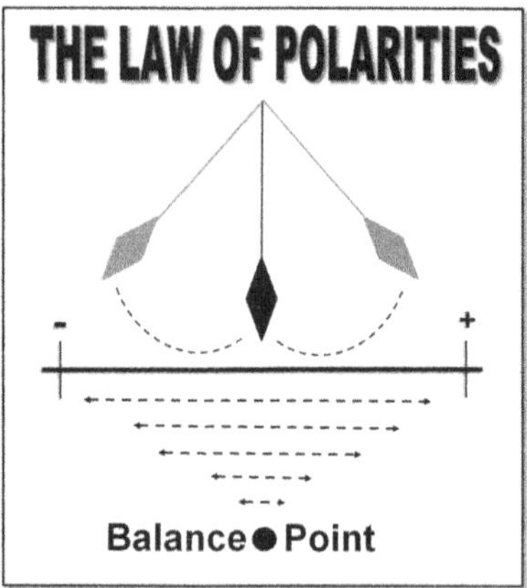

Duality is a construct whereby incarnated souls learn from experiencing polar opposites. But duality is also a spectrum with an infinite number of points between the polar opposites. We learn balance by traveling along the spectrum until we find the middle point.

Duality exists so that we can experience polar opposites. In order to learn how to be in a balanced state, we start our life incarnations at the extreme opposite ends of a spectrum, experiencing one pole in one life and the opposite in another life. Each consecutive lifetime may begin at a point closer to the middle based on the wisdom we have gained from past life experiences. Like a pendulum that swings back and forth, each arc is shorter and eventually the weight comes to rest in the center. This is when our duality fully shifts to a monad and our lesson is complete. Some souls will progress through this exercise quickly while for others it may take many lifetimes.

A good example of this is when I first transitioned from a female gender role to a male gender role. I swung very far to the masculine side at first, wanting to be all–male and eschewing femininity to the point of not even listening to female vocalists. However as the years passed, I gradually grew more balanced in my identity until now I identify myself as very androgynous.

Some transsexuals who are undergoing surgical processes, transition from their birth assigned pole to the opposite pole.

Other individuals undergo surgical processes that augment their birth–assigned pole. For example some women undergo breast enlargement, which they believe enhances their femininity and men have penile enlargements to enhance their masculinity.

Masculine and feminine qualities are attached to dualistic characteristics, such as in the Tao concept of *yin* and *yang*. The *yin–yang* symbol is the Tao representation of duality as shown in the following figure:

YIN	YANG
Feminine	Masculine
Passive	Active
Receptive	Creative
Dark	Bright/Light
Soft	Hard
Moon	Sun
Night	Day
Water	Fire
Black	Red & White
North	South
Even	Odd
Cold	Hot
Death	Life
Winter	Summer
North	South
Quiet	Excited
Tranquil	Restless
Slowness	Rapidity
Substantial	Non-substantial
Shady/cloudy, north slope, south bank	Sunny, south slope, north bank
North side of a hill (away from sun)	South side of a hill (facing sun)
Emotion	Intellect

(Continued next page)

YIN	YANG
Intuition	Logic
Creation	Destruction
Magnetic	Radiating
The Void	The Creation
Being	Doing
Cyclical	Linear
Simultaneous	Sequential
To Give	To Receive
Diffused Awareness	Focused Consciousness
Introvert	Extrovert
Submissive	Dominant
Compassion	Aggression
Calm Quiet Environment	Stimulating Energizing Environment
Prefers Rest & Balance	Prefers Socializing
Lower Blood Pressure	Higher Blood Pressure
Solid	Hollow
Abstract	Tangible
Natural	Synthetic
Conserve, Store	Change, Transform
Store Vital Substances	Digest & Excrete Impurities
Earth-centric	Spirit-centric
Chronic Conditions	Acute Conditions
Fatigue/Tiredness	Insomnia
Damp	Dry
Lethargic	Restless
Underactive	Overactive
Weak Musculature	Tight Musculature
Lack of Thirst	Thirsty
Curled Up	Stretched Out
Empty Pulse	Full Pulse
Body	Head
Lower Body	Upper Body
Anterior	Posterior
Right Brain	Left Brain
Left Side of Body	Right Side of Body

The dark swirl represents *yin*, the feminine, and the light swirl represents *yang*, the masculine. The Wikipedia article on *Yin* and *Yang* says:

"Yin and yang are actually complementary, not opposing, forces, interacting to form a whole greater than either separate part; in effect, a dynamic system. Everything has both yin and yang aspects. Either of the two major aspects may manifest more strongly in a particular object, depending on the criterion of the observation."[1]

We can change our perception from "either–or" thinking to unitary and inclusive thinking if we view *yin–yang* as complements of the same quality. In this way, we can move away from black and white thinking into spectrum thinking allowing for multiple shades of grays where polar opposites begin to blend and overlap. Eventually, the circle melts into a continuum of merged qualities. There is no longer a boundary between one and it's opposite.

Kenneth Kramer, in his book *The Sacred Art of Dying*[2], discusses the concept of multiple souls. He says that Confucian philosophers believed that individuals had dual souls. One soul, called the higher or *Yang* soul, is less dense and remains in the home after death. Relatives place incense and food on the home altar for the departed *Yang* soul. The other soul, called a lower or *Yin* soul, which is denser, stays with the body after death. Relatives sweep the grave site once a year to honor the departed *Yin* soul.

Similar to the characteristics of *yin* and *yang*, gender characteristics have also been applied to the left and right hemispheres of the human brain. Popular brain lateralization theories attribute masculine characteristics to the left brain and feminine characteristics to the right brain. However, the brain is "wholistic". If a portion of the brain is injured, another region can oftentimes assume its functions. The figure below lists the typical characteristics associated with the left and right brain:

LEFT BRAIN	RIGHT BRAIN
2-Dimentsional	Multi-Dimensional
Logical	Random
Linear	Holistic
Sequential	Intuitive
Rational	Holistic
Analyzes	Synthesizes, Imagines
Objective	Subjective
Parts	Wholes
Symbolic	Spatial
Differences	Similarities
Processes over Time	Processes over Space
Temporal	Global
Future Oriented	Present Moment
Step-By-Step Reasoning	Mystical
Logical, Thinking	Dreamer, Musical
Mathematical	Creative
Verbal	Visual
Pattern User	Pattern Seeker
Splits	Lumps
Organize, Plan	Spontaneous, Fluid
Sequential	Simultaneous
Counting, Measurement	Shapes, Motions
Tracks Time	Free Association
Technique	Inspiration
Effort	Flow
Expressive	Receptive
Routine, Predictability	Novelty
Controls Right Side of Body	Controls Left Side of Body

Jung believed that the *anima* and *animus* was developed through projection. This process begins when a newborn projects onto the mother and continues into adulthood when a romantic partner is projected onto.

In *Dancing in the Eye of Transformation: 10 Keys to Creative Consciousness,* Sylvia Brailler says:

"Making a conscious connection with [the anima and animus] aspect of ourselves is one way to come into a more balanced place and to acknowledge our true nature as androgynous souls. The power of androgyny lies in

> *rediscovering the opposites within one's self and in reintegrating the parts of ourselves that have been lost to us through societal sex–role behavioral training."*[3]

But what if someone is already androgynous or has a third gender identity? Who is their inner soul? Wouldn't an androgynous individual need both an *anima* and an *animus* to be balanced? Or might there be a third energy, unidentified by Jung, which would be the projection and inner soul of an androgynous individual?

The progression towards wholeness begins with acknowledging the traditional and stereotypical bigender standards for males and females. Through discovery and development of the qualities of both ends of the bigender system, an individual cultivates a sense of self that can access all qualities, be they masculine or feminine (monism).

An individual's perfect partner is someone who complements their physical form and their *anima/animus.* In combination, the *anima* and *animus* are known as syzygy (siz′ə jē), the Divine Couple. Syzygy represents wholeness and completion. The conjunction of the two creates a new whole without the loss of the individual. And as in synergy, the sum of the partnership is greater than the sum of its parts (individual halves).

> "Many of us have experienced gender wounding that has prevented us from living the full expression of our hopes and desires for our lives. To heal men and women, it will require not only healing male energy in men, and female energy in women, but it will require that women integrate healed masculine energy and men integrate healed feminine energy within themselves.
>
> Men do not always primarily exhibit the male polarity and women do not always primarily exhibit female polarity tendencies. The true nature of the yin and yang principles is not indicated by physical form. All people are a balance of the two polarities. Any person of either sex can be a mirror for growth."
>
> *–Sylvia Brailler, Dancing in the Eye of Transformation: 10 Keys to Creative Consciousness*

GENDER CLASSIFICATION MODELS

If the ideal system of gender classification were to be created, how many categories would it have? Many indigenous cultures around the world recognize three gender categories:

1. Male
2. Female
3. Neither male nor female and both male and female

Some cultures reserve the third gender for male–bodied two spirits and add a fourth gender for female–bodied two spirits. Chapter 10 is devoted to Two Spirits and third gender cultures.

Kenneth Ray Stubb, the "Sexual Shaman", identifies seven categories of gender: a Mars man, a Venus woman, a transgender male, a transgender female, an androgynous male, an androgynous female, and a genderless individual.

In *Sexing the Body: Gender Politics and the Construction of Sexuality*[4], Anne Fausto–Sterling, professor at Brown University and a leading expert in biology and gender development, proposed a classification system of five sexes based on biological differences of the body.

1. Males
2. Females
3. Herms (True hermaphrodites*) Individuals who possess one testis and one ovary.
4. Merms (Male pseudohermaphrodites*) Individuals who have testes and some aspects of the female genitalia but no ovaries.
5. Ferms (Female pseudohermaphrodites*) Individuals who have ovaries and some aspects of the male genitalia but lack testes.

**Note: the term hermaphrodite is no longer used in referring to humans. The correct term would be intersex individuals.*

Bem Sex Role Inventory

Sandra Bem, a psychologist at Cornell University, created the Bem Sex Role Inventory (BSRI) [5] in 1974. It measures feminine, masculine, and androgynous traits of individuals as mutually exclusive dimensions. The BSRI consists of sixty questions, twenty each on feminine, masculine, and neutral items. Each question is rated on a seven point scale. Based on their responses, individuals are classified as having one of four gender–role orientations: masculine, feminine, androgynous, or undifferentiated. Bem viewed androgynous individuals as being more flexible and mentally healthy than either masculine or feminine individuals and undifferentiated individuals as being less competent. The Bem Sex Role Inventory is available online at http://garote.bdmonkeys.net/bsri.html.

Center for Gender Sanity Model

The Center for Gender Sanity created the model[6] illustrated in the figure below in 2009 to illustrate the common labels used to categorize various aspects of gender and sexuality. All four continua are independent. The cultural expectation is that males occupy the extreme left ends of all four scales and females occupy the right ends. But that simply does not work in the real world. An individual may be at any point along all four continua. There are as many combinations as there are people. I like this layout, as shown below, because even though it is linear, it shows how the piece parts of identities differ yet are related.

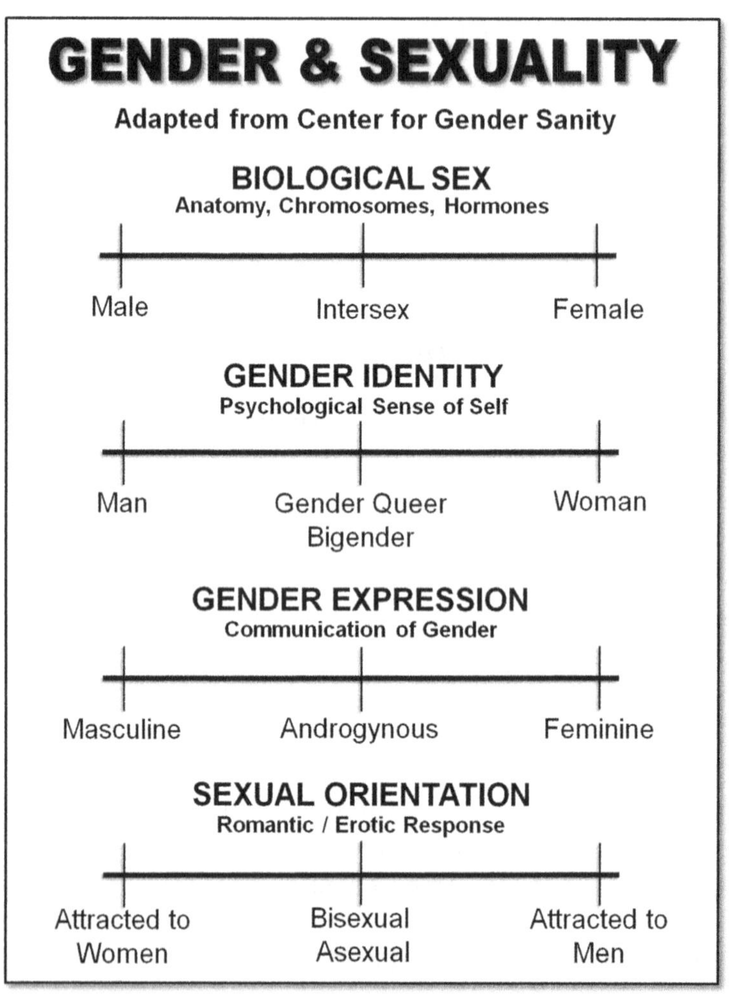

Sam Killermann's Genderbread Person

The Social Justice Advocate's Handbook: A Guide to Gender[7] by Sam Killermann is an excellent book on gender identity published in 2013. Killermann developed a different perspective on gender development than the standard linear scales seen thus far. His model, portrayed by the genderbread person, illustrates the difference between sex, attraction, gender identity, and gender expression. His illustration can be viewed on page 70 in his book.

He also includes a linear scale but the scale resembles the function of an equalizer, allowing the degree of bass, treble, and high notes to vary by degree. He is illustrating that dual characteristics of gender and sexuality exist in each individual but they can vary by degree.

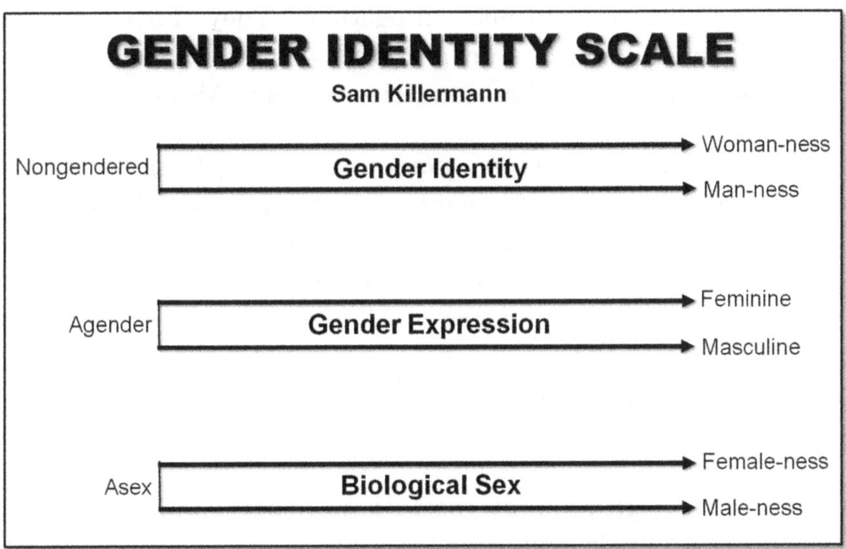

Bornstein's Sex and Gender Chart

My New Gender Workbook published in 2013 by Kate Bornstein is one of my favorite books on gender and sexual identity. She says:

> *"Gender is real easy to sum up in one word: categorization. Anything that categorizes people is gender. Sex is f*cking: any way, shape, or form, alone or with others."*[8]

She created a great illustration to demonstrate the difference between sex and gender. Unfortunately I was unable to obtain permission to use it here but you can view it in her book on page 49.

Hill and Mays' Gender Planet

The Gender Book by Mel Reiff Hill and Jay Mays is another great book on gender identity. It is succinct, all inclusive, and presents identity concepts in fresh new ways. They have created perhaps the most accurate representation of gender identity thus far by eliminating linear continua altogether. They have overlaid multiple gender identities on a globe called the Gender Planet. Identities are like individual countries. Hill and Mays say:

> *"Imagine gender as a planet. All people grow up somewhere on that planet, most in Ladyland or Manlandia. Lots of people are comfortable where they're born and stay in that same area their whole lives. Some people, though, are citizens of Manlandia but are born in Ladyland. Just like in the real world, you can't tell someone's citizenship by looking at them; it's very personal."*[9]

Below is my graphic interpretation of their "planet" theory. I used different labels and added a sexuality planet (that doesn't exist in their book). To see the original graphic representation refer to page 12–13 in *The Gender Book.*

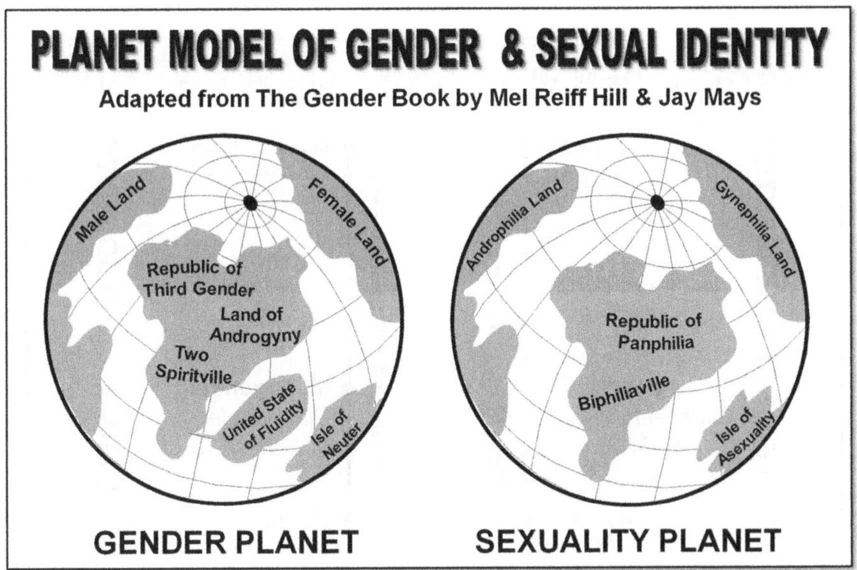

Stephen's Vertical Model

Most of the linear models previously created have been on a horizontal axis. However what would happen if we changed the scale to a vertical axis? Moving to a vertical axis, as illustrated below, changes perception of gender and sexual identity a bit. Here we can perceive an all–encompassing identity on one end of the spectra and neutral or non–existent identity on the other end. In the middle of the spectra lie a mono–identity and a bi–identity. The problem with presenting identity on a vertical scale is that it implies there is a hierarchy and with hierarchy comes judgment of bad or good, higher or lower, and more or less than.

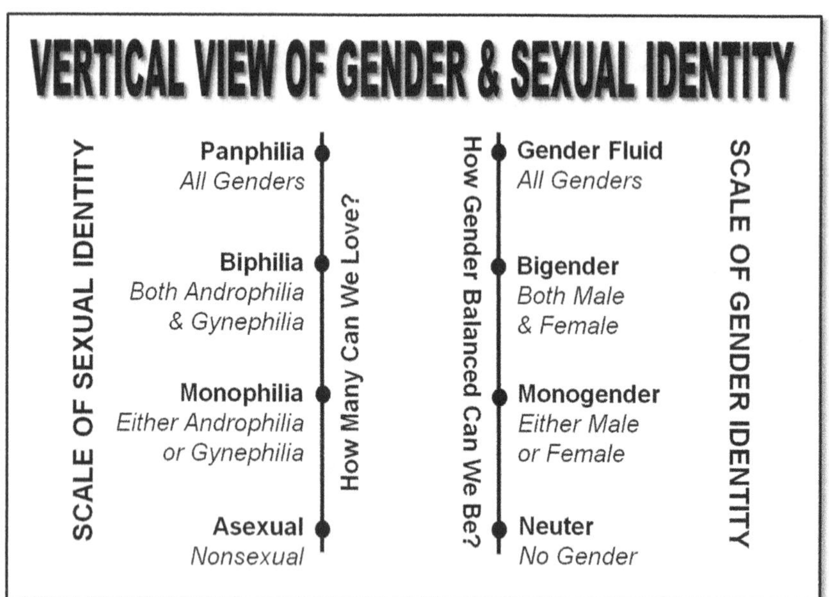

Stephen's Holographic Model of the Soul

The planet model of gender and sexual identity as illustrated in the Hill and Hays Gender Planet section above implies that all similar types of identity live together in one region. However, in the real world, individuals of differing identities live interspersed among one another.

I have been working on a circular model for many years. My model is an illustration of a holographic soul that has all aspects of gender and sexual identity available as points in space. The probability of manifesting identity at any one point is dependent on intention and attention. Since all souls are spun off from of a common universal energy, they are all connected even though individual paths of evolution are unique.

A hologram is a three–dimensional image created by photographic projection. The term is taken from the Greek words "*holos*" (whole) and "*gramma*" (message). It is representative of two different principles: 1) all the parts of the whole are connected and each part contains the whole and 2) the whole can be reproduced from any part.

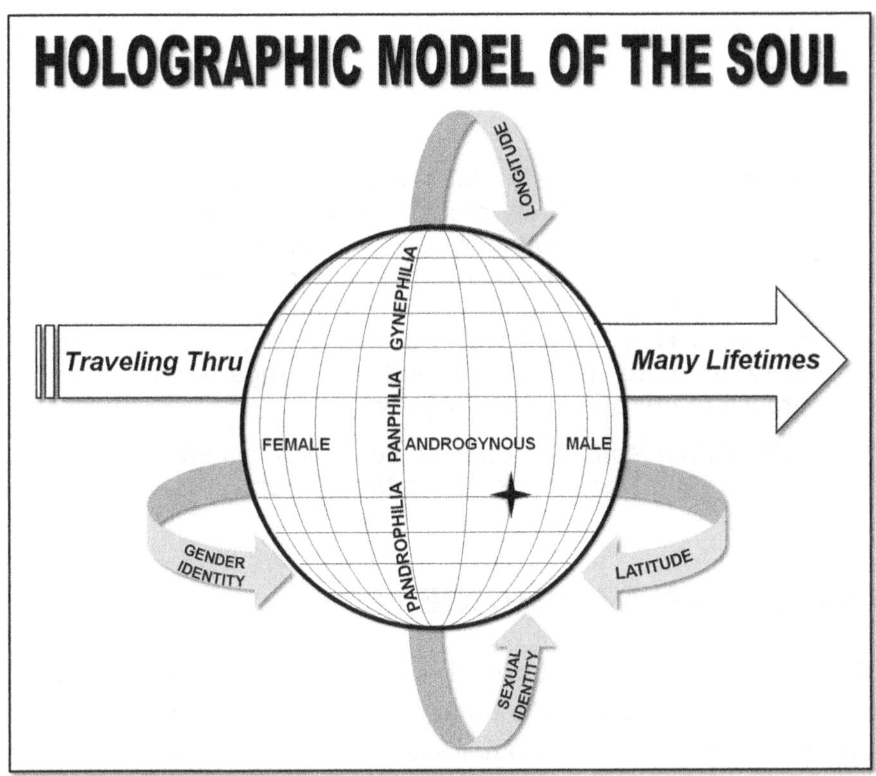

Picture your soul as a holographic globe, as illustrated above, with longitudes that represent a continuum of sexual identity as and latitudes that represent a continuum of gender identity. Just as you can live at any longitude and latitude coordinates on Earth, your identity can reside at any longitude and latitude of identity on the Soul Globe. Since a hologram is three–dimensional, points can also exist on the surface of the sphere or they can lie deep within the interior. With free choice and fluidity of identity available to you at all times, you can spend an entire lifetime on one point or move from point to point throughout one lifetime. Or you might spend multiple lifetimes at one point. Meanwhile, our Soul is traveling through many lifetimes experimenting with multiple variations of identity like choosing an outfit to wear from a wardrobe. To complete the picture of a holographic soul, other continua such as race, creed, culture, ancestry, age, ability, socioeconomic status, and spirituality can be overlaid on the holographic soul.

"Eliminating the binary does not mean that someone cannot identify as purely male or purely female. It means that no one has to. Gender does not paint the picture of who I am. Who I am paints the picture of my gender. Why not use all of the colors on the palette? The binary not only serves to limit who we can be. It also limits our ability to unite as a group and work together for the purpose of our own human dignity."

–Stephanie Mott, Executive Director, Kansas Statewide Transgender Education Project

GENDER IN LANGUAGE

The binary gender system provides social rules so we know how to treat others. However, if the binary gender system is replaced, not only do we need to adjust our social rules and etiquette, but our language as well. In this section, we will look at options for a gender neutral English language.

In Indo–European, Afro–Asiatic and Niger–Congo languages personal pronouns have gender distinctions between male and female. Austronesian, East Asian, Uralic, and many Niger–Congo languages do not have gender distinctions in personal pronouns.

English may be easier to convert to gender neutrality than other languages such as Spanish or French, where all nouns have specific genders. Although English does not have grammatical gender, there are still many words that imply binary genders. These words can be replaced with non–binary words.

Today there are many proposed alternatives that adjust the English language to be more inclusive of gender identity options. Some of these alternatives are:

1. Use of "they", "them", "their", "theirs", and "themselves" to represent singular pronouns. (This is the predominant style I have used in this book.)

2. Alternate back and forth between genders, a form some authors use in their writing.
3. Use of one of the new pronoun systems that have been invented as shown in the tables below:

PRONOUNS

MODEL	SUBJECT	OBJECT	POSSESSIVE	REFLEXIVE
Male Gender	He	Him	His	Himself
Female Gender	She	Her	Her	Herself
Compact	S/he	Him/r	His/r	Him/herself
No Gender	It	It	It	Itself
No Gender	That	That	Thats	Thatself
No Gender	One	One	One's	Oneself
Singular They	They	Them	Their	Themself
US Regional Dialect	Yo	Yo	Yos	Yoself
Futurama	Shklee	Shklim	Shklir	Shklimself
Germanic	Ze	Zir, Zem, Hir, Mer	Zir, Zes, Hir, Zer	Zirself, Zemself, Hirself
Humanist	Hu	Hum	Hus	Humself
Mary Orovan	Co	Co	Cos	Co
Spivak	E or Ey	Em	Eir	Emself
No Gender	E	Het	Het	Hetself
No Gender	Jee	Jem	Jeir	Jemself
No Gender	Per	Per	Per	Perself
No Gender	Sie	Hir	Hir	Hirself
No Gender	Thon	Thon	Thons	Thonself
No Gender	Ve	Ver	Vis	Verself
No Gender	Xe	Xem	Xyr	Xemself
No Gender	Yon	Ton	Yos	Tonself
No Gender	Zhe	Zhim	Zher	Zhimself

COMMON TERMS

TERM	REPLACED BY
Brother/Sister	Sibling
Nephew/Niece	Nibling
Uncle/Aunt	Ommer
Boy/Girl/Daughter/Son	Kid/Child
Father/Mother	Parent
Husband/Wife	Spouse
Waiter/Waitress/Steward/Stewardess	Server
Handsome/Beautiful	Attractive

TITLES

TITLE	REPLACED BY
Mr/Miss/Ms	M, Misc, Mre, Msr, Mx, Pr, Sair

In 2013, Sweden officially adopted a new gender–neutral pronoun, "*hen*", which is a modified version of the Swedish words "*han*" and "*hon*," that mean "he" and "she" respectively.

As our social consciousness continues to evolve, the day may arrive soon when it will be correct etiquette to ask individuals during introductions, not only their preferred name, but their preferred pronoun when being addressed.

> "Gender should never be polarized. It is a rainbow that is far too splendorous in its diversity. The expression of one's whole gender must be intuitive, fluid, and in a perpetual state of becoming. Widespread occurrences of hermaphroditism in plants, animals and humans provide graphic evidence of Spirit expressing its diversity beyond the cultural constructs of bipolar gender. Some Native American elders believe that there is an abundance of transgender people being born at this time who can help heal our world."
>
> *–Holly Boswell, The Spirit of Transgender*

NOTES:

[1] *Wikipedia.* "*Yin* and *Yang*." Last modified July, 2014. http://en.wikipedia.org/wiki/Yin_and_yang

[2] Kramer, Kenneth. *The Sacred Art of Dying: How World Religions Understand Death.* Paulist Press, 1988.

[3] Brailler, Sylvia. *Dancing in the Eye of Transformation: 10 Keys to Creative Consciousness.* Triple Muse Publications, 2006.

[4] Fausto–Sterling, Anne. *Sexing the Body: Gender Politics and the Construction of Sexuality.* Basic Books, 2000.

[5] Bem, Sandra Lipsitz. *Bem Sex–Role Inventory: Professional Manual.* Consulting Psychologists Press, 1981.

Bem, Sandra Lipsitz. "Bem Sex–Role Inventory" Mental Measurements Yearbook with Tests in Print, 1981.

[6] Center for Gender Sanity "Diagram of Sex and Gender." Reprinted by permission of the Center for Gender Sanity. http://www.gendersanity.com/diagram.html

[7] Sam Killermann *The Social Justice Advocate's Handbook: A Guide to Gender.* Impetus Books, 2013.

[8] Bornstein, Kate. *My New Gender Workbook: A Step–by–Step Guide to Achieving World Peace Through Gender Anarchy and Sex Positivity.* Routledge, 2013.

[9] Hill, Mel Reiff and Jay Mays. *The Gender Book.* Marshall House Press, 2013.

CHAPTER 7:
SEXUAL IDENTITY
The Consciousness of Sexuality

PANSEXUALITY

The word "pan" comes from the Greek word for "all". Pansexuals are sexually and romantically attracted to individuals of all gender identities. They understand that there is a much wider gender spectrum than just males and females. In other words, being attracted to an individual's soul, energy, and inner beauty supersedes the importance of the physical body.

(Symbol: Designer Unknown)

SEXUALITY 101

Sexual identity, which is the self–concept of sexuality, has three aspects: psychological, behavioral, and spiritual. Sexual identity includes the components of gender, romantic identity, and sexual expression. Identity may be broken down into the following components:

1. ***Sexual Orientation*** – What genders (or none), one is romantically or sexually attracted toward.
2. ***Sexual Orientation Identity*** – Concept of how one identifies (or not) with various sexual orientations.
3. ***Sexual Behavior*** – Sexual acts performed by the individual.

I will not be using the term "sexual preference" because that implies that sexuality is a choice. Sexuality, while it may change over time, is never a personal choice. From a metaphysical perspective, we have come into this particular lifetime with an orientation that will help us learn a specific lesson. I prefer to use the term "sexual identity" instead because sexuality is not only who you love but how you perceive yourself loving them.

Most models of sexual identity are based on what genders or biological sexes an individual has attraction to: same, the opposite, both, or neither. Because there are so many more variations of gender identity than the traditional two of male and female, it is too confusing to base sexual identity on whether someone is "like" you or "not like" you. I prefer terms that describe sexual identity based on who the target of affection is. These terms describe an individual's sexual desires independently of their own gender identity. It is especially helpful to use the following terms in order to eliminate confusion when referring to sexual identity of trans* individuals. The list of terms based on target of affection are:

- ***Androphilia*** (from Greek "andro", male + "philia", love) – attraction to males and/or masculinity.

- ***Gynephilia*** (from Greek "gunē", women, + "philia", love) – the attraction to females and/or femininity.
- ***Androgynephilia*** – the attraction to both males and females.
- ***Panphilia*** – the attraction to all individuals and is not based on the other person's gender.

These four terms should replace "heterosexual" (attracted to opposite–gender individuals), "homosexual" (attracted to same–gender individuals), "bisexual" (attracted to both genders), and "pansexual" (attracted to all genders).

Following is a list of sexual identities. I tried to make the list as inclusive as I could. Many identities may seem very similar to others, but each one is a bit unique in definition to the individual that claims it as a label. These sexual identity terms are defined in the glossary at the back of the book.

Sexual Identity Options

Akoiromantic	Homosexual
Ambiphile	Idemromantic
Ambiromantic	Lesbian
Androphile	Lithromantic
Androgynephile	Lithsexual
Androgynoromantic	Monoromantic
Androromantic	Monosexual
Antiromantic	Neutroisromantic
Aromantic	Queer
Asexual	Questioning
Autochorissexual	Non-heterosexual
Autosexual	Not specified
Banjee	Omniromantic
Bicurious	Omnisexual
Biphilia	Panphilia
Biromantic	Panromantic
Bisexual	Pansexual
Celibate	Polyamorous
Chameleosexual	Polyromantic
Cupioromantic	Polysexual
Demiromantic	PoMosexual
Demisexual	Questioning
Ex-gay	Quoiromantic
Gay	Recipromantic
Greyromantic	Requiesromantic
Gynephile	Same Gender Loving
Gynoromantic/Gyneromantic	Sapiosexual
Hetero-Flexible	Skolioromantic
Homo-Flexible	Skoliosexual
Heteroromantic	Transromantic
Heterosexual	Versatile
Homoromantic	Wtfromantic

Sexual identity is being further differentiated by whether an individual is sexually attracted or romantically attracted to others. An individual may have a different sexual identity than a romantic identity. For example they might be romantically gynophilic but sexually androphilic. Sexual attraction is based on physical attraction — who do you want to have sex with?

Romantic attraction is based on emotional attraction — who do you want to fall in love with? The two states can be mutually exclusive. You can have sex without romantic attachment and you can love another without sexual expression.

Another dimension of sexuality is how an individual behaves with sexual partner(s). There is a range of identities and practices but predominant among them are the following three classifications of sex roles. These categories originated from sex between men and referred to sexual positions but now they can be considered actual roles, which include social, psychological, and sexual identity. These terms are also used in specific sexual communities such as the BDSM community.

- ***Top*** – An individual who penetrates. Also implies the dominant individual in a relationship.
- ***Bottom*** – An individual who is penetrated. Also implies the submissive individual in a relationship.
- ***Versatile*** – An individual who alternates between penetrating and receiving, or being dominant and submissive. The slang term for this is “switching”. “Flip flopping” is switching during one sexual encounter.

SEXUAL IDENTITY CLASSIFICATION MODELS

Sexual orientation is very difficult to measure. Sexual orientation measurement can be based on many different phenomena, such as: sexual arousal, brain scans, eye tracking, body odor preference, finger length ratio and right or left handedness. Some tools used to determine sexual orientation include self–reporting, surveys, interviews, physical arousal measurements, sexual behavior, sexual fantasy, and erotic arousal patterns.

In the following section I will share the sexual identification and classification models that have been developed by different sexology experts. Most all of them are based on a linear model of identification. However, while reading this section, keep in mind that Alfred Kinsey, a biologist, zoologist, and entomologist who specialized in human sexuality, said:

> *"Not all things are black nor all things white. It is a fundamental of taxonomy that nature rarely deals with discrete categories."*

Ulrichs's Classification

Karl Heinrich Ulrichs[1], a writer and the earliest pioneer of the gay rights movement, believed homosexual individuals were "spiritual hermaphrodites" with the mind and soul of one sex and the body of the other, thus creating a third sex. He developed a sexual orientation classification system for homosexuals in the 1860s. The term "homosexual" had not yet been created, so Ulrichs used his own terms. The categories were:

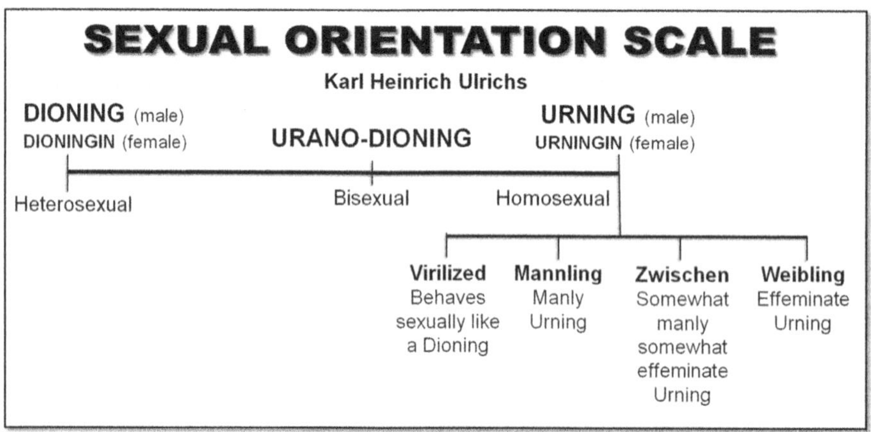

Hirschfeld's Sexual Orientation Classification

Magnus Hirschfeld[2], a physician and sexologist, developed a sexual orientation classification system in 1896. It measured the strength of an individual's sexual desire on two independent ten–point scales: A (homosexual) and B (heterosexual). An individual could be at any point on each of the two scales. For example, an entirely heterosexual identity would be an A0–B10. An entirely homosexual identity would be an A10–B0. Someone strongly attracted to both males and females (a bisexual) would be an A10–B10. Someone attracted to neither (an asexual) would be an A0–B0.

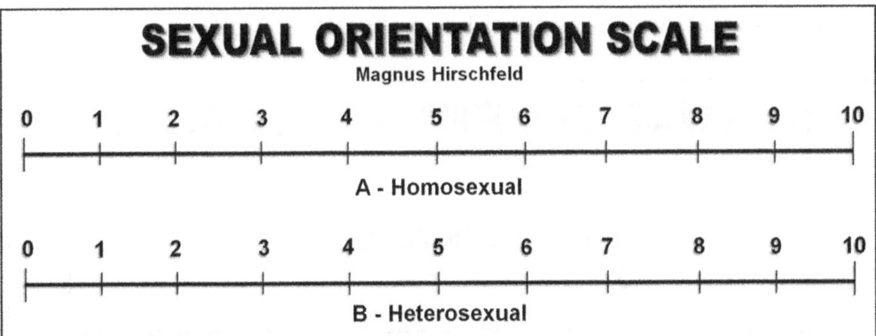

Kinsey Scale

Alfred Kinsey, Wardell Pomeroy, a sexologist, and Clyde Martin, an assistant to Kinsey, developed The Kinsey Heterosexual–Homosexual Rating Scale[1] in 1948. This scale allowed for the possibility of degrees between exclusively heterosexual or homosexual. The scale is based on the relative amounts of heterosexual and homosexual experiences and responses an individual has had. An individual whose identity stayed stationary at one point on the scale would be an example of static sexuality. An individual whose identity moves to various points on the scale at different points in time would be an example of fluid sexuality.

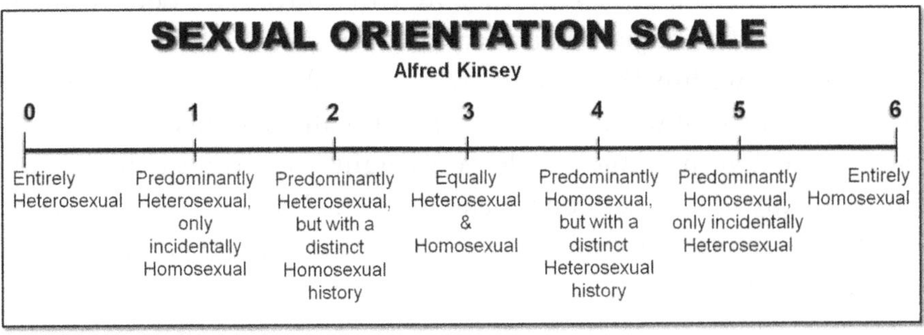

Shively/DeCecco Scale of Sexual Orientation

M.G. Shively and J.P. DeCecco created a Scale of Sexual Orientation[3] in 1977. The two scales assess two dimensions of sexual orientation: the physical and the affectional.

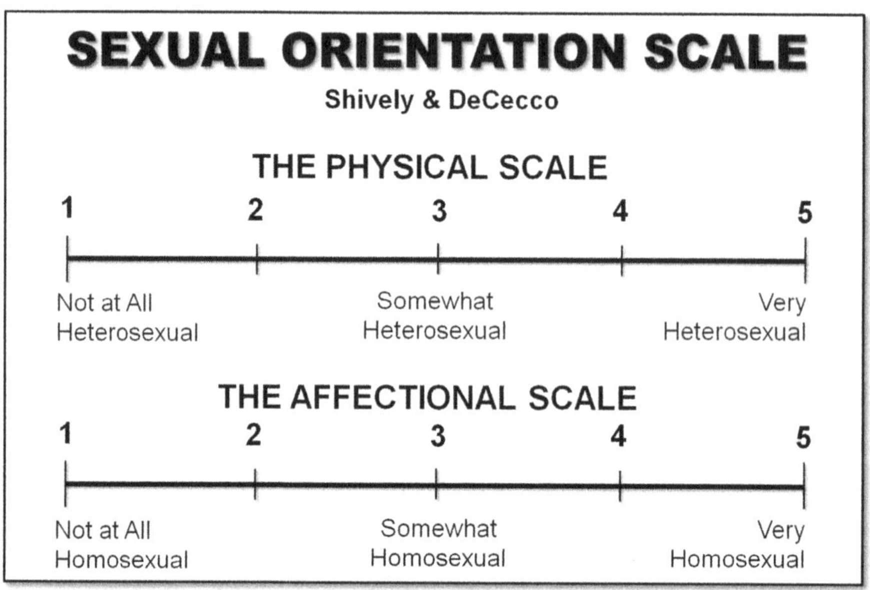

Klein Sexual Orientation Grid

Fritz Klein, a psychiatrist and founder of the American Institute of Bisexuality, developed the Klein Sexual Orientation Grid (KSOG) [4] in 1978. It has a seven point scale to assess seven different dimensions of sexuality at three different points in an individual's life: the past (from adolescence to twelve months ago), the present (within the last twelve months), and the ideal (what an individual would most desire). The result includes twenty–one values and five possible labels of straight, bi–straight, bi–bi, bi–gay, and gay. The questions focus on sexual attraction, behavior, fantasies, emotional and social preference, lifestyle, and self–identification.

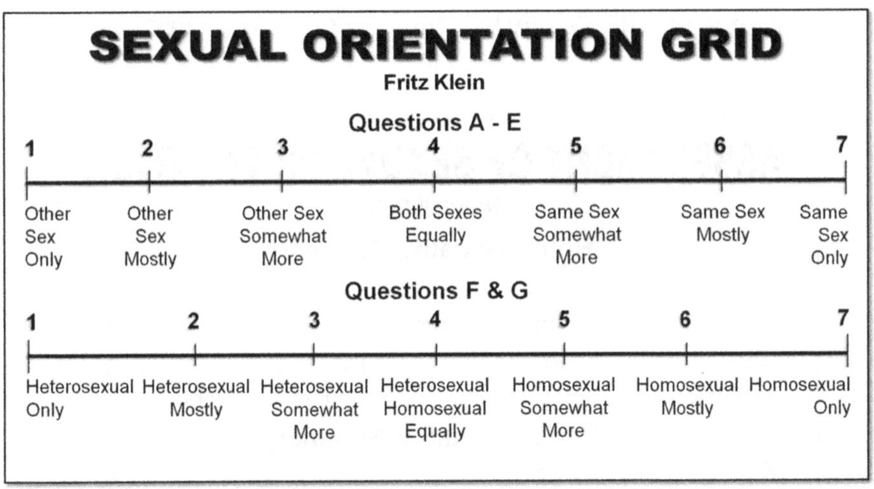

Coleman Assessment of Sexual Orientation

Eli Coleman, the director of the Program in Human Sexuality at the University of Minnesota, developed a Clinical Assessment of Sexual Orientation[1 and 5] which is based on nine dimensions: current relationship status; self–identification identity; ideal self–identification identity; global acceptance of one's current sexual orientation identity; physical sexual identity; gender identity; sex–role identity; sexual behavior identity, fantasies, and emotional attachments; and the individual's past and present perception of their sexual identity compared to their idealized future. The results are categorized based on the labels of heterosexual, bisexual, or homosexual.

Sell Assessment of Sexual Orientation

Randall Sell, professor at the Joseph L. Mailman School of Public Health at Columbia, developed the Assessment of Sexual Orientation (SASO) [6] in 1996. It consists of twelve questions: six questions about sexual attraction, four about sexual behavior, and two about sexual orientation identity. Sexual orientation is evaluated on four separate scales (homosexuality, heterosexuality, bisexuality, and asexuality) by rating the degree of each by the ranking "not at all", "slightly", "moderately", or "very" as shown below:

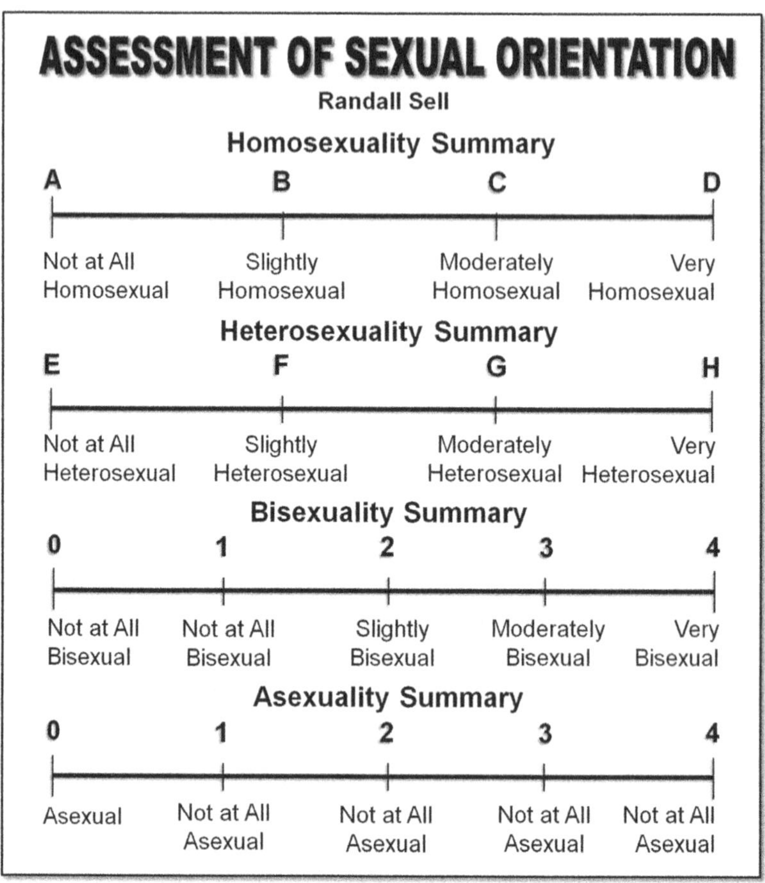

Epstein Sexual Orientation Inventory

Robert Epstein, a research psychologist, developed the Sexual Orientation Inventory (ESOI) [7] in 2006. It consists of a series of eighteen questions. Numerical results are given on a scale of nine to thirteen in the following categories:

- Mean Sexual Orientation
- Sexual Orientation Range
- Sex Drive
- Same Sex Attraction

- Opposite Sex Attraction

The lower an individual scores, the more heterosexual their orientation is. The higher an individual scores, the more homosexual their orientation is. The wider the range of scores, the greater sexual flexibility is and the more choice there may be in expressing sexual orientation. The ESOI test is available at http://mysexualorientation.com/take/.

SEXUAL IDENTITY FLUIDITY

Sexual identity can change throughout an individual's life. However, when and why it does change seems like a complete mystery. According to Sigmund Freud, neurologist and founder of psychoanalysis, and Wilhelm Fliess, an otolaryngologist, all humans are born bisexual but through psychological development a monosexual form becomes dominant while bisexuality remains latent.

For statistics on sexual orientation changes and sexual identity fluidity, read the paper at http://mygenes.co.nz/PDFs/Ch12.pdf.[8] The research in this paper indicates that fluidity is more common among women than among men, more common among transsexuals than non–transsexuals, more common among homosexuals than heterosexuals, and more common among bisexuals than either homosexuals or heterosexuals.

One study based on 106 transsexual clients found that 32.8 percent male–to–female transsexuals and 17.5 percent female–to–male transsexuals[9] reported changes in who they were sexually and romantically attracted to during or after gender transition procedures such as surgery and hormone therapy. The rate of change in sexual orientation after surgery was quite higher than the rate of change of those who did not have surgery. The reason for this change in sexual orientation is still unknown, however, it has been established that it is not related to hormone therapy. Gender identity and sexual orientation are supposed to be independent of each other however with so many transsexual cases of change in sexual orientation during transition more research needs to be done to understand the correlation between the two.

A form of "forced" sexual orientation change, referred to as "ex–gay" therapy, is a combination of methods that aim to change a homosexual orientation. This therapy may include behavioral, cognitive, psychoanalytic, medical, and religious techniques. In some parts of the world, efforts to change a person's sexual orientation may even include the extreme action of corrective rape. Some U.S. states are now outlawing the use of "ex–gay" therapy mostly because it has been proven to be ineffective.

> "Sexual orientation develops across a person's lifetime. For some the focus of sexual interest will shift at various points through the life span."
>
> *–American Psychological Association*
>
> "For some people, sexual orientation is continuous and fixed throughout their lives. For others, sexual orientation may be fluid and change over time."
>
> *–Centre for Addiction and Mental Health*

BISEXUALITY

Bisexuality is a sexual identity in which an individual feels sexual attraction towards both males and females. There are two types based on how they happen in time:

1. ***Concurrent*** – An individual is attracted to both males and females simultaneously.
2. ***Consecutive*** – An individual is attracted to both males and females but at different times in their lives.

Some bisexuals may feel more strongly attracted to one gender than the other. William Masters and Virginia Johnson, sexuality research pioneers, used the term "ambisexual" to refer to a person who is sexually attracted to both men and women to the same degree. Some consecutive bisexuals may even identify as homosexual or heterosexual because they have not yet encountered the other phase of their bisexuality.

> "Those who condemn another's sexual orientation merely reveal the absence of depth in their own sexual lives. Because when you have had the highest form of sexual experience — one that is soul-sourced and soul-driven — you immediately recognize that gender is entirely irrelevant. The soul doesn't care about body parts. It simply loves what it does."
>
> *–Jeff Brown, Love It Forward*

ATTRACTOR FACTORS

There are many questions that we can ask ourselves about what attractor factors draw us to a specific individual or repels us from another. What makes one individual seem more attractive than another? Do we respond differently depending on who we are with or what environment we are in? Is attraction related to mirroring? Is attraction a function of entrainment? Why do we immediately like or not like a person? Are we attracted to individuals with lower, equal, or higher vibrations? Are we attracted to individuals that we agreed to meet during this incarnation to learn specific lessons with?

Here is a list of questions we might ask when we examine what properties make up the phenomenon of charisma and magnetism:

- Is it mindset? A positive attitude?
- Is it a mood, a result of an emotional state?
- Is it love, the result of an open heart?
- Is it intent, affirmations successfully manifested?

- Is it self–confidence and self–esteem?
- Is it chemical, a reaction to pheromones?
- Is it genetics, an inherited trait?
- Is it karmic, a result of many lives lived?
- Is it destiny, being endowed with charisma to learn the specific lessons associated with it?
- Is it energy from the sprits, guides, and angels that surround us?
- Is it the speed at which a person's energy vibrates?
- If it is derived from a higher vibration, how does an individual raise his/her vibration?
- Is it increased through energy medicine exercises?
- Is it increased through grounding and running energy?
- Is it increased through doing personal work?

If charisma or magnetism is the interaction of energy, is it true that "like attracts like" as in the Principle of Attraction? Or is it true that "opposites attract" like the basic principle of Physics?

Indeed, there are not easy or clear answers to these questions. Perhaps it would be far easier to just say that our attraction to others is magical and leave it there.

We may be attracted to certain people's energy because of their charisma, magnetism, charm, personality, appeal, allure, and/or rapport. Like no two snowflakes are the same, no two individuals have the same energy imprint. Therefore we can be attracted to one identical twin and not the other.

Charisma is a word from the Greek language that means "favor freely given" or "gift of grace". Individuals that are considered charismatic have a special attractiveness or charm about them. Charisma, or the art of attracting, can be understood from two different perspectives:

1. As a function based on physical chemistry. Attraction is a function of the Physical Body.

2. As a function based on spiritual connections. Attraction is a function of the Energy Body.

THE CHEMISTRY OF ATTRACTION

The Physical Body has a system of chemicals. These chemical secretions can trigger social responses in members of the same species therefore a preponderance of our attraction may be chemically based.

Oxytocin has been nicknamed the "cuddle chemical". It has several different functions. One, it is very present in mothers, especially when going into labor or nursing newborns. It encourages the mother to cuddle her child. The second function of oxytocin is associated with sexual arousal. It is triggered through physical and emotional events. It peaks during orgasm and women are more sensitive to it than men.

PEA (phenylethlamine) has been nicknamed the "infatuation chemical" by Diane Ackerman, in her book *A Natural History of Love*[10]. PEA peaks in the body when two people are attracted to each other or fall in love, when people are faced with danger, or during thrilling activities. PEA is an amphetamine–like chemical that produces feelings of pleasure, euphoria, and excitement.

Sex pheromones are secreted chemicals that trigger sexual responses in members of the same species. In addition, there are aromatic pheromones that can be purchased and worn in order to attract sexual partners.

> "The meeting of two personalities is like the contact of two chemical substances. If there is any reaction, both are transformed."
>
> –*Carl Jung*

THE SPIRITUALITY OF ATTRACTION

Charisma may also be a result of an attraction to a magnetic Energy Body. It would seem that we would naturally be attracted to Energy Bodies that emitted a lot of light, similar to how moths are attracted to the flame and insects are attracted to light bulbs.

The highest level of vibration is love. The more open and loving our hearts, the higher we vibrate. The more personal work we have done to come to love ourselves, the higher we vibrate. The higher we vibrate, the more we will attract others especially those of like vibration.

Another spiritual aspect of attraction is based on our previous connections with other souls. Even though we may not consciously remember other souls we meet while incarnated, subconsciously we will react to them based on subconscious memories. We may have contracted to love certain souls in this lifetime. We may have incarnated to be with specific souls that we love. It is no accident who we meet, who we connect with, and what the nature of that connection will be. Older souls are attracted to an individual's soul, heart, and spirit vibrations, instead of their age, ethnicity, socio–economic status, education, religion, or gender.

Sex and intimacy are therapeutic for high frequency individuals. High frequency people see sex as an intense exchange of positive energy, a clearing of negative energies, and a sharing of spiritual forces.

SACRED SEXUALITY

Sacred sex should not be taboo because it is an expression of love — love for others, love for one's self, or maybe even just the love of sex. When two people feel an affinity or powerful love towards each other, they want to express their love through touch. If the chemistry is right, especially in the limerence[11] stage, a couple may have the feeling of wanting to physically merge, to swallow up the partner, or be swallowed up by the partner.

In *Soul Psychology*, Joshua David Stone says that:

"The ego is making love only to the Physical Body; the

spirit is making love to the spirit living within the Physical Body."[12]

He explains that the sharing of fluids between two individuals creates a spiritual bond or cord of energy that may be difficult to break during a lifetime. So when choosing a partner consider what karmic bonds you are creating and with whom.

In *Repetition*[13], Doris Eliana Cohen, says that when a male and female join together in orgasm, the experience is not only sexual but also spiritual. When two individuals share orgasm, they're uniting as one and transcending their differences.

In Judaism, the *Shekhina* is the Divine Feminine, the feminine aspect of God. At the beginning of the Shabbath, two candles are lit by the woman of the home, kindling great arousal in the upper world. It is a mitzvah (good deed) for a Kabbalist to make love to his wife on the Shabbath. This act of uniting the Divine Masculine and the Divine Feminine makes God one [whole and balanced]. As above, so below. As it is on Earth, so it is in Heaven.

TYPES OF LOVE

The ancient Greeks identified five different types of love:

1. ***Eros*** – Romantic and Sexual
2. ***Philia*** – Friendship
3. ***Storge*** – Kinship
4. ***Agape*** – Divine
5. ***Xenia*** – Hospitality

The Chinese identified an additional category called *Ren*, which is benevolent love that focuses on duty, action and attitude. In Judaism, *Chesed* is a form of love described as loving–kindness. Impersonal love is a love for objects, causes, principles, or goals.

For simplicity, I have divided love into four states:

1. ***Romantic*** – Sexual love of lovers, significant others, and spouses.
2. ***Platonic*** – Non–sexual love of friends and family.
3. ***Spiritual*** – Altruistic, unconditional love, loving kindness, and being in service.
4. ***Loveless*** – The absence of love.

The states of love can overlap. For example, it is possible for someone to have romantic, platonic, and spiritual love towards a significant other. In fact, I believe that experiencing the first three states of love with another person would be the ultimate in a relationship.

The Heart Wheel

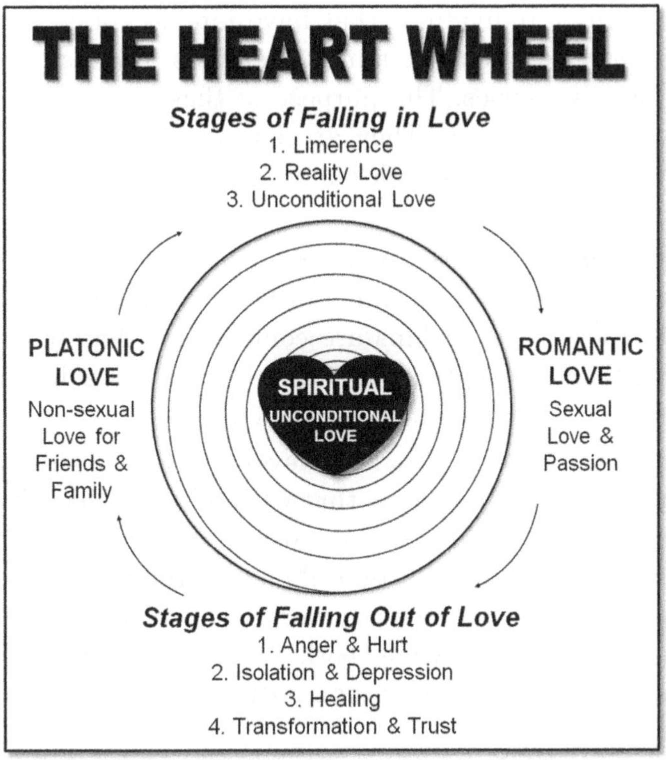

THE HEART WHEEL

Stages of Falling in Love
1. Limerence
2. Reality Love
3. Unconditional Love

PLATONIC LOVE
Non-sexual Love for Friends & Family

SPIRITUAL
UNCONDITIONAL LOVE

ROMANTIC LOVE
Sexual Love & Passion

Stages of Falling Out of Love
1. Anger & Hurt
2. Isolation & Depression
3. Healing
4. Transformation & Trust

From a state of "No Love", we wander onto the Heart Wheel experiencing different states of love, with the ultimate goal of spiraling into the Center, which is the highest state of love, that of Unconditional Loving Kindness.

In addition to types of love there may also be levels of love relationships to consider. Nicolya Christi, in her book *Contemporary Spirituality for an Evolving World*[14], has identified four levels of romantic love:

1. ***Companions*** – Unawakened and unconscious individuals that form relationships based on convenience; neediness; loneliness; fear; need for security, safety, acceptance; or need

for a mother/father figure. Sex involves the Physical Body only.

2. ***Soul Mates*** – Individuals that have intense connections. Soul mates may be partners, family members, friends, associates, pets, or adversaries. The purpose of these relationships is to work out life lessons. They are based on soul contracts and karma from past lives. Sex may or may not be involved in these relationships.
3. ***Twin Souls*** – Spiritually awakened individuals that form relationships that are a union of heart, body, mind, soul, and spirit. These relationships are conflict–free, highly conscious, unconditional, accepting, and usually last for a lifetime. Sex involves the Physical and Energy Body.
4. ***Twin Flames*** – The highest level of relationship that an incarnated soul can have is that with a twin flame. Every soul has a twin flame but they are usually not incarnated at the same time. The union of twin flames is the unification of one soul that was split in two in order to evolve over lifetimes. The union only occurs when both souls are completely self–actualized and their Earth incarnations are complete.

SEXUAL ENERGY

Sexual energy is one of the most powerful energies humans can generate, reflect, and absorb. However, sexual energy doesn't always have to be used for the sexual act or for the goal of orgasm. Many Eastern practices teach the tantra of love, sex, and yoga. These practices defer orgasm so sexual energy can be diverted to creativity, play, prayer, and manifesting desires.

When the two energies of sexuality and spirituality are combined with one intention and one action, a tremendous amount of energy can be generated and released. The intention becomes the energetic expression and the action becomes the physical expression. This can be done in solo sex or sex with partners. Experiment with releasing a wish to manifest something into the Universe with the energy of an orgasm!

SACRED INTIMATES

A sacred intimate has been called by many names: erotic priest, priest of love, sacred prostitute, qadishtu, hierodule, heteratae, courtesan, friend with benefits, healer, sexual shaman, sex worker, sex therapist, and sensual masseur.

A sacred intimate is a professional that works erotically and energetically with those seeking healing, guidance or transformation in their erotic and spiritual lives. The primary gifts a sacred intimate contributes are presence and service. They are in service by: listening deeply, teaching techniques, performing emotional clearing, fulfilling fantasies, countering negative self–talk, and doing erotic healing. A sacred intimate helps others remove the stigma and shame from sex and their body parts. The sacred intimate provides a safe and sacred space to heal, teach, and help others explore their sexual issues.

Some of their work may include hugs, erotic massage, role play, bondage, or any other actions that will meet the needs of the client while not crossing the professional and personal boundaries of the sacred intimate. Sacred intimate work is about healing, reclaiming, rejoicing and celebrating beautiful erotic spirit.

If you find yourself without a partner but would like to explore your sexuality in safe and sacred space, here are a few ways:

- Participate in erotic massage exchanges
- Learn tantric yoga
- Go to sex therapy
- Engage a surrogate sex partner or sacred intimate

SACRED SEX RULES

In any encounter between two people there should be consent and agreement on what the ground rules are. Too many rules will restrict your freedom of expression, but a few basic ones will protect the participants involved. An agreement on ground rules provides a safe and sacred place. Some sacred sex rules are:

- Follow the Wicca Rede of respect: "If it harms none, do what ye will."
- Exorcise shame.
- Trust in and be guided by the flow of the heart.
- Use the mind as an erogenous zone, not as a referee or judge.
- Keep interactions sacred by not gossiping about them to others. What happens during intimacy stays in intimacy.

It is important to keep your own energy systems pure. Having a daily practice of grounding and protection is a must. In addition, carefully consider who you choose to exchange intimate energy with. You may even consider doing an energetic purification after being intimate, especially if the energy you assumed doesn't feel right to you. (If you are not familiar with grounding, protection, and clearing practices, I recommend reading the books listed in footnote 15. There are two acceptable motives for intimate energy exchanges (IEE):

1. You are with a partner of equal or higher energetic vibration.
2. You are with a partner of lower energetic vibration as an act of service for them.

ENERGETIC SEX

Sex isn't only about inserting tab A into slot B. Much more is happening on the energetic level. In fact two individuals can merge energetically without involving physical bodies. The energetic body can be caressed, massaged, and made love to.

Making love takes place not only physically but also energetically and emotionally. Making love energetically means using the Energy Body to connect. This is a wonderful option for many trans* individuals whose current Physical Body may not be the way in which they want to make love to another. Trans* individuals may be grieving body parts that aren't available so making love energetically is a solution that bypasses the physical genitalia.

The mind is the most erotic organ in your body. That is why fantasy is so powerful. So making love energetically consists of using your mind to:

1. ***Set intention***. Your intention will involve what you want to experience with your partner.
2. ***Set attention***. Focus on the energetic exchange more than on the specific body parts.

I have created a ceremony of making love energetically. It will be included in the sequel to this book, which is a workbook on the alchemy of gender and sexuality.

> "Sexual union should be like a rite, a ritual performed in mindfulness with great respect, awe, and love. We must look upon ourselves and the other as a human being, with the capacity of becoming a Buddha."
>
> –*Thich Nhat Hanh*

NOTES:

[1] Ritter, Kathleen Y. and Anthony I. Terndrup. *Handbook of Affirmative Psychotherapy with Lesbians and Gay Men.* The Guilford Press, 2002.

[2] Hirschfeld, Magnus. *The Homosexuality of Men and Women.* Prometheus Books, 2000.

[3] Shively, M. G. & DeCecco, J. P. "Components of Sexual Identity." *Journal of Homosexuality*, 2, 1977.

[4] Klein, Fritz. *The Bisexual Option: Second Edition.* American Institute of Bisexuality, Inc. 1993.

[5] Gonsiorek, John C. Ed. *A Guide to Psychotherapy with Gay and Lesbian Clients.* Routledge, 1985.

[6] Randal L. Sell. "Preliminary Testing of The Sell Assessment of Sexual Orientation." http://www.lgbtdata.com/uploads/1/0/8/8/10884149/ms003_sell_details.pdf

[7] Mysexualorientation.com "Straight, Gay, or Inbetween?" Last modified 2012. http://mysexualorientation.com/take/

[8] Whitehead, Neil and Briar Whitehead. *My Genes Made Me Do It.* "Chapter 12. Can Sexual Orientation Change?"

[9] Auer, Matthias, Johannes Fuss, Anasthasia Athanasoulia, Guenter Stalla, and Caroline Sievers. "Changes in Sexual Orientation in Gender Identity Disorder: Evaluation of Their Association to Sex Reassignment Surgery and Cross–sex Hormone Treatment." http://www.endocrine-abstracts.org/ea/0032/ea0032P333.htm

[10] Ackerman, Diane. *A Natural History of Love.* Vintage, 1995.

[11] Limerence was defined by psychologist Dorothy Tennov as the near–obsessional form of romantic love. It is the involuntary cognitive and emotional state of intense romantic desire for another person that is experienced in the initial stages of a new relationship.

[12] Stone, Joshua David. *Soul Psychology: Keys to Ascension.* Light Technology Publishing, 1995.

[13] Cohen, Doris Eliana. *Repetition: Past Lives, Life, and Rebirth.* Hay House, 2008.

[14] Christi, Nicolya. *Contemporary Spirituality for an Evolving World: A Handbook for Conscious Evolution.* Bear & Company, 2013.

[15] Recommended Books on Grounding, Protecting, and Clearing:

Eden, Donna. *Energy Medicine Kit.* Sounds True Incorporated, 2005.

Friedlander, John and Gloria Hemsher. *Basic Psychic Development: A User's Guide to Auras, Chakras & Clairvoyance.* Weiser Books, 2012.

Linn, Denise. *Sacred Space: Clearing and Enhancing the Energy of Your Home.* Wellspring/Ballantine, 1995.

CHAPTER 8:
CHANGING GENDER
Transitioning Gender in One Lifetime

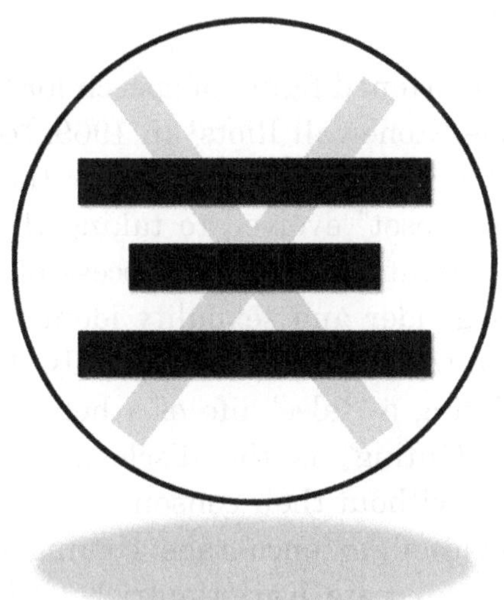

TRANSSEXUALITY

A symbol for transsexual transformation consists of the Greek letter "X". As a symbol with 3 bars, it represents the 3 phases of a transsexual's life: the pre-transition, the transition, and post-transition. "X" is the Roman symbol for "10", which is the number of completion. "X" represents the perfectly balanced human, one line being the spiritual, active, and male side and the other line being the earthly, passive, and female side. "X" represents the union of dualism. "X" represents a cross over, as in transitioning from one gender to another. "X" is short for the prefix "ex", which means a formerly held position, as in ex-male or ex-female.

(Designed by Drake)

IDENTITY TRANSITIONS

In this chapter I will present information on transitioning sexual and gender identity within one lifetime. In the next chapter I will discuss transitioning sexual and gender identity over multiple lifetimes in the form of reincarnation.

STAGES OF COMING OUT AND IDENTITY ACCEPTANCE

"Coming out" is a shortened figure of speech for "coming out of the closet". Prior to the Stonewall Riots[1] in 1969, "coming out" really meant coming out into the gay world. After the Stonewall Riots, "coming out of the closet" evolved to taking the "skeleton out of the closet". Today coming out is the process of individuals going public about their gender and sexuality identity. In other words, they disclose their true identity with family, friends, and work peers instead of living a "false" life of a heterosexual or of birth assigned gender. "Outing" is the disclosure of an individual's alternative identity without their consent.

The first individual to encourage coming out was German homosexual rights advocate Karl Heinrich Ulrichs in the 1800s. He introduced the idea of self–disclosure as a means of emancipation claiming that visibility would help change public opinion. His thoughts were echoed by Magnus Hirschfeld, a physician and sexologist, in the early 1900s. Hirshfeld encouraged coming out in order to favorably influence legislators and public opinion.

Individuals may come out about identities of:

- ***Sexual Identity*** – An individual may identify as gay, lesbian, bisexual, pansexual, or asexual.
- ***Gender Identity*** – An individual may decide to transition from birth assigned gender to the gender with which they identify.
- ***Intersex Identity*** – An individual may decide to disclose the status of their biological body as being intersex. Like trans*

individuals, they may decide to transition to the gender with which they identify if it does not match their birth assigned gender.

Coming out has many possible consequences to consider such as: social stigma, trans*phobia or homophobia, gender sexism and heterosexism, issues with family and friends, job discrimination, financial loss, blackmail, legal actions, restrictions associated with children, criminalization, violence, or in some countries even capital punishment.

On the other hand, closeted individuals must deal with shame, repressing and hiding their feelings, low self–esteem, isolation, lack of support, and an increased risk of suicide. Some trans* individuals may prefer to live in stealth. Others may transition and quietly assimilate into a life where no one knows about their past.

Choosing to come out is not only a psychological process but a rite of passage including emancipation from oppression and social stigma. Models of coming out have been created and are discussed below. Not all individuals will complete all of the stages described or complete them in the order they are listed. Some stumbling blocks, such as the use of alcohol and drugs to ease the pain of rejection and low self–esteem, may slow the process towards integration and self–actualization of one's identity.

All of the models listed below have detailed explanations of each stage or phase associated with the labels. The explanations can be found in the source documents I have listed in the footnotes at the end of the chapter.

All of the models are similar and the common thread that runs through them is that there is a progression from a lack of awareness of identity to an immersion into identity on a personal and community level and finally a complete integration of identity. Based on this, identity models can apply to any individual regardless of gender and sexual identity. There are additional steps of identity development for individuals that have alternative gender and sexual identities (non–binary gender and non–heterosexual orientation) because of the lack of acceptance of these identities in our culture. There is a need to gather strength to break away from the traditionally accepted "norm".

As we journey from childhood to adulthood, we must find and define our identity. It is most important to realize that these models are useful for us to understand the journey of individuation. And it is also important to realize that individuals cannot be lumped together and fit into a model. Each of us has a unique and important journey that may not fit the linear models at all.

> "It's not really coming out, which suggests opening a door and stepping through. It's more like a long, long walk through what began as a narrow corridor that starts to widen."
>
> *–George Takei*

Cass's Identity Formation Model

Vivienne Cass, a clinical psychologist and sex therapist, created the Identity Formation Model in 1979 for lesbian, gay, bisexual, and transgender individuals that come out. This was the first model to treat LGBT* individuals as something other than "deviant". Her model consisted of six stages of identity formation: Identity Confusion; Identity Comparison; Identity Tolerance; Identity Acceptance; Identity Pride; and Identity Synthesis. [2 and 3]

Coleman's Stages of Identity Development

Eli Coleman, the director of the Program in Human Sexuality at the University of Minnesota, developed a similar developmental model of coming out in 1981–1982. His model consisted of five stages of identity development: Pre Coming Out; Coming Out; Exploration; First Relationship; and Integration. [2]

Sophie's Stages of Lesbian Development

Joan Sophie, a therapist, created a general stage theory of lesbian identity development in 1985–86. Her model consisted of four stages of identity formation: First Awareness; Testing and Exploration; Identity Acceptance; and Identity Integration.[4]

Hanley–Hackenbruck Stages of Coming Out

Peggy Hanley–Hackenbruck, a psychiatrist, developed a model of coming out in 1988. Her model consisted of three stages: Prohibition; Ambivalence–Practicing or Compulsion–Exploration; and Consolidation–Integration.[5]

Troiden's Stages of Coming Out Model

Following on the heels of Cass, Richard Troiden, a sociologist, developed a model of coming out in 1989. His model consisted of four stages of identity development: Sensitization; Identity Confusion; Identity Assumption; and Commitment.[2]

Grace's Stages of Identity Development

John Grace, a social worker, developed a model of coming out in 1992. He believed that a complete understanding of homophobia must be understood before gay and lesbian development dilemmas could be explained. So he identified four homophobic areas in which personality development and identity formation is negatively impacted: personal/active, personal/passive, institutional/active, and institutional/passive. His model consisted of five stages of identity formation: Emergence, Acknowledgement; Finding Community; First Relationships; and Self–Definition and Reintegration.[2]

Niolon's Stages of Coming Out Model

Richard Niolon, professor at the Chicago School of Professional Psychology, developed a model with five stages of coming out. His stages consisted of: Self–Recognition; Disclosure to Others; Socializing with Others; Positive Self–Identification; and Integration and Acceptance.[6]

D'Augelli's LGB Identity Development Model

Anthony D'Augelli, professor of human development at the University of Connecticut, identified six unordered, independent, and interactive processes of identity development for gay, lesbian, and bisexual (LGB) individuals in 1994. His model consisted of six processes: Exiting Heterosexual Identity; Developing Personal LGB Identity Status; Developing a LGB Social Identity; Becoming a LGB Offspring; Developing a LGB Intimacy Status; and Entering a LGB Community.[7]

Fassinger's Gay and Lesbian Identity Development Model

Ruth Fassinger, psychologist and previously professor at CSU Stanislaus and JFK University, created a Model of Gay and Lesbian Identity Development in 1996 for lesbians but later updated it in 1997 to include gay men. Her model is in two parts. The first part, called "Process 1: Individual Identity" is based on self–awareness and acceptance. The second part, called "Process 2: Group Identity" is based on community roles. Both parts have the same four phases: Awareness; Exploration; Deepening/Commitment; and Internalization/Synthesis.[8]

Lipkin Homosexual Identity Model

Arthur Lipkin, an instructor and research associate at the Harvard Graduate School of Education, combined the three models of Cass, Coleman, and Troiden in 1999 to create a mega–model of five stages: Pre–Sexuality; Identity Questioning; Coming Out; Pride; and Post–Sexuality.[9]

Worthington et al.'s Heterosexual Identity Development Model

Heterosexuals also get their identity model, developed by Roger L. Worthington, Holly Bielstein Savoy, Frank R. Dillon, and Elizabeth R. Vernaglia. This team of psychologists identified six influences on heterosexual identity development: biology; microsocial context; gender norms and socialization; culture; religious orientation; and systemic homonegativity, sexual prejudice, and privilege. Their model, created in 2002, consisted of five statuses that are included in the Heterosexual Identity Development Model: Unexplored Commitment; Active Exploration; Diffusion; Deepening and Commitment; and Synthesis.[10]

Lev's Transgender Emergence Model

Arlene Istar Lev, a social worker, therapist, and educator, released a Transgender Emergence Model in 2004. Her model consisted of six stages: Awareness; Seeking Information and Reaching Out; Disclosure to Significant Others; Exploration (Identity and Self–Labeling); Exploration (Transition Issues and Possible Body Modification); and Integration (Acceptance and Post–Transition Issues).[11 and 12]

Evans's Transgender Identity Development Model

In 2010, Nancy Evans, professor at Iowa State University, published a Transgender Identity Development Model that she shared in her book *Student Development in College: Theory, Research, and Practice*. Her model consists of six stages: Existing Traditionally Gendered Identity; Developing a Personal Transgender Identity; Developing a Transgender Social Identity; Becoming a Transgender Offspring; Developing a Transgender Intimacy Status; and Entering a Transgender Community.[13 and 14]

Stephen's Trans Identity Acceptance Model*

I created a transition model based on my personal evolution through sexual identity development and gender transition. I noticed that there were distinctive steps in my evolution. They consisted of six stages:

STAGE	LABEL & EMOTION	DESCRIPTION
1	Awakening Denial	Attempt to conform to family and society's expectations. Trying to cope.
2	Searching Anger	Experimentation with various gender roles and with multiple genders as sexual partners. Acts of self-sabotage and self-destruction due to unhappiness and inauthenticity.
3	Transition Acceptance	Resolving confusion over identity and committing to a resolution that matches my true identity.
4	Withdrawal Depression	A cocoon period to incubate my changes and integrate the new self while in isolation.
5	Emergence Growth	Exiting the incubator to assimilate the new self in the world. Building self-esteem, self-empowerment, and support systems.
6	Integration Blossoming	Fully living out loud as a holistic soul sharing newly found gifts with the world and being in service to others.

An even shorter synopsis of my journey can be illustrated in only three stages:

STAGE	LABEL	DESCRIPTION
1	Construction	Making myself conform to who I was expected to be based on family and societal expectations.
2	Deconstruction	Trying to destroy myself due to the self-loathing of living with a false identity.
3	Reconstruction	Remaking myself to align with my true identity.

I believe that the highest risk of suicide occurs at Stage 2 when an individual is not able to fully live in their true identity. In other words, they collapse under the pressure of family and society and the pain of not living authentically.

THE TRANSSEXUAL MEDICINE WHEEL

Another form of a transition model is a circular model called the medicine wheel. The concept of the medicine wheel originated with the North American indigenous tribes who also called it a medicine hoop. Medicine wheels were used for healing, spiritual rituals, prayer, meditation, visual reminders of higher principles, and physical connection points to the Spirit World. The medicine wheel is also used as a cosmological model of the four directions. It represents the concept that all things are interrelated. As a round wheel it is the circle of life reminding us that everything in the universe cycles through phases and returns to begin again. Traveling the circumference of the medicine wheel is a journey of self–empowerment.

I created a Transsexual Medicine Wheel, which represents the transition of a transsexual individual to the life and body of desire. Each direction on the wheel has an archetypal animal that represents the qualities associated with that point in space and time. There are many animals that represent survival and transformation and can be great symbols for individuals with non–conforming identities such as:

- The crab, turtle, and lobster that have hard shells of protection but a soft inner being.
- The chameleon that can change its appearance to adjust to its surroundings.
- The snake that sheds its skin when it no longer fits.
- The caterpillar/butterfly and the tadpole/frog that transform as they develop.
- The coyote who is the traditional trickster and shapeshifter.

- The phoenix that perpetually rises out of the ashes of destruction.

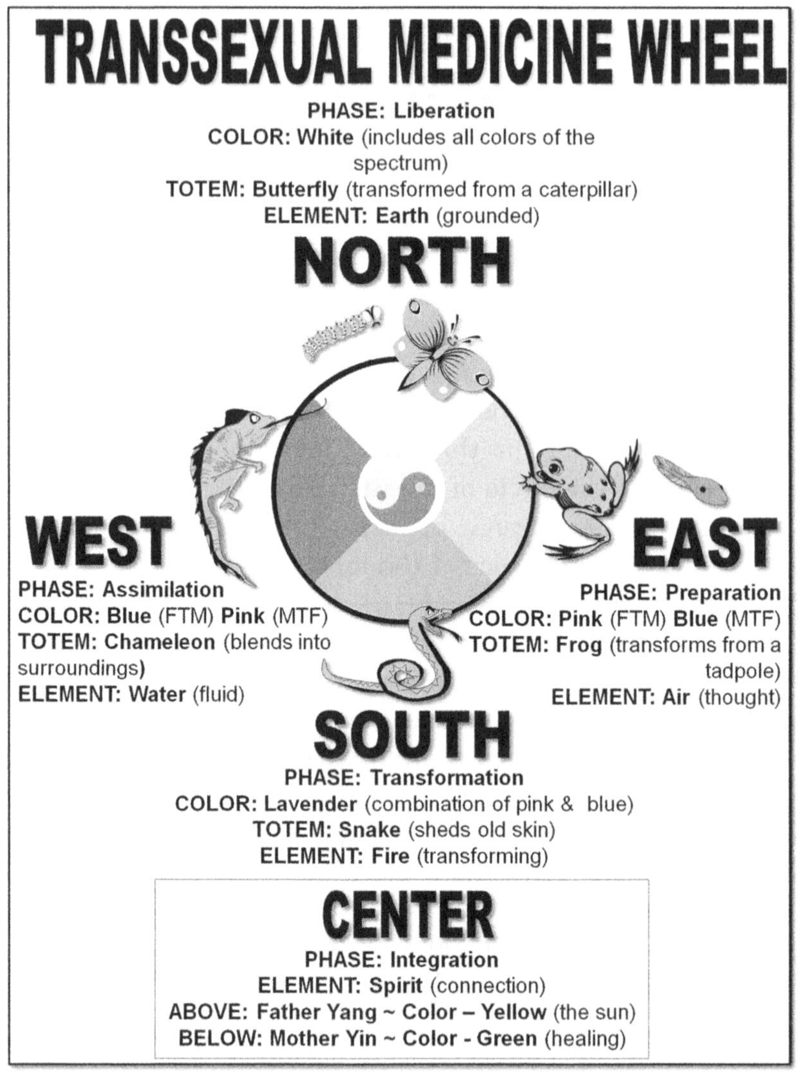

On the Transsexual Medicine Wheel, shown in the illustration above, the journey begins in the East direction. Here is the place of Preparation. The element Air represents the thought process that has led to the beginning of the transformation. The totem is the Frog, which is an animal that knows the process of transformation, having begun life as a tadpole. The color is pink for female–to–male transsexuals and blue for male–to–female transsexuals, representing the traditional colors of female and male for the Old Self that began with a birth assigned gender.

In the South, the Transformation begins with realization that the past no longer serves. It is released as a new way of viewing the world is acquired. The element Fire represents the birth of the new self through combustion and passion. The totem is the Snake, which is an animal that knows how to shed its skin when it no longer serves it. The color lavender represents a blend of masculine blue and feminine pink.

Moving to the West, the Assimilation phase begins. This is a process of adaptation of the new self into the world. The element of Water represents the fluidness required to connect and interact with the world. The totem is the Chameleon, which can change its appearance an adjustment to environmental conditions. The color is blue for female–to–male transsexuals and pink for male–to–female transsexuals, representing the traditional colors of male and female for the new self in the gender of choice.

Moving to the North, finally Liberation is felt as jubilation. Having successfully manifested a new life is a source of joy and empowerment. The element of Earth represents the feeling of being completely grounded by growing roots into a place of belonging. The totem is Butterfly, which is a symbol of transformation itself. It begins life in one form as a caterpillar, spends transformation time in a cocoon, and then emerges as a beautiful butterfly. The color, white, is a composite of all colors in the spectrum.

The final direction is the Center. It is the place of integration. The self is now in right relationship to itself in the Inner World and itself in the Outer World. The self has learned to go with the flow and be in balance. The element of Spirit represents the connection to the Below, who is Mother Yin and to the Above, who is Father Yang. The color for Father Yang is yellow, representing the sun. The color for Mother Yin is green, representing the healing energy of the earth. After the journey around the wheel, home will always be in the Center. Periodically, when it is necessary, a journey to any of the directions may be required to recalibrate, but a rapid return to the Center will always follow.

TRANSSEXUAL CLASSIFICATION MODELS

Biology is no longer destiny due to the advances of Western medicine and surgical techniques. Now consciousness powers gender identity instead of the sex organs of the Physical Body. Transsexuals, who have undergone or seek to undergo genital reassignment, are only a portion of the trans* population. Many trans* individuals do not wish to change their sexual anatomy. The following section is specifically about transsexuals.

There are two distinct categories of transsexual individuals:

1. Those who completely cross over and fully identify as opposite the birth assigned sex.
2. Those who do not completely cross over but identify somewhere between the two polar opposites of male and female. These individuals make up the third gender.

Harry Benjamin's Sex Orientation Scale

Harry Benjamin, an endocrinologist and sexologist, developed the Sex Orientation Scale (SOS) for biological males in 1966. It was the first attempt to classify transvestites and transsexuals. Dr. Benjamin understood the nature of gender identity and gender expression as a spectrum with many more variations than shown on his scale. Following is a summary of his seven documented types: [15 and 16]

TYPE	TITLE
0	Normal Sexual Orientation
I	Pseudo Transvestite
II	Fetishistic Transvestite
III	True Transvestite
IV	Non-Surgical Transsexual
V	True Transsexual - Moderate Intensity
VI	True Transsexual - High Intensity

Watson Gender Disorientation and Indecision Scale

Very similar to the Harry Benjamin Sex Orientation Scale is the Gender Disorientation and Indecision Scale created by Robin Watson. Following is a summary of the five groups: [17]

GROUP	LABEL
1	Low Intensity Transvestite
2	Medium Intensity Transvestite
3	Transvestitic Transsexual
4	Moderate Intensity Transsexual
5	High Intensity Transsexual

Blanchard Classification System of Transsexuals

Ray Blanchard, sexologist and head of the gender program at Toronto's Centre for Addiction and Mental Health, typecast male–to–female transsexuals into two categories in the 1980s. He said that non–homosexual transsexuals exhibit autogynephilia, which is a term applied to males that are aroused by thoughts of being a woman. Blanchard divides male–to–female transsexuals into two categories: [18 and 19]

- ***Homosexual Transsexual*** (Androphilic) – attracted to males.
- ***Non–Homosexual Transsexual*** (Gynephilic, Bisexual, and Asexual) – attracted to females, both males and females, or neither.

I am not quite sure why Blanchard and others find it necessary to divide transsexual individuals into categories based on who their sexual partners are. The two identities of gender and sexuality should be considered independently of each other. Until recently, medical treatment was not approved for transsexuals who would end up "gay". In other words, treatment was only approved if a transsexual would appear heterosexual after gender/genital reassignment. This is no longer a requirement for individuals seeking treatment and hopefully the medical profession is honoring it.

Pauly's Body Image Scale

Ira Pauly, a psychiatrist, with Thomas Lindgren, then a medical student, developed the Body Image Scale in 1975. This scale is used to rate transgender individuals' feelings about thirty body parts on a five–point scale ranging from very satisfied to very dissatisfied.[20]

Stephen's Classification System of FTMs

Due to a lack of classification models for female–to–male transitions, I have created the following model of four groups.

GROUP	LABEL	CHARACTERISTICS
0	Gender Fluid	Non–committed to either male or female gender. May change social presentation at will or live part time as male and part time as female.
1	Social Trans	Identifies as male in female body. Presents as full time male but does not undergo hormone therapy or surgery.
2	Chemically Trans	Identifies as male. Presents as full time male. Undergoes hormone therapy (testosterone) but does not undergo surgery.
3	Surgically Trans - Partial	Identifies as male. Presents as full time male. Undergoes hormone therapy (testosterone). Undergoes some surgical alteration of the body such as mastectomy and/or hysterectomy.
4	Surgically Trans - Complete	Identifies as male. Presents as full time male. Undergoes hormone therapy (testosterone). Undergoes complete surgical alteration of the body including mastectomy, hysterectomy, and male genital construction.*

*Male genital construction consists of various options including:

- ***Vaginectomy, Hysterectomy, and Oophorectomy*** – Removal of the vagina, uterus, fallopian tubes, and ovaries.
- ***Metoidioplasty*** – The clitoris (enlarged from testosterone therapy) is released from the surrounding skin so it is more accessible.
- ***Testicular Implants*** – The labia majora is used to create a scrotum via tissue expanders and implants.
- ***Phalloplasty*** – Construction of a penis by taking a graft of tissue from the forearm, thigh, or abdomen and extending the urethra.

By contrast, male–to–female genital construction usually consists of: orchiectomy and penectomy (removal of testes and penis), vaginoplasty, clitoroplasty, and labiaplasty (construction of vagina, clitoris, and labia).

TRANSITION PROCESSES

Before the 20th century there were not many options for transsexual identified individuals. I believe that some individuals that were self–identified or labeled as gay or lesbian before the 20th century, may have actually been trans* identified. With new technical and medical processes available, there are much better options available today. Modifications can be made on multiple levels. The present day transsexual individual can change gender in eight ways:

1. Psychologically
2. Sociologically
3. Aesthetically
4. Hormonally
5. Surgically
6. Legally

7. Financially
8. Professionally

As mentioned in Chapter 2 on biological influences on gender, sex is determined by five factors:

- Chromosomes
- Gonads (Ovaries and/or testicles)
- Hormones
- Primary sex characteristics
- Secondary sex characteristics

During a gender transition, chromosomes cannot be changed, gonads can be reconstructed, and hormones can be changed which alters secondary sex characteristics.

The genital reassignment process typically begins with a period of feminization or masculinization through hormone replacement therapy. Male–to–female transsexuals take estrogens, antiandrogens, and sometimes progestogens. Female–to–male transsexuals take androgens (testosterone). Hormone replacement therapy will continue for the rest of the individual's lifetime.

Some medical professionals require a minimum of six months of counseling and/or living full time in the target gender before they will administer hormone replacement therapy. Some medical professionals require a minimum waiting period of two years before they will perform surgery. This is an integration period where the trans* individual can live full time in the target gender.

Living full time, sometimes called "going fulltime" or "living 24/7–3D", means that an individual lives 24 hours a day, 7 days a week, 365 days a year in the new gender role. Living part time means living in the new gender role privately while living in the gender role of birth assigned sex publically. Living in the transitional period is not an easy time. There is the fear of discovery as well as physical pain from the binding of breasts, the tucking of penises, or the use of prosthetics.

Any trans* individual is on their own personal journey that fits their personal identity and situation. They may or may not decide to undergo any physical or social transformations. They may undergo some transition processes and not others. Or they may undergo a complete transition. In other words, "trans" means to "cross". In this case, the implication is that an individual is crossing from one pole to the opposite pole. However, many individuals do not make the complete transit. They may find their place to be somewhere in between the binary poles.

The following figure illustrates the continua between the male and female poles and what physical steps might be taken to transition from one pole to another.

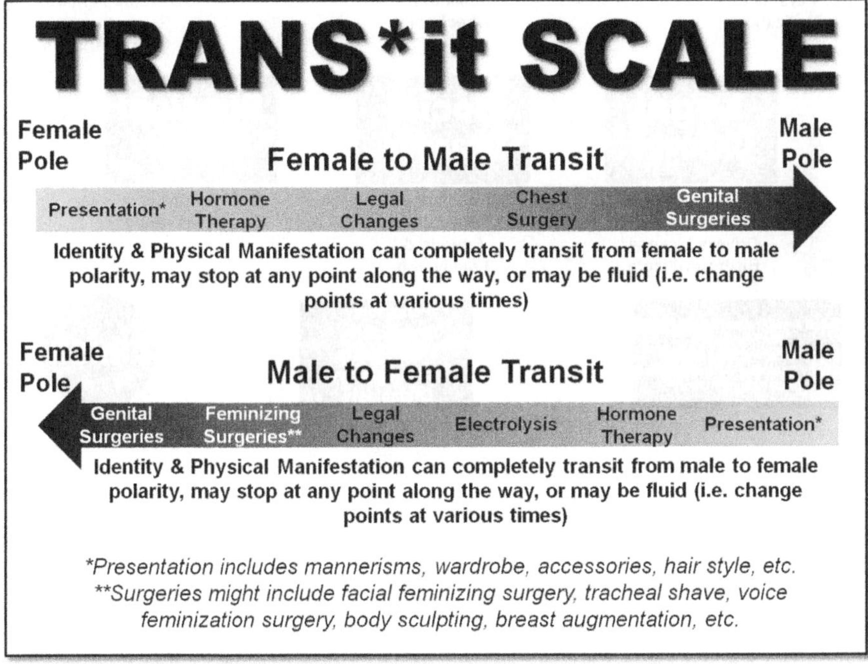

The two figures below illustrate how complex the transition process is. The diagrams may look like a board game but it is hard to illustrate a three–dimensional process in a two–dimensional format. That is why so many models are criticized for being linear. It is the constraint of the medium we are communicating in. If this book were a hologram, the illustrations could be represented in three dimensions.

The stages shown below may be done concurrently or consecutively. The entire process may last only a year or two or might take many years to complete.

A journey for an MTF individual might consists of these steps:

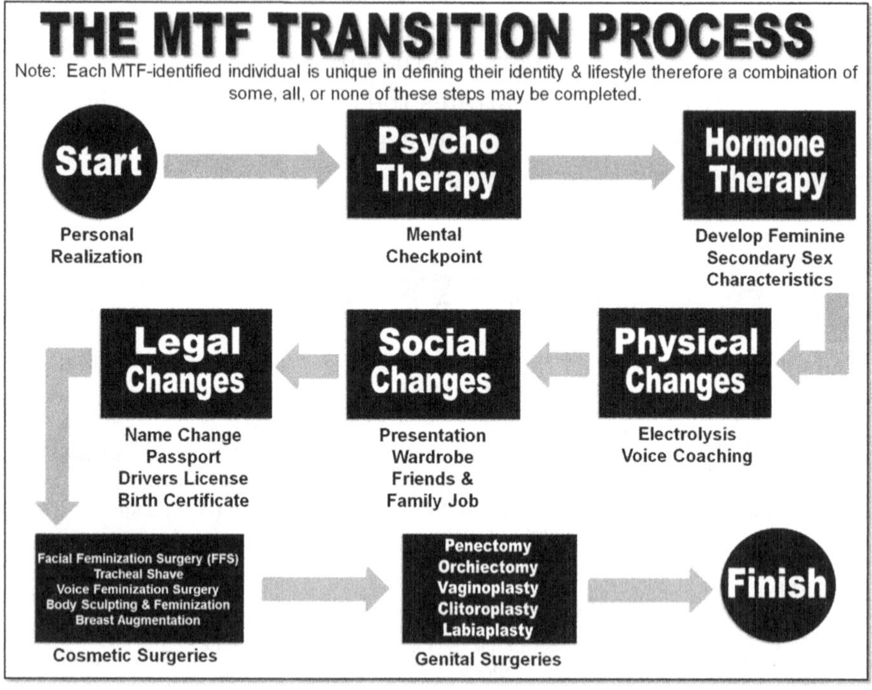

A journey for an FTM individual might consists of these steps:

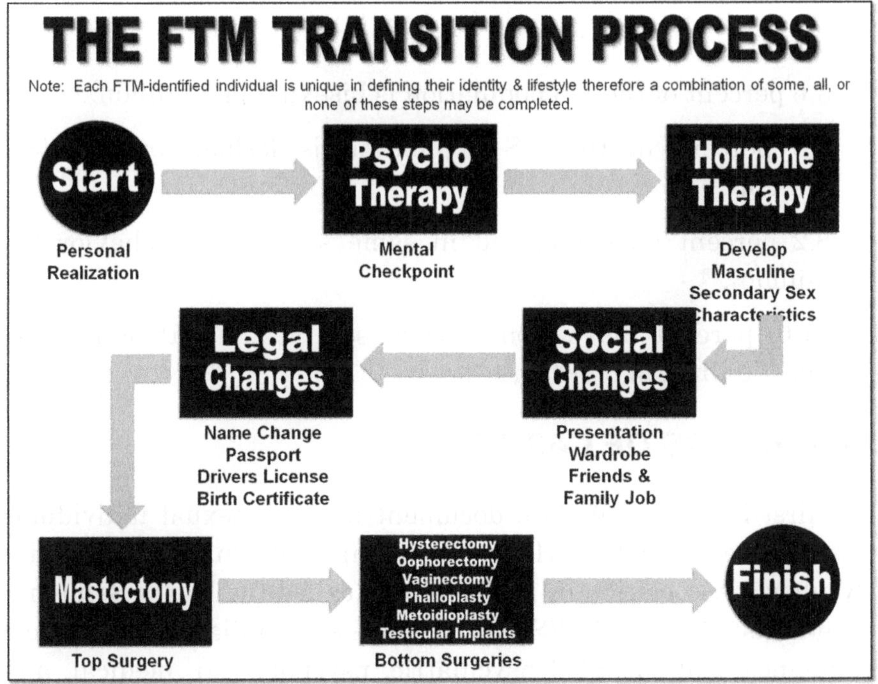

The rate of occurrence of transsexual individuals is not accurately known due to confusion over the true definition of trans* and availability of individuals willing to disclose this identity. Estimates from clinical papers range from 1 in 7,400 to 1 in 42,000 in birth assigned males and 1 in 30,040 to 1 in 104,000 in birth assigned females. The Amsterdam Gender Dysphoria Clinic estimates that occurrence is 1 in 10,000 birth assigned males and 1 in 30,000 birth assigned females based on more than forty years of statistics. Olyslager and Conway estimated the worldwide occurrence is as high as 1 in 4,500 birth assigned males and 1 in 8,000 birth assigned females.[21] In 2011, the Human Rights Council estimated 0.3 to 1 percent of the United States population is trans*.[21] Trans* activists, as well as Bulloughs, report that the incidence of transsexuality is actually 1 in 50,000 and occurs equally amongst male– and female–bodied individuals.[22]

To compare the rate of trans* occurrence to the rate of alternative sexual orientation, the Human Rights Council estimates the following statistics from 2011:

- 3.6 percent of the US population is bisexual (4.2 million).[23]
- 3.3 percent of the US population is lesbian or gay (3.7 million).[23]
- 8.2 percent have engaged in same–sex sexual behavior (19 million).[23]
- 11.0 percent have some same–sex sexual attraction i.e. questioning (25.6 million).[23]

STANDARDS OF CARE (SOC)

The first Standard of Care document for transsexual individuals was created by the Harry Benjamin International Gender Dysphoria Association in 1979 and was called the Harry Benjamin Standards of Care (HBSOC). It was a compilation of clinical guidelines that included psychiatric, psychological, medical, and surgical requirements and procedures for the care and comfort of transgender individuals.

The Harry Benjamin International Gender Dysphoria Association has now evolved to the World Professional Association for Transgender Health (WPATH) organization. They publish an updated version of standards called "Standards of Care for the Health of Transsexual, Transgender, and Gender–Nonconforming People"[24]. The most current edition can be obtained at their website www.wpath.org. Although WPATH guidelines may be the most well–known there are other sets of guidelines published outside of the United States.

"The overall goal of the SOC [Standards of Care] is to provide clinical guidance for health professionals to assist transsexual, transgender, and gender nonconforming people with safe and effective pathways to achieving lasting personal comfort with their gendered selves, in order to maximize their overall health, psychological well-being, and self-fulfillment. This assistance may include primary care, gynecologic and urologic care, reproductive options, voice and communication therapy, mental health services (e.g., assessment, counseling, psycho-therapy), and hormonal and surgical treatments. While this is primarily a document for health professionals, the SOC may also be used by individuals, their families, and social institutions to understand how they can assist with promoting optimal health for members of this diverse population."

-WPATH, Standards of Care for the Health of Transsexual, Transgender, and Gender-Nonconforming People

I would like to add my personal perspective to the care of trans* individuals. I have noticed that most healers and therapists assume that the male and female sides of a trans* individual need to be balanced. I feel that this perception comes from a basic belief that if an individual wants to transition from one gender to another then they are in some way putting down or denying the gender assigned at birth. However, a trans* individual probably knows more about male–female energy balance than any cis individual because they are living with these two energies since birth. I invite the healers and therapists providing services to trans* individuals to broaden their perspective beyond what seems obvious and realize that trans* individuals have many dimensions in addition to the male–female paradigm.

NOTES:

[1] The Stonewall Riots was a violent confrontation between police and patrons at the Stonewall Inn, a gay bar in New York City. This confrontation occurred on June 28, 1969 and was the result of a police raid on the bar that included arrests and physical harassment of the gay patrons. The riots lasted 5 days and was the first time that gay, lesbian, and trans* people fought back against discrimination and harassment.

[2] Ritter, Kathleen Y. and Anthony I. Terndrup *Handbook of Affirmative Psychotherapy with Lesbians and Gay Men.* The Guilford Press, 2002.

[3] Cass, V. "Homosexual Identity Formation: A Theoretical Model". *Journal of Homosexuality,* 4 (3), 1979.

[4] Sophie, Joan. "A Critical Examination of Stage Theories of Lesbian Identity Development". *Journal of Homosexuality,* Vol. 12 (2), 1985–86.

[5] Hanley–Hackenbruck, Peggy. "Psychotherapy and the 'Coming Out' Process". *Journal of Gay & Lesbian Psychotherapy,* Vol. 1 (1), 1989.

[6] *Psychpage.com.* "Stages of Coming Out." http://www.psychpage.com/learning/library/gay/comeout.html

[7] *Iwu.edu.* "D'Augelli's Model of Lesbian, Gay, and Bisexual Identity Development." https://www.iwu.edu/studentlife/lgbt/d_augelli_2010.pdf

[8] *UNC Charlotte.* "Theories on LGBTQ Development." http://safezone.uncc.edu/allies/theories

[9] Lipkin, Arthur. *Understanding Homosexuality, Changing Schools: A Text for Teachers, Counselors, and Administrators.* Westview Press, 1999.

[10] Worthington Roger L., Holly Bielstein Savoy, Frank R. Dillon, and Elizabeth R. Vernaglia. "Heterosexual Identity Development: A Multidimensional Model of Individual and

Social Identity." Sage Publications, 2006. http://www.sagepub.com/dimensionsofmulticulturalcounselingstudy/articles/section6/Article98.pdf. Also see http://rethinkhighered.blogspot.com/2012/03/student–development-theory-gender-and.html

[11] Lev, Arlene Istar. *Transgender Emergence: Therapeutic Guidelines for Working With Gender–Variant People and Their Families.* The Howorth Clinical Practice Press, 2004.

[12] *UNC Charlotte.* "Theories on LGBTQ Development." http://safezone.uncc.edu/allies/theories

[13] Evans, Nancy. J., Deanna S. Forney, Florence M. Guido, Lori D. Patton, and Kristen A. Renn. *Student Development in College: Theory, Research, and Practice.* Jossey–Bass, 2009.

[14] Wollenschleger, Marc. "Gender and Sexuality Development." http://studentdevelopmenttheory.wordpress.com/gender-and-sexuality/

[15] *Genderpsychology.org.* "Dr. Harry Benjamin's Gender Disorientation Scale." http://www.genderpsychology.org/transsexual/benjamin_gd.html

[16] Benjamin, Harry, *The Transsexual Phenomenon.* Warner Books, 1977.

[17] Genderpsychology.org. "Watson Table." http://genderpsychology.org/transsexual/watson.html

[18] Blanchard, R. "Typology of Male–to–female Transsexualism". *Archives of Sexual Behavior*, 14, 1985.

[19] Blanchard, R. "The Concept of Autogynephilia and the Typology of Male Gender Dysphoria". *Journal of Nervous and Mental Disease*, 177, 1989.

[20] Pauly, Ira B. and Thomas W. Lindgren. "A Body Image Scale for Evaluating Transsexuals". *Archives of Sexual Behavior,* Nov 4 (6), 1975.

[21] Olyslager, Femke and Lynn Conway "*On the Calculation of the Prevalence of Transsexualism*" Last modified Sep 6, 2007. http://ai.eecs.umich.edu/people/conway/TS/Prevalence/Reports/Prevalence%20of%20Transsexualism.pdf

[22] Bullough, Vern L. and Bonnie Bullough. "Gender Identity Disorders: Evaluation and Treatment." *Journal of Sex Education and Therapy* 16 (1), 1990.

[23] Gates, Gary J. "How Many Lesbian, Gay, Bisexual, & Transgender People?" Last modified April 2011. http://williamsinstitute.law.ucla.edu/wp-content/uploads/Gates-How-Many-People-LGBT-Apr-2011.pdf

[24] *Wpath.org*. "Standards of Care." http://www.wpath.org/site_page.cfm?pk_association_webpage_menu=1351&pk_association_webpage=4655

CHAPTER 9:

REINCARNATION

Transitioning Gender over Multiple Lifetimes

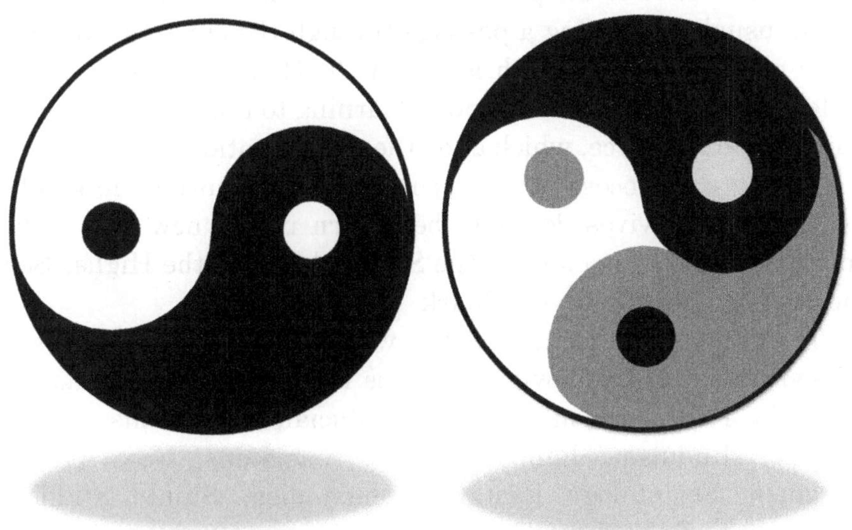

YIN YANG YUEN

The symbol on the left is the *Taijitu* (diagram of supreme ultimate) and represents the concept of *Yin* (Female) and *Yang* (Male). It is the classic symbol for the balance and harmony of opposite energies. The symbol on the right, called the *Yin Yang Yuen*, was designed to include a third gender.

(Yin Yang Yuen Designer Unknown)

GENERAL INFORMATION ON REINCARNATION

Our past lives have a huge influence on who we are in our current lives. Therefore, I am devoting an entire chapter to the subject. I am not providing evidence to prove or disprove the existence of reincarnation. It is up to each of us to decide for ourselves what our truth is. My truth is that reincarnation does indeed exist. My focus here is solely about past life influences on gender and sexual identity.

Reincarnation is the process of a soul living successive lives on Earth, usually including a passage through the spiritual world or inner planes between death and rebirth. There is a point in this cycle when a soul achieves enough learning to remerge with Great Spirit/Creator/Source, which ends the reincarnation cycle.

During the process of reincarnation, the essential energy of a living being survives death to be reborn into a new body. This energy is often referred to as the Spirit, the Soul, the Higher Self, the True Self, or the Divine Spark.

Today about 75 percent of the world's population believes in reincarnation. The following religious faiths and cultures have a belief in reincarnation: Baha'i, Confucianism, Druids, Druze, Gnostic, Hinduism, Jainism, Native Americans, New Ageists, Paganism, Scientology, Rastafari, Shamanism, Shinto, Sikhism, Spiritism, Sufi, Taoism, Theosophy, Wicca, and Yoruba. Judaism does, too, but only in the Kabbalah and Orthodox sects. Buddhism does as well, but the concept of what is reincarnates differs from other reincarnation belief systems. Unitarian Universalists are divided with some believing in reincarnation and some not. The Christian faith believed in reincarnation until the fourth century when Constantine struck all references to it from the Bible and Christian literature. Islam and Zoroastrianism do not have any belief in reincarnation.

The information I present here is based on dozens of books by past life therapists that have regressed thousands of souls. We are all very familiar with the process of life from cradle to casket but there is a plethora of theories about the process of casket back to cradle.

The life of a soul originates in the fifth dimensional world. A contract is created during a pre–birth life selection process. Then as the soul moves through the birth canal, amnesia occurs, which erases or hides from consciousness all of the soul's past life memories. During an incarnation on Earth, lessons are learned with free will allowing choices along the journey. After death, a soul has a post life review. This is not for judgment purposes but to review what was or was not accomplished. The results of the review will determine the lessons to be set up for the next incarnation. The soul resides in the fifth dimension until it is ready for the next incarnation. The following figure illustrates how the cycle of life occurs within the reincarnation cosmology.

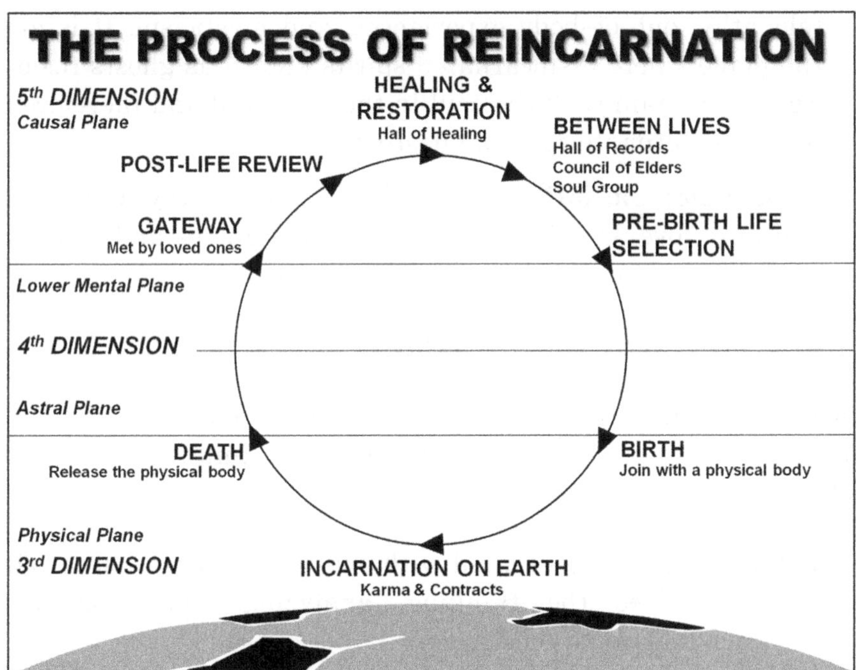

PLANES OF EXISTENCE

There are many models that describe the planes of existence. Here I am defining only three major ones that I refer to relation to reincarnation:

1. **Third–dimension (3D)** is everyday life that exists on the physical plane of Earth. The energy on this plane is dense and has a low vibration rate making items and bodies visual and tangible.
2. **Fourth–dimension (4D)** is the astral plane just beyond our physical existence. Recently departed souls often pause here before traveling forward into the spiritual realm because they can more easily send an energetic communication to loved ones left on Earth. We can access the 4D world through telepathy, out–of–body experiences, and mysticism. It is also the plane where disincarnated spirits known as ghosts reside. Ego can remain with the soul in the 4D world and therefore it is not the ultimate spiritual destination.
3. **Fifth–dimension (5D)** is the realm of pure energy, pure soul, and pure love. Our Higher Self, spiritual guides and teachers reside here. This is the place of life between lives.

LEVELS OF CONSCIOUSNESS

There are three levels of consciousness that exist in the incarnated mind.[1] All three have different functions as listed below:

1. **The Conscious** is associated with everyday consciousness. The conscious does the thinking, analyzing, imagining, and learning, and makes decisions.
2. **The Subconscious** is hidden or unconscious from our everyday awareness. It makes no decisions of right or wrong and accepts what has been impressed on it. The subconscious stores emotional complexes, long–term memory, instinct, habits, behavior patterns, belief systems, and controls physiological

body functions. The subconscious is the level that is accessed when recalling past lives in a regression session.

3. **The Superconscious** belongs to the Higher Self or the Collective Conscious. It is also called the higher consciousness, objective consciousness, Buddhic consciousness, cosmic consciousness, God–consciousness, and Christ consciousness. The superconscious is responsible for creativity, intuition, and spiritual awareness. It vibrates at a very high frequency. The superconscious is the level that is accessed when recalling life between lives in a regression session.

BRAIN WAVE STATES

There are five levels of brain wave activity[2] as defined in the figure below. When in the alpha state we can access the Fourth Dimension and when in the theta state we can access the Fifth Dimension. Alpha and theta states can be activated through chanting, dancing, praying, repetitive percussion sound, shamanic journeys, trance, and hypnosis. An individual can access memories of past lives while in the alpha state. The theta state is required to access memories of the life between lives. Children's brains remain in an alpha state until about age seven, so they can easily have vivid memories of past lives. Hypnosis and shamanic journeys are two common ways to alter the brain wave state in order to tap into past life memories.

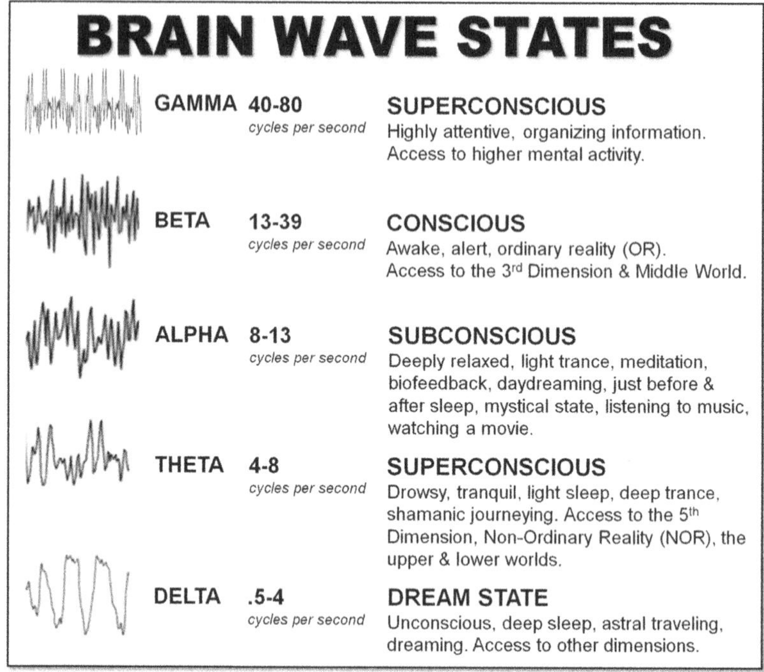

BRAIN WAVE STATES
GAMMA 40-80
cycles per second
SUPERCONSCIOUS
Highly attentive, organizing information. Access to higher mental activity.
BETA 13-39
cycles per second
CONSCIOUS
Awake, alert, ordinary reality (OR). Access to the 3rd Dimension & Middle World.
ALPHA 8-13
cycles per second
SUBCONSCIOUS
Deeply relaxed, light trance, meditation, biofeedback, daydreaming, just before & after sleep, mystical state, listening to music, watching a movie.
THETA 4-8
cycles per second
SUPERCONSCIOUS
Drowsy, tranquil, light sleep, deep trance, shamanic journeying. Access to the 5th Dimension, Non-Ordinary Reality (NOR), the upper & lower worlds.
DELTA .5-4
cycles per second
DREAM STATE
Unconscious, deep sleep, astral traveling, dreaming. Access to other dimensions.

TIME FREQUENCIES

Time is linear only when we are incarnated in the third dimension. In other dimensions, past, present, and future time are different vibrations of energy all pulsating at the same time. [3] The past vibrates at a slower energy than the present and the future vibrates at a faster energy than the present. We can access other points in time by "tuning" our awareness just like tuning into a specific radio station.

Karma is the energetic wave that affects all lives simultaneously. Energy that is released through thoughts, emotions, and actions in any one of our lives, affects all of our other lives. This is why revisiting specific events in past lives can be a very healing experience and affect present and future lives.

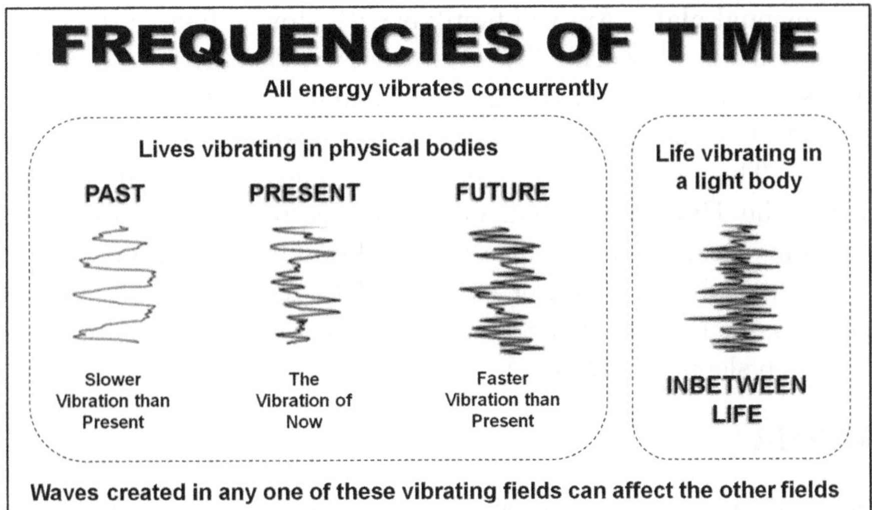

THE HIGHER SELF

The soul is holographic energy consisting of waves of light and color. When we are born, a portion of our soul energy steps into the Physical Body, while the remainder stays in spirit form on the fifth dimensional plane. The fifth dimension portion of our spirit is called the Higher Self.[4] Other terms for the Higher Self are Holy Spirit, Holy Ghost, Universal Consciousness, and Superconsciousness. When we die, our soul is released from the confines of the Physical Body and increases its vibration in order to reunite with its self in spirit. While incarnated, one of the ways to access our Higher Self is through a between lives regression. This experience can propel our emotional, physical, and spiritual health toward greater wisdom.

THE AKASHIC RECORDS

The deep subconscious mind retains the memories of every thought, feeling, motive, desire, and behavior of every experience from every incarnation. Memories are also stored in the Akashic record, which is the register of everything which has ever occurred. The Akashic records are stored in ether on the fifth dimensional plane. Are you familiar with storing files in the cloud in the electronic world? The Akashic records are the cloud that stores the files of every thought, word, and action that ever or will ever exist. "*Akasha*" is a Sanskrit word meaning "sky", "space" or "ether". The Akashic records have been referred to as the Cosmic Mind, the Universal Mind, or the Collective Unconscious. The Akashic records can be accessed through meditation, astral journeying, dream work, or hypnosis. The most famous reader of the Akashic records was Edgar Cayce. He would read them while in a deep sleep–like trance.[5]

KARMA

"Karma" is a Sanskrit word meaning "action", "effect", or "destiny". Karma can be likened to the Law of Cause and Effect.[6] Karma is a sum of all that an individual has done, is currently doing, and will ever do. The effects of all past deeds create present and future experiences. Thus we have responsibility for our own lives. In our current lives, not only are we are working on the karma that we created in past lives, but we are creating karma that will affect our future lives.

ACCESSING PAST LIVES

Memories of past lives may come to us in many ways by moving into altered states of consciousness such as:

- Déjà vu
- Spontaneous memories
- Recurrent dreams
- Recurring phobias
- Hypnotic regression
- Psychic readings
- Meditation and visualization
- Identification and conscious awareness of the clues listed below

By being aware, we will notice clues to our past lives that show up in in our everyday lives. Chances are excellent that if you are in great attraction to, or great resistance to, persons, places, or events, it is associated to a past life memory. Clues to our past lives present themselves in many ways such as:

- Feeling connected to certain historical time periods
- Being fascinated with a geographical location or climate
- Resonating with art, artifacts, music, dance, books, or movies
- Feeling connected to other cultures, heritage, and ancestry
- Having an awareness of words, language, and phrases that you use
- Examining your taste in clothing style and home décor
- Examining your food preferences and eating habits, and your preferences in aromas
- Feeling connected to certain vocations, avocations, hobbies, and education
- Identifying allergies, physical pain, health issues, injuries, diseases, and surgeries
- Identifying scars, tattoos, birth marks, and body type
- Examining relationships to friends, lovers, family, workplace acquaintances, animals, and pets
- Possessing knowledge, skills, or talent beyond current experience especially at the level of a prodigy or genius
- Recalling childhood memories, likes, aversions, and play themes
- Feeling connected to causes that you are passionate about
- Experiencing recurring dreams, themes, habits, mannerisms, patterns, preferences, personality traits, emotions, reactions, sensations, trauma, or fears

- Examining origins and meanings of your name and/or nickname
- Experiencing déjà vu, synchronistic experiences, or strong feelings about individuals you meet

PAST LIFE REGRESSION (PLR)

Experiences from past lives can have a major impact on the current lifetime. Many of us have experienced at least one hundred or more lifetimes before this incarnation. This influence remains hidden from consciousness unless past life recall is activated.

Past Life Regression Therapy (PLRT) is a therapeutic process used to access the subconscious mind and cellular memory of birth, past lives, and life between lives. This technique is effective in locating the original source of past trauma and transforming the core issues that affect daily life functioning and cause physical pain or illness.

One of the most effective ways to access the subconscious mind is through hypnosis. A hypnotherapist trained in past life regression can be an excellent facilitator in helping a person journey to a past life or life between lives. A good past life therapist will know what questions to ask during a session and how to use intervention techniques in cases where traumatic past life memories are encountered.

There are two intentional ways to explore a past life. The first is by receiving a past life reading from another person, such as a psychic, who "reads" the past life experiences or "reads" the Akashic record of the client. The second way is to be regressed by a past life therapist so that a past life is experienced directly. I have experienced both methods and I have found that the second method of being regressed to a past life is much more powerful. Directly experiencing a past life provides a potent kinesthetic and visual experience which often includes an emotional release and subsequent healing. In addition, the experience is so vivid there is little doubt that it is not real. Past life experiences provide many "Aha!" moments. I remember saying to myself "Oh, now I know why I do that." Or "Oh, now I know why I feel like that." A person may want to visit a past life for many different reasons such as:

- Curiosity
- Exploring past life connections to current relationships
- Discovering contracts or vows made in previous lifetimes that affect this lifetime. (These contracts can be cancelled or renegotiated as desired.)
- Discovering overt acts of past lives that affect karmic lessons in this lifetime. (These overt acts can be atoned for thus changing or fulfilling karmic lessons now.)
- Discovering past talents and bringing them to the present life to increase creativity and/or peak performance
- Discovering the soul's pre–life contract and purpose for this lifetime
- Discovering the soul's overall purpose thereby gaining clarity and focus

Here is a list the typical questions that are asked in a Past Life Regression session:

1. Who are you?
2. What are you wearing?
3. What is your skin color?
4. What is your gender?
5. How old are you?
6. What is your name?
7. Where are you?
8. What do you see around you? What is the landscape like?
9. What is the weather or climate?
10. What is the name of the place you're in?

11. What is the date?
12. What is the time of day?
13. Do you hear anything?
14. Do you smell anything?
15. What are you doing?
16. Why are you doing it?
17. How do you feel about doing it?
18. Is anyone with you?
19. If so, who are they and why are they with you?
20. How do you feel about them?
21. Do you recognize them in your current lifetime?
22. How does this past lifetime relate to your current life?
23. Did you create contracts in this lifetime?
24. What was your vow at death, if any?
25. What issues were addressed at your post–life review?

BETWEEN LIVES REGRESSION (BLR)

In the spiritual dimension of the between lives, there is a planning stage where the upcoming physical lifetime is arranged. The beings that will be involved work together to develop situations which will allow for lessons to be learned. These lessons are based on past situations and are necessary for the development of the souls involved. As a soul is born, amnesia prevents memory of these agreements. This is intentional because the learning situations would not be fully authentic otherwise.

A between lives experience is a visit to the fifth dimensional world. This experience is facilitated through a hypnotic state. Here there are many different places to visit. They include the Hall of Wisdom (the place of life reviews), the Hall of Records (also known as the Akashic Records), the Hall of Justice (home of the

Council of Elders), the Hall of Healing (a place of rejuvenation), and the home of your soul group and teacher(s).

Here is a list the typical questions that are asked in a Between Life Regression session:

1. What is your guide's name?
2. What percentage of soul energy did you bring into this current life?
3. What percentage of masculine, feminine, and androgynous energy do you have in this life?
4. How are you doing with this amount of soul energy?
5. Who are the members of your soul family?
6. What is the purpose for your choice of body, particular talents, life circumstances, etc.?
7. What is the purpose for your choice of current family and other significant people?
8. What are the gifts from your family of origin?
9. How does your council of elders feel you are progressing in this life?
10. What is the primary purpose of your current life?
11. What life themes are you working on?
12. What is the overall mission of your immortal soul?
13. What are the challenges or patterns of your suffering?
14. What is the purpose of your physical illness or limitation? How can it be let go?
15. What red flag is there (caution note that you need to be aware of)?
16. What are the next steps to take in fulfilling your life purpose?

Experiencing a between life regression helps individuals understand their spiritual purpose and provides information on why they chose to experience specific issues in their current life. This understanding helps remove victim consciousness that may be causing pain and suffering. As an individual accepts responsibility for their free will and understands how they can shape their own destiny, self–empowerment increases exponentially.

PAST LIFE INFLUENCE ON GENDER AND SEXUAL IDENTITY

There is no text dedicated to the subject of past life and between life regressions of individuals with alternative gender identities and only one on individuals with alternative sexual identities. So I am going to extensively share passages that I have found in my research of nearly 100 books on reincarnation. Note that in these passages I use the words and labels of the authors, which are not necessarily the same ones I would use.

In 1890, theosophist Susan E. Gay, in her "Theosophical–Feminist Manifesto[7]" article wrote that "men who were manly" and "women who were very feminine" were the least developed souls. Another theosophist writer, Frances Swiney[7], wrote that all souls were essentially feminine but had to pass through a masculine state on their soul journey.

In the 1880s, theosophist Charles Webster Leadbeater[7] stated that the soul changed sex, over many lives, in order to learn lessons and evolve, but it generally stayed in the same sex from three to seven incarnations before changing gender.

Theosophist Charles Lazenby[7] believed that after six lives as the same gender, the seventh life would be a transitional phase in an intermediate gender in which individuals' physical bodies belonged to one sex but their thoughts and desires belonged to the other. After this life they would live another six lives in the opposite gender of the first six lives.

Author Alois Schwaiger[7] believed that there is a male and female component within everyone. She said that at death, the male side dies but the female side returns to its origin before being reincarnated again.

In *Repetition: Past Lives, Life, and Rebirth*[8], Doris Eliana Cohen stated that gay men have suffered some form of sexual abuse or trauma at the hands of another male, while lesbians have suffered trauma, sexual abuse, or conflict with their mother in their current or past life.

Walter Semkiw, a doctor, reincarnation researcher, and director of the Institute for the Integration of Science, Intuition and Spirit, states that research on reincarnation indicates that a soul changes gender about 10 percent of the time. This figure was supported by Ian Stevenson, a psychiatrist at the University of Virginia and a reincarnation research pioneer, who devoted his life to doing scientific research on children who had spontaneous past life memories. The past lives of these children could be factually validated in over 1200 cases. Walter Semkiw says that most individuals maintain the same gender from one lifetime to another and it is based on the soul's innate masculine or feminine quality. As a result, he says:

> *"If a soul changes gender and is not prepared for change, it is possible that gender disorders, such as transsexualism, may occur."*[9]

Ian Stevenson wrote numerous books on reincarnation based on his life's work. He said:

> *"The condition in which a person of one anatomical sex believes that he should be a person of the opposite sex is known as gender identity confusion. If the person affected experiences concern and anxiety over his condition he is said to have gender dysphoria. Among Hindus and Buddhists the interpretation of gender dysphoria is simple: the person affected was a member of the opposite sex in his previous life."*[10and 11]

Stevenson believed that homosexuality is a choice made by an individual before reincarnating and that:

"The homosexual psyche is fundamentally different from the heterosexual. As a rule, it is far more balanced and whole, with a relatively equal blending of male and female energies. Homosexuality has two purposes, a major and a minor. The minor purpose is simply the Higher Self's thirst for diverse experience. Homosexuality's major purpose arises from its relative balance of male and female energies, which generates a more harmonious and flexible field of sexual energy than is common among heterosexuals."[10 and 11]

Stevenson adds that:

"Heterosexuality, homosexuality, and bisexuality are equally normal, valid, and important sexual orientations when expressed in partnerships based on mutual respect. If the body is the soul made flesh, then sexuality is the conduit through which soul challenges find expression, leading either to traumatic defeat or sublime triumph. The homosexual population in any culture serves as the sexual barometers of their society. Homosexuals reflect back to the larger culture any imbalances or flaws in its sexual life, including gender roles; traditions of appropriate masculine and feminine behavior; the rigidity or looseness of accepted sexual behavior; customs of romance, courtship, and marriage; sexual repression and pathology, and so on. Homosexuals ... are particularly involved in pulling society forward on its sometimes begrudging evolution path."[10 and 11]

In *Messages from the Masters*, Brian Weiss, a psychiatrist who has regressed thousands of individuals, says:

"The soul has no sex, no hormones, no biological tendencies. The soul is pure, loving energy."[12]

He continues to say that we all switch sexes over the course of our many lifetimes although he believes there is a tendency to specialize in one sex or the other.

In *Past Lives Future Lives: Accounts of Regression and Progression through Hypnosis*, Bruce Goldberg, a hypnotherapist, says that a soul must change sex at least once in order to complete the karmic cycle, however, a soul lives most of its lives as only one sex.[13]

In *The Idiot's Guide to Life after Death,* Diane Ahlquist says:

> *"People who believe in reincarnation typically think that when you make the transition back to Earth you can return as either male or female, no matter which sex you were when you died or which gender you may have been in your other lives. It may take you becoming female to have an understanding of what you did wrong as a male a lifetime ago, and vice versa."*[14]

She also believes that when an individual is gay or lesbian they are "confused" because the soul was so used to being one sex that it fights being born into another sex. She goes on to cite that bisexuals are:

> *"...able to adjust more to the new body than someone who's homosexual; they just can't adjust 100%. ...having leftover gender characteristics from former lives doesn't mean you're gay or bisexual. It simply means that perhaps you're still feeling residuals from having lived as the opposite sex. You subconsciously remember certain activities you once enjoyed and carry them into this lifetime."*[14]

In *Return from Heaven*, Carol Bowman explains that beliefs of a particular culture influence the reincarnation patterns within that culture. Some cultures, such as in Burma and Thailand, believe it is possible to change sex in the next life so there are a high number of sex change cases. Other cultures, such as the Lebanese Druse and the Alaskan Tlingit, do not believe that it is possible to change sex from one incarnation to the next so there are few sex–change cases found there.[15]

In *Discovering Your Past Lives*, Glenn Williston and Judith Johnstone suggest that all souls experience both male and female lives and that:

> "*We choose homosexual roles to focus our attention on the balance between masculinity and femininity if we have been identifying too strongly with either one in past lives.*" [16]

In *I Am All over That*, Shirley MacLaine, the well–known actress and spiritual journeyer, writes that one of the explanations for homosexuality and transgenderism is:

> "*...a profound identification with a recent incarnation as a member of the opposite sex.*"[17]

She says:

> "*Resistance to reincarnational understanding is because we feel threatened by our sexual identity. We just don't like to contemplate seriously that we might have been a member of the opposite sex in a previous incarnation. Questions of sex and spiritual understanding of the soul are intertwined.*"[17]

Shirley MacLaine helped to popularize the idea of reincarnation in the Western world in the 1980s. In *Out on a Limb* she states:

> "*The sexual preference of individuals plays an important part in the requirement for understanding that we are all basically the same because we have all experienced being both sexes; our souls are basically androgynous. High spiritual understanding knows no sexuality differences because the elements of both sexes are simultaneously present.*"[18]

In the book, one of her teachers, John, explains to Shirley that:

"The ancient prophets and Christ figures such as Jesus and Buddha were not so much celibate as they were vibrating at an even and perfectly balanced frequency. Their yin and yang were so evenly distributed that sexuality was of no interest to them because there was no conflict and therefore no tension."[18]

In *Dancing in the Light,* Shirley MacLaine states that:

"Really advanced souls are androgynous because they reflect the complete and perfect balance of the yin and the yang in the soul itself."[19]

Lynn Kear wrote *We're Here: An Investigation into Gay Reincarnation,* which is the only book I could find that talked exclusively about reincarnation for individuals with alternative sexual identities. In the book there are a number of case studies. Here is a quote from one of them, called Sam:

"Homosexuals in this society get treated real quickly to the contradictions. It puts them on a road where they're thinking more. They're questioning what's happening around them. Homosexuality allows people to see contradictions. It allows us to question one part of humanity. Then we go on and question others. I think if there is ever to be a link between intelligence and homosexuality then I think it's due to that initial contradiction. We have the ability to question what goes on around us and to answer those questions."[20]

In *Reincarnation Key to Immortality*, Marcia Moore, an astrologer, and Mark Douglas stated that some individuals feel like they are born into the wrong body because of their haste to return to Earth. [21] Those that feel as though they are born in the wrong body may also die at an early age to search for a more suitable form in which to incarnate. Perhaps this is one reason that the suicide rate in the trans* population is so high. They also propose that a life in which a child dies young may be a "trial run" in a new gender since switching polarities is so difficult and takes several lifetimes. However, another perspective on childhood death states that children who incarnate into a short life are usually old souls that have volunteered to teach specific lessons to others, especially their parents and families.

In *Bringing Your Soul to Light*, Linda Backman states that individuals need both female and male incarnations to develop the androgyny of the soul. She has regressed thousands of clients and has never encountered a client who described all of their past lives as having been lived as only one gender. She says:

> *"Our androgynous soul is balanced and gender neutral. Changing gender from incarnation to incarnation, we come to understand which traits and behaviors are healthy and unhealthy in either sex. Our soul strives toward androgyny, toward carrying a pure balance of equal parts."*[22]

She points out that:

> *"If a culture or relationship is androgynous rather than patriarchal or matriarchal, it will display a lack of rigid gender roles and create a milieu where the people involved can comfortably display opposite–sex characteristics or be involved in activities that are commonly associated with the opposite gender."*[22]

In *A Case for Reincarnation*, Christine Hartley says:

> *"In the final state of at–one–ness there will be neither male nor female. Each soul will be beyond the division of the sexes, having acquired the capabilities of both in order to attain perfection one must have experienced every aspect of life."*[23]

In *Light Emerging*, Barbara Brennan states:

"Many individuals may choose a male or female body without the traditional sexual attraction toward the opposite sex, simply because that is not the type of life experience needed by the individual in that particular lifetime. There are no judgments in the spiritual world as to how one chooses to express one's sexuality. Rather, the goal is to express one's sexuality with love, truth, wisdom, and courage."[24]

She states that homosexuality can be the result of two circumstances: free choice to create circumstances for life experience or a trauma that resulted from the karma of past actions.

In *Your Soul's Gift*, Robert Schwarz says to examine an individual's pre–birth plan by looking at the circumstances in which they were born: the time period; the culture, norms, and mores; the race, religion, and economic status; and the attitudes of the key players in the formative years. Any or all of these might contain opposing forces that causes a dynamic tension. This tension has great purpose to trigger and subsequently guide spiritual evolution.

Gender identity and sexual identity are two dynamics where tension can create a schoolroom of learning situations. To examine the purpose of a life, look beyond the details of specific situations to the bigger picture of metaphors, concepts, and themes that are being played out. Chances are very good that concepts other than learning the difference between male and female or the difference between loving males and females are involved such as learning about the self through empowerment, assertiveness, and esteem, or learning to relate to others by working as a group for freedom, justice, and human rights. A child with gender or sexual identities that differ from those of the parents have chosen these parents with care. It may be that they volunteered to assist the parents to learn acceptance and understanding. It takes a lot of courage on the part of both child and parents to live out these lessons.

A soul might choose a gay sexual identity for various reasons. In *Your Soul's Gift,* the spirit guide of one case named Staci said:

1. *"About twenty percent of all souls enjoy playing in self–expression as homosexuals. For them it offers a safe journey through the experiences they desire. They become more and more comfortable in embracing that form and play in it for many more lives."*[25]
2. *"An experience in a prior life, where, because of its sexual role, the soul was enslaved, injured, or killed and does not wish to experience that again [may cause it to come] back as the opposite sex but [it] is not yet ready to love the opposite sex and so loves the same."*[25]

A soul chooses to incarnate with a specific sexual identity to learn about contrasts of opposites. Another spirit guide says:

"...the playing with the opposite sex in terms of heterosexuality provides unique experiences. In your planetary system there is a school of opposites, defined often as contrasting experience. When male is in relationship with female, there are many opportunities to embrace various learning concepts that would not occur in conscious thought or be observed by the individual without the contrast of the opposite sex."[25]

In some planetary systems there are more than two and as many as five genders. The guide continues to explain:

"These other planetary systems give access to many other lessons that are not able to be experienced or contained in your system. A large part is not describable to you because you do not have the words." [25]

In *Destiny of Souls* and *Journey of Souls,* Michael Newton writes about his regression sessions with thousands of clients. He describes, through his clients' regressions, how we work with our spirit guides to set up details of our upcoming life. We choose our time of birth, our parents, our bodies, and many other details. This is not the same concept as immutable destiny, for during our journey on Earth we have free will at each moment. Our path has been pre–arranged but the decisions we make at every twist and turn of the path influences not only our journey but our time line for accomplishing tasks. Based on Newton's work with his clients, he has identified two reasons for an individual to select a specific gender and sexual identity:

1. Younger souls choose the body of one particular gender about 75 percent of the time because they are more comfortable in that gender. Older souls alternate gender choices evenly.
2. Individuals choose a gay or lesbian sexual orientation in order to experience a more difficult road. There may be a karmic need of the soul:

   "to accelerate personal understanding of the complex differences in gender identity as related to certain events in their past."[26 and 27]

   Gay and lesbian individuals are older souls that have decided to learn about rising above public opinion "*to find self–esteem and self–identity.*"[26 and 27]

In *Messages from the Body*, Michael J. Lincoln lists two core reasons for an individual to have an intersex condition:

1. *"Experience–expansion. Their soul opted for a truly challenging and broadening experience for this lifetime. They will add it to their whole soul history in a manner that is designed to increase their capacity to teach and heal."*[28]
2. *"Karmic balancing. They now have to learn from the consequences of their abusive patterns in past lives. They will come out of it a much richer soul in experience."*[28]

In *Problematic Patterns*, Michael J. Lincoln discusses the reasons for an individual to have a transsexual or intersex condition as:

> *"They are experiencing a reaction to being in the wrong gender, in relation to the yin–yang (female–male) ratio in their soul. That is, they are a soul which is strongly one component (yin or yang) that has selected a body of the other gender, and for some reason that is not acceptable to them. Most of the time, it is because they have forgotten why their soul chose it for this life once they were here."*[29]

Although bound by ethical obligations to remain nonjudgmental, some individuals in the helping professions do judge, and whether or not it is intentional, they can be emotionally abusive to their clients. An example of this occurs in *One Sex to the Other: Reincarnation and the Dual–Gender Soul.* Author Amy Shapiro discusses a regression session with a female–to–male transsexual, who had never incarnated in a female body until this life. In her book she quotes Rev. Sue Likegord as saying this about him:

> *"The way that we create our karma for ourselves is through desire and he always desired to be male. But the soul also has a higher purpose. You learn something from every lifetime, so that the soul extracts the wisdom from experience. I hope that he will sometime be able to take a female lifetime without cutting off his breasts."*[30]

It is important to interview potential doctors and therapists in order to insure that they will be supportive of your journey. As incarnated beings, none of us have the perceptual capability to understand the grand spiritual plan for any other soul and so should not judge another soul's journey.

MY RESEARCH RESULTS

In *Reliving Past Lives: Evidence under Hypnosis,* Helen Wambach, a psychologist, researched 1,088 regression cases and tabulated the distribution of the recalled past lives based on sex, race, and socioeconomic class. She then correlated the data with the population–growth curve. She found that irrespective of the gender of the individual regressed; the past lives of her subjects were distributed quite evenly across gender. Her results of 50.6 percent male and 49.4 percent female is an almost exact correspondence with the gender distribution in the actual population.[31]

During the research phase of this book I completed seventy–eight past life regressions. The intention set during the session induction was to visit the past lives that had the most influence on the client's current life. In other words, what past life set the karma that influences the present life situations? In sessions with trans* clients, the intention of discovering why a life in a trans* body was chosen was also set.

Below is a chart of my results:

Subject	# Sessions	% Male Past Lives	% Female Past Lives	% Unknown Past Lives
Cis Straight Male	4	75%	8%	17%
Cis Gay Male	4	88%	13%	0%
Cis Straight Female	38	38%	60%	2%
Cis Bisexual Female	1	0%	100%	0%
Cis Lesbian Female	7	63%	38%	0%
Trans FTM	19	75%	17%	8%
Trans MTF	4	0%	100%	0%
Intersex	1	50%	50%	0%
Total	**78**	**58%**	**37%**	**6%**

My sample is too small to derive any realistic statistics from but the results are still interesting to look at.

- Of 27 male–identified individuals, only 4 (15%) did not experience a male past life. Of 50 female–identified individuals, 12 (24%) did not experience a female past life.
- The majority of all regression clients had lives as ordinary farmers, merchants, and hunters. Most of them were lives in low or middle socio–economic status. Some of them had lives as warriors and one or two remembered lives as tribal kings.

All of my trans* clients stated that their life purpose was to help others. None reported that incarnating into a trans* body was the result of "bad" karmic actions in past lives. There was no single universal reason identified by my clients for choosing specific gender and sexual identities. Each client had unique and personal reasons for their choice of this lifetime.

THEORIES ON WHY INDIVIDUALS INCARNATE WITH SPECIFIC GENDER AND SEXUAL IDENTITIES

In general there are four basic reasons to reincarnate:

1. ***Desire*** – The desire to be incarnated with specific souls.
2. ***Growth*** – The desire to progress the soul's evolution through lessons.
3. ***Karma*** – To pay retribution, compensate, or balance previous actions.
4. ***Service*** – To help others.

Below is a list of my theories of why gender and sexual identities are chosen:

THEORY #1: Individuals may reincarnate so quickly from a past life that they bring their memories and habits with them into the current life. These habits and memories may or may not match up with the birth assigned sex. In addition, individuals may be experiencing "soul remembering" of past lives lived as males, females, or third gender individuals.

THEORY #2: Individuals choose a specific gender or sexual identity in order to fulfill or balance karma. The individual may have inflicted or suffered some form of sexual abuse, trauma, or misuse of power in a past life. Balancing past karmic actions is not a punishment for those actions but rather provides opportunities to learn and grow from past experiences.

THEORY #3: Individuals choose a specific gender or sexual identity in order to avoid reliving painful past life experiences of enslavement, injury, or death in a particular gender or sexual identity.

THEORY #4: Individuals choose a specific gender or sexual identity based on timing issues such as the desire to be sexually available or unavailable to a specific mate.

THEORY #5: Individuals choose a new gender or sexual identity that is unfamiliar to them after spending many consecutive lives in another form.

THEORY #6: Alternative gender and sexual identities may be chosen by older souls for accelerated learning purposes.

THEORY #7: Individuals choose a new gender or sexual identity as a metaphor for learning about bringing other polarities into balance.

THEORY #8: Old souls are more comfortable being androgynous and pansexual, which is the balanced state of the soul in the spirit world.

THEORY #9: Individuals choose a specific gender or sexual identity simply because that is what they like.

THEORY #10: A soul may volunteer to take on specific gender or sexual identities in order to assist others with their lessons. An individual may take on specific roles to help "teach" parents, siblings, children, or society about gender and sexual diversity possibilities and how to be tolerant of diversity. An individual that has chosen a path of alternative gender or sexual identity can stand as an example of courage, freedom, self–empowerment, and independence. In addition, souls with non–conforming gender and sexual identities are introducing a new wave of consciousness on Earth.

Choosing gender and sexual identities is a multi–dimensional event and can be based on more than one reason. The one thing that is certain is that an individual chooses gender and sexual identity based on their own soul's needs and desires. Each soul is living a unique journey and so there is never only one simple reason why someone is one way or another.

Since there are so many unique soul paths there are many combinations of options to experience at the Earth School. An individual may choose to experience a transgender life. Should it be male–to–female or female–to–male? The experiences of each are completely different. An individual may choose to experience a gay life. Should it be in a male body or a female body? Again the experiences will be completely different. An individual may choose an intersex body. Each point on the gender and sexual identity spectrum provides its own unique experience and lessons. Can we truly say we are evolved souls until we have experienced each of these variations?

PAST LIFE ASTROLOGY

In past life astrology (PLA) an individual's chart is analyzed for clues to past lives. This analysis will not likely give specific details of a past life as a regression session does but it will give the meaning and influence of past lives on present lives by showing the life themes, life purposes, soul issues, and unfinished karma that is present in the current life. Below are some specific references from astrologers about gender and sexuality choices.

In *Past Life Astrology,* Judy Hall says that:

"When Uranus is placed in the Eighth House it often indicates old ambivalence and ambiguity around gender and sexuality. The soul may have changed gender between lives or have chosen to explore different modes of expressing sexuality."[32]

An example of how past life astrology works on a chart of a trans* identified individual is available in *Yesterday's Sky* by Steven Forrest. He includes an analysis of Christine Jorgensen's astrological chart. Christine Jorgensen was the first highly publicized transsexual in the United States. An ex–GI, she had genital reassignment surgery in the 1950s. Steven Forrest says this about her transition:

"Was a physical sex change actually necessary to this process? As an evolutionary astrologer, all I can say is that she had some deep unfinished business with both genders. I would add that, given the humiliations of the karmic past, her way forward lay in feeling the energized and powerful aspects of her own possibilities. It lay in the category of making a radical, Plutonian free choice in the direction of her own healing as she understood it. The interaction of flesh with spirit, of body with mind, is a complex phenomenon. It is folly to ignore any element of the system. Ultimately, the manifest physical world proceeds from the reincarnating, ever–learning mind. It is there, in deep mindfulness, that our most profound work must occur."[33]

In *Pluto: The Evolutionary Journey of the Soul*, Jeff Green says that switching genders from recent past lives may affect internal security and create some self–image difficulties. He lists the following indicators of gender switching between lives on the chart:

- Pluto is in the Fourth or Tenth House
- South and North Nodes are in the Fourth or Tenth Houses

- South and North Nodes are in Cancer or Capricorn

The Fourth House, Cancer, and the Moon correlate to the Jungian concept of *anima* and *animus*. An individual that has Pluto in the Fourth House may find it hard to feel secure in their birth assigned sex because most of these individuals have been relating to themselves in the opposite sex in the most recent prior lives. The more times an individual returns to a gender, the less adjustment is needed.

An individual that has Pluto in the Tenth House in almost all cases has switched gender in the most recent prior life. They switch gender because further evolutionary growth cannot occur until a state of balance is re–established. The sudden switch in gender can create emotional issues. Identifying the source or reason for these feelings helps with the integration process.

Jeff Green also refers to Christine Jorgensen as an example of an individual who "*refused to accept this gender switch*" and had genital reassignment surgery instead. Her chart had Pluto in the Tenth House the South Node in Capricorn. He comments about her:

> *"Her determination to have this gender switch reversed served as an inspiration and example for others who feel the same need."*[34]

Please note that Christine Jorgensen is just one example. Based on my theory that individuals choose gender and sexual identities based on many different reasons or motives, her case may not apply to other individuals who on the surface may seem similar. Each individual is unique unto their self. The above astrological influences are not present in my birth chart, which means that my soul's reasons for choosing this lifetime are different.

Observation Point

My Past Life Regression Session

(Drawing as I experienced myself in my previous life.)

My most recent past life was as a German gay man in the death camps during WWII. I recalled being forced to assist the medical doctors during their experiments on Jewish inmates. I carried the message to my current life that one, it is not safe to be a gay man (because you will be persecuted for it) and two, it is not safe to be a female because of the experiments I witnessed. Thus I am still resolving issues of gender and sexual identity into this life.

I consider my life to be a gift of learning about empathy, sensitivity, femininity, and masculinity. I remember asking why I had the life in the camps as a gay man and the answer I received was that it was not a punishment but that I had volunteered to be there in order to support other souls that in so much pain. As a result I believe that the purposes of our lives are multi-dimensional. I am healing myself as well as holding space for others as they heal.

NOTES:

[1] Stone, Joshua David. *Soul Psychology: How to Clear Negative Emotions and Spiritualize Your Life* Wellspring/Ballantine, 1999.

[2] Hunter, C. Roy. *The Art of Hypnosis: Mastering Basic Techniques.* Crown House Publishing, 2010.

Immrama Institute. "Brainwave States." http://www.immramainstitute.com/brainwave-technology-for-health-wellness/brainwave-states-alpha-theta-delta-beta-gamma/

[3] Chadwick, Gloria *Future Lives: Discovering & Understanding Your Destiny.* Sterling, 2008.

[4] Roman, Sanaya. *Spiritual Growth: Being Your Higher Self.* HJ Kramer, 1992.

[5] Todeschi, Kevin J. *Edgar Cayce on the Akashic Records: The Book of Life.* A.R.E. Press, 1998.

[6] Mack, Joshua. *Karma 101: What Goes Around Comes Around and What You Can Do About It.* Fair Winds Press, 2002.

[7] Stemman, Roy. *The Big Book of Reincarnation: Examining the Evidence that We Have All Lived Before.* Hierophant Publishing, 2012.

[8] Cohen, Doris Eliana. *Repetition: Past Lives, Life, and Rebirth. Hay House, 2008.*

[9] Semkiw, Walter. "Principles of Reincarnation: Understanding Past Lives." http://www.iisis.net/index.php?page=semkiw-reincarnation-past-lives-principles

[10] Stevenson, Ian. *Children Who Remember Previous Lives: A Question of Reincarnation.* McFarland, 2000.

[11] Stevenson, Ian. *Life before Life: Children's Memories of Previous Lives.* St. Martin's Griffin, 2008.

[12] Weiss, Brian. *Messages from the Masters: Tapping into the Power of Love.* Warner Books, 2001.

[13] Goldberg, Bruce. *Past Lives, Future Lives: Accounts of Regression and Progression through Hypnosis.* Ballantine Books, 1988.

[14] Ahlquist, Diane. *The Idiot's Guide to Life after Death.* Alpha, 2007.

[15] Bowman, Carol. *Return from Heaven: Beloved Relatives Reincarnated Within Your Family.* HarperTorch, 2003.

[16] Williston, Glenn and Judith Johnstone. *Discovering Your Past Lives: Spiritual Growth Through a Knowledge of Past Lifetimes.* Thorsons Pub, 1995.

[17] MacLaine, Shirley. *I Am All over That: And Other Confessions.* Atria Books, 2012.

[18] MacLaine, Shirley. *Out on a Limb.* Bantam, 1986.

[19] MacLaine, Shirley. *Dancing in the Light.* Bantam, 1986.

[20] Kear, Lynn. *We're Here: An Investigation into Gay Reincarnation.* Retropolitan, 1999.

[21] Moore, Marcia and Mark Douglas. *Reincarnation Key to Immortality.* Arcane Books, 1968.

[22] Backman, Linda. *Bringing Your Soul to Light: Healing Through Past Lives and the Time Between.* Llewellyn Publications, 2009.

[23] Hartley, Christine. *A Case for Reincarnation.* Robert Hale Ltd, 1972.

[24] Brennan, Barbara. *Light Emerging: The Journey of Personal Healing.* Bantam, 1993.

[25] Schwarz, Robert. *Your Soul's Gift: The Healing Power of the Life You Planned Before You Were Born.* Whispering Winds Press, 2012.

[26] Newton, Michael. *Destiny of Souls: New Case Studies of Life between Lives.* Llewellyn Publications, 2000.

[27] Newton, Michael. *Journey of Souls: Case Studies of Life between Lives.* Llewellyn Publications, 1994.

[28] Lincoln, Michael J. "*Messages from the Body: Their Psychological Meaning (The Body's Desk Reference).*" Talking Hearts, 2006.

[29] Lincoln, Michael J. "*Problematic Problems: (Behavioral, Psychological and Psychiatric–Their Emotional Meaning).*" Talking Hearts, 2007.

[30] Shapiro, Amy. *One Sex to the Other: Reincarnation and the Dual–Gender Soul.* BookSurge Publishing, 2006.

[31] Wambach, Helen. *Reliving Past Lives: Evidence under Hypnosis.* Barnes & Noble Books, 2000.

[32] Hall, Judy. *Past Life Astrology: Use Your Birthchart to Understand Your Karma.* Godsfield, 2006.

[33] Forrest, Steven. *Yesterday's Sky.* Seven Paws Press, 2008.

[34] Green, Jeff. *Pluto: The Evolutionary Journey of the Soul.* Llewellyn Publications, 1985.

CHAPTER 10:
TWO SPIRIT AND THIRD GENDER CULTURES

Alternative Gender and Sexual Identity Societies

TWO SPIRITS

This graphic symbol has two feathers representing the two spiritual energies, Male and Female, on a background of the yin-yang symbol. The circle is a symbol of sacred cycles that have no beginning and no end.

(Designed by Drake)

NORTH AMERICAN TWO SPIRITS

A Two Spirit holds the energy of both male and female in one body. They are considered to be a third gender in most Native American tribes. The third gender is comprised of individuals that have a gender identity that is neither male nor female or both male and female, thus they are able to walk between the worlds. Some tribes thought of male–bodied Two Spirits as a third gender and female–bodied Two Spirits as a fourth gender. Two Spirits were very accepted because individuals were not forced into a binary–gender role model. Individuals who were in relationship with third gender individuals were not considered gay or lesbian.

Many tribes did not force children into a gender role based on the sex of the Physical Body. They instead allowed the child to choose. In one such ceremony, a bow and arrow and baskets are placed together. A child was free to choose which object they wanted and that which they chose became indicative of what their gender identity would be. The child would be raised according to this indication.

Another reason that Two Spirits were so well–accepted and even honored in Native American culture is because of the trust the people placed in Great Spirit/Creator. The people were very spiritual and saw every single element on Earth in relationship to Great Spirit/Creator, therefore Two Spirits were ordained by Great Spirit/Creator. Thus, they had special talents and were given special treatment.

More than 155 North American indigenous tribes honored dual–sexed or third gender individuals.[1] Two Spirits often became healers, counselors, therapists, spiritual priests, shamans, medicine people, prophets, marriage counselors, and matchmakers.

The original non–native North American term for Two Spirits was "*berdache*"[2], which originated from the French word "*bardaj*", a derogatory term for a cross–dresser, passive homosexual, male prostitute, or young feminine boy. The root "*barda*" comes from Arabic meaning "captive, captured" and from the Persian word "*bardaj*" meaning "seized, prisoner". This term was also inaccurate since most of the tribes that recognized dual–sexed and third gender individuals had a term for them in their own language.

The modern term "Two Spirit" was created at the third annual Native American/First Nations Gay and Lesbian Conference in Winnipeg Canada in the 1990s to replace the term "*berdache*". It is translated from the Anishinabe/Ojibwe term "*niizh manitoag*", which means having two spirits, male and female, in one body.[3]

The Western labels of "transsexual", "homosexual", "cross dresser", "transvestite", and even "transgender" do not accurately describe a Two Spirit. While the definition of Two Spirits implies that the individuals are androgynous with both male and female hearts and souls, there are additional criteria associated with the concept. The traditional role of the Two Spirit in tribal life was characterized by the following:

- Two Spirits presented as the opposite gender of their birth assigned sex or as both genders in temperament, dress, lifestyle and social roles. The dress of traditional Two Spirits was usually a mix of male and female articles.
- Two Spirits assumed the work roles of either the opposite gender as their birth assigned sex or both genders.
- Female–bodied Two Spirits usually had female sexual partners and male–bodied Two Spirits usually had male sexual partners but occasionally female sexual partners. Two Spirits usually did not have sex with other Two Spirits, as they were considered brothers or sisters.
- Two Spirits were more than individuals that identified as lesbian, gay, bisexual, or transgender. Two Spirits also had to have a major spiritual component associated with their identity that was sanctioned through visions and dreams.

Two Spirits held distinct social roles in the tribe. Besides performing jobs that were considered to be strictly male or female, male–bodied Two Spirits might also be medicine persons, diviners, matchmakers, undertakers, ceremonialists, war nurses, and child caretakers. Female–bodied Two Spirits might also have roles as medicine persons, chiefs, traders, hunters, warriors, guides, skilled craft artists, or prophets. In many tribes, it was considered a great honor or very lucky to be named by a Two Spirit. Often having a Two Spirit in the family was a guarantee of wealth because they were skilled at doing the jobs of both males and females.

Unfortunately, the introduction of Christianity by missionaries and the influx of white settlers virtually destroyed the acceptance of Two Spirits in North American native life. However, based on the belief of the circle of life, our return to indigenous consciousness is imminent. There are many signs already pointing to an increase of interest in indigenous spirituality. The survival of Mother Earth depends on this return to Earth–based spirituality. And with it comes the resurrection of the third gender.

Modern Two Spirits should have the following characteristics:

- *Possess non–conforming gender and sexual identities.* Two Spirits have an even balance of male and female energy. They express themselves outside the traditional binary gender roles in temperament, dress, lifestyle, and social roles. They may specialize in non–traditional gender role work by taking on roles viewed as belonging to the "opposite" of their birth assigned sex.

- *Be a member of an indigenous culture.* Indigenous means living naturally or being native to an area. It is an innate awareness of belonging to a specific geography. The indigenous–identified soul is consciously aware of the spirit of being native. To North American Indians, being a Two Spirit means having Native American bloodlines.

- *Hear the call of Spirit.* Two Spirits are spiritually connected through beliefs, visions, and dreams. They may take on roles of a medicine person, spiritual counselor, and/or teacher. They are trained to have knowledge in ritual, ceremony, and spiritual culture.

"The concept of a 'transsexual' is a Western one, clearly linked with a medical procedure and based on the notion that there are two opposite sexes. It is therefore not an apt description of *berdaches*. Within Western thought, with its numerous dichotomies of paired opposites, there is little tolerance for ambiguities outside of the categories of 'women' and 'men'. As a result, gender nonconformist people who feel dissatisfied may conclude that they have only one alternative, to transfer themselves from one sex to the other. Many transsexuals, as products of our culture, make this transfer completely, by surgical reassignment and hormones. Many lead happier lives. But others do not make so happy an adjustment, and may feel no more comfortable as a woman than as a man. Their unhappiness, I would suggest, is the result of a restricted social value, which sees only two opposite possibilities."

–Walter Williams, The Spirit and the Flesh

North American Tribe Terms for Two Spirit Identities[2]

Acoma Kokwima
Aleut/Kodiak–Achnucek
Apache–Nde'isdzan
Blackfoot–Ake'skassi, Saahkómaapi'aakíikoan, Sahwo'mapi akikwan
Cheyenne–Heemaneh
Cree – Ayekkwe, Aayahkwew
Crow – Boté, Baté, Badé
Diné (Navajo) – Nadle, Nadleeh
Hopi – Hovo, Ho'va, Hho'ua, Kwasaitaka, Korosta, Korowista
Lakota (Sioux) – Winkte, Winkte Winyan
Mohave – Alyha, Hwame
Ojibwa (Chippewa) – Agokwa, Ogokwe, Okutitakwe
Omaha – Mexoga
Pauite – Dubuds
Shoshoni–Taikwahni Tainnapa', Taikwahni Wa'ippe'
Yuma–Kwe'rhaame
Zuni – Ihamana, Lhamana, Katsotse

"He [a *winkte*] told me, 'if Nature puts a burden on a man by making him different, it also gives him a power.'

We think that if a woman has two little ones growing inside her, if she is going to have twins, sometimes instead of giving birth to two babies they have formed up in her womb into just one, into a half man–half woman kind of being. We call such a person a *winkte*.

Winktes were men who dressed like women, looked like women and acted like women. They did so by their own choice or in obedience to a dream. They were not like other men, but the Great Spirit made them *winktes* and we accepted them as such. They were supposed to have the gift of prophecy, and the secret name a *winkte* gave to a child was believed to be especially powerful and effective. In former days a father gave to a *winkte* a fine horse in return for such a name."[4]

–John Fire, Chief Lame Deer (Lakota)

"The Creator created very special beings when he created two-spirited people. He gave certain individuals two spirits. We're a special people and that's been denied since contact with the Europeans. What heterosexuals achieve in marriage, we achieve in ourselves."

–Sue Beaver (Mohawk)

Famous Two Spirits

Hosteen Klah (1867–1937) A Diné (Navajo) *nadle* who was a weaver and medicine person. Their weaving was exhibited at the Chicago' World Columbian Exposition.

Lozen (1850s–1889) A female-bodied Apache warrior, prophet, and healer.

Osh-Tisch/Finds Them and Kills Them (1800s) A Crow *baté*.

Pine Leaf (? - 1854) A female-bodied Crow warrior and chief. They had at least four female wives.

Running Eagle (? - 1850) A female-bodied Piegan warrior who had a female partner.

Silver Heels/Nonhelema (Not a Man)/The Grenadier Squaw (1700s) A female-bodied Shawnee warrior chief who preached peace.

Water Sitting Grizzly/Qangon/Bowdash/Kaúxuma Núpika (early 1800s) A Kootenai "Manlike Woman" and prophet.

We'wha (1849–1896) A Zuni *lhamana* and perhaps the most well-known of Two Spirits. They were a guest of President Cleveland in Washington DC. For more information about We'wha, read *The Zuni Man-Woman* by Will Roscoe[5].

Yellow Head/Ozaawindib (early 1800s) An Ojibwa warrior who identified as female.

THIRD GENDER CULTURES AROUND THE WORLD

To review, third gender[6] is a category of individuals whose gender identity is neither male nor female or both male and female. The term "third" is usually understood to mean "other". Some anthropologists have described cultures with as many as four and up to seven genders. As noted in Chapter 3, third gender status has been legalized in some countries.

Following is a tour of third gender cultures around the world: [6]

(Note: You, the reader, may have noticed a preponderance of reference to male–bodied individuals, not only in the medical references but also the historical references. In most cultures female–bodied individuals are nearly invisible. They are rarely spoken of in history books. This includes women in virtually any profession other than prostitution and motherhood.)

AKAVA'INE *(Cook Islands),* ***FA'AFAFINE*** *(Samoa),* ***FAKAFEFINE and FAKALEITI*** *(Tonga),* ***MĀHŪ*** *(Hawai'i),* ***and WHAKAWAHINE*** *(New Zealand)* **– *SOUTH PACIFIC***

The Māori of the Cook Islands call transgender individuals "*akava'ne*" or "'*akava'ine*", which means to "act like a woman". Sometimes "*laelae*" is also used when referring to effeminate men. The *akava'ines* were a part of Māori culture until the 1800s when the Christian missionaries arrived. Today, homosexuality is illegal in the Cook Islands.

A male–bodied third gender individual in Samoa is called a "*fa'afafine*". The Samoan slang word is "*mala*". They are very dedicated to the communal family. *Fa'afafine* may have sex with male or females but since they are members of a third gender, this is not considered a homosexual relationship. However, it is taboo for a *fa'afafine* to have sex with another *fa'afafine.*

An effeminate male in Tonga is called a "*fakaleiti*", however they prefer to call themselves "*leiti*" or "ladies".

In Hawai'i, a *māhū* is a third gender individual. In modern day Hawai'i, "*māhū*" is used as a slang word for transvestite and transgender individuals. "*Aikane*" is a term for a man who is the lover of another man.

The Māori of New Zealand call transgender individuals "*whakawahine*". Other terms used are "*hinehi*" or "*hinehua*".

BAKLA** (Tagalog), **BAYOT** (Cebuano), **BANTUT** (Tausug), **AGI** (Ilonggo), **BINABAE, BADING – PHILIPPINES

These terms all refer to third gender identities in the Philippines, which also include effeminate gay men and transwomen. Gender–variant female–bodied individuals are called "*lakin–on*" or "tomboy".

FEMMINIELLO – ITALY

The term "*femminielli*" or "*femmenielli*" describes feminine male–bodied individuals in Neapolitan culture. These individuals might be gay men or transwomen. *Femminielli* are believed to bring luck. It is popular practice to have a *femminiello* hold a newborn baby or participate in games. Campania *femminiello* hold a privileged position in traditional local events. The marriage of the *femminielli* is a secret and sacred ceremony held annually in Torre del Greco, where the highest priests of the Uranian religion participate.

HIJRA, ARAVANI, AND JOGAPPA – INDIA AND PAKISTAN

Hijras are born as male–bodied or intersex individuals, dress in feminine clothes, and have a gender identity of neither male nor female. "*Hijra*" may be considered derogatory so "*khwaja saraa*", "*khasuaa*", "*khusaraa*", or "*kinnar*" can be used instead. *Kothis* are regarded as feminine men or boys who take a feminine role in sex with men, but do not live in the kind of intentional communities that *hijras* usually live in. *Hijras* are considered to be a third gender identification, however, their social status is low. *Hijras* belong to a special caste. Even though third gender status has been legalized in India, Pakistan, and Nepal, they third gender individuals still are the victims of discrimination and violence. Some *Hijras* undergo *nirwaan*, which refers to the removal of penis, testicles, and scrotum.

Hijras usually live together in groups headed by a guru. They perform, dance, and sing for family functions. Bahuchara Mata, a

Hindu goddess, is the patroness and Lord Shiva is a patron of *hijras*. For their faithful devotion, they are granted the ability to confer blessings on people during auspicious occasions like childbirth and weddings.

In south India, *hijras* are devoted to the Hindu god, Aravan. They are called *aravani* or *ali*.

Another third gender sect in southern India is the *jogappa*. They worship the Hindu goddess Yellamma (Renuka) who is believed to have the power to change one's sex.

Sanskrit texts list various types of males who are impotent with females including *sandha* (transgenders), *nisarga* (intersexed), and *mukhebhaga*, *kumbhika* and *asekya* (three different types of homosexual men). *Kliba* is also a Sanskrit word that describes third gender individuals.

KHANITH/XANITH – MIDDLE EAST

The Arabic term "*khanith*" or "*khaneeth*" originates from the written Arabic words "*mukhannath*" ("effeminate"), which refers to transgender individuals. "*Khuntha*" ("hermaphrodite") refers to intersexed individuals. The word is an insult in the Middle East. *Khanith* are considered to be the bottom in homosexual relationships. They keep their status as men as long as they are legally married to a female and consummate the marriage. Their clothing is between that of a male and a female.

KATHOEYS – THAILAND

In Thailand, males with varying degrees of femininity are called "*kathoeys*" ("ladyboys"). Other terms used in Thailand are: "*sao praphet song*" (having a female identity), "*phet thi sam*" (having a third gender identity), and "*phu–ying praphet thi sorng*" (woman of the second kind). The term "*kathoey*" may be considered derogatory especially in the form of "*kathoey–saloey*".

MUXE – MEXICO

Mixed gender identities originate from the Aztec priests and Mayan gods who were androgynous. Catholicism brought by the

Spanish conquerors wiped out almost all traces of third gender identities except for the *muxe* (or *muxhe*), who are males with feminine characteristics in the state of Oaxaca, which is predominately populated by the Zapotec people. Other Zapotec communities have similar third gender roles, such as the *biza'ah* of Teotitlán. The word "*muxe*" is derived from the Spanish word for woman, "*mujer*". *Muxe* are not considered homosexual but third gender. Their male partners are called "*mayate*". They may be transvestites ("*vestidas*") or wear male clothes with make–up ("*pintadas*"). *Muxe* may be accepted in village communities but may be discriminated against in large cities. *Muxe* cook, clean, look after children, take care of elders, as well as dance, sing, and entertain.

TRAVESTI AND CHUQUI CHINCHAY – LATIN AND SOUTH AMERICA

A *travesti* is a male with a feminine gender identity in South America. *Travestis* do not identify as transsexual women. They may present as female and modify their bodies with hormones or silicone injections, but do not seek genital surgery or identify as a female. Like the *hijra*, *travestis* often are seen as a lower social class.

In the Incan Andes, third gender individuals who served the jaguar deity, Chuqui Chinchay, were called "*quariwarmi*", which meant "men–women". They were shamans that performed rituals and their androgynous attire was representative of their function as intermediaries between dualities such as masculine and feminine, present and past, living and dead.

TWO SPIRITS AND THIRD GENDER INDIVIDUALS IN SPIRITUAL ROLES

Medicine people and shamans have the ability to walk between many worlds including that of the masculine and the feminine. Experiencing both male and female roles dramatically increases empathy and understanding that can be used in healing work.

In Siberia, shamans–to–be must spend time living in both genders. This includes dressing as a member of the "opposite" birth assigned sex. Many shamans adopt androgynous roles for the rest of their lives. Consequently, they are considered to have special magical powers and responsibilities. Siberian shamans, who were are "*chuckchi*" ("soft man"), are shamans first and individuals with alternative gender identities second. They are considered more powerful than other shamans. The Russian term "*schupan*" means "a gender transformed shaman".

Daan van Kampenhout, author of several books on shamanism, describes Siberian shamanic costumes as being androgynous so that the wearer understood the total of all human experience, through living as both a male and a female. He says:

> *"As part of the training of the shaman–to–be, he or she was expected to live for some time as a member of the opposite sex. During this period, the aspirant had to think, act and dress like a man if she was a woman, like a woman if he was a man. Often, a person who successfully passed this part of their shamanic examination would choose to continue living as a member of the other sex. In some parts of Siberia, this was even expected of all male shamans. Many traditional shamanic cultures offered their homosexual members the possibility of living with a partner: a gay or lesbian could become a shaman and change sex, afterwards being able to marry a person of the same biological sex. Usually such transformed shamans would be looked upon with awe, fear or suspicion. They were considered to have very strong and special magical powers and carried distinctive and important responsibilities, yet their shaman costumes were androgynous."*[7]

In Borneo, the highest level shamans are those who have been transformed into women. They are called "*manang bali*" (which means "changed shaman from male to female"). Third gender male–bodied shaman–priests, also called "*basir*", "*bajasa*", and "*bissu*", function as healers, ritual leaders, and perform spiritual ceremonies. They receive their powers from female spirits.

Shamans of the pre–Christian Philippines, called "*bayguin*", were usually male–bodied individuals with feminine nature and demeanor.

In Burmese Buddhism, *acaults* are cross–gender males that are considered to be sacred beings with special ceremonial roles as shamans and seers.

In Mesopotamian Sumer, *gala*, *assinnu*, *ur.sal*, and *kur.gar.ra* were third gender individuals who served the goddess Inanna/Ishtar. They were sacred prostitutes, dancers, musicians, and actors. In Babylon they were called "*kalbu*".

In ancient Syria, Phoenicia, and Canaan, *Qedeshim* were feminine–identified men who worshiped Asherah. They often castrated themselves in her honor.

Galli or *gallae* were the Greco–Roman priests of Cybele and Attis. They dressed as neither male nor female and were castrated.

Megabyzoi were effeminate priests that greeted pilgrims arriving at the temple of the Greek/Roman Goddess Artemis/Diana.

To learn more about male–bodied individuals, who devoted themselves fully to Goddess worship, read *Transgender Spirituality: Man into Goddess*[8] by Sakhi Bhava.

Another spiritual role that gays fill is called the "gatekeeper". The Dagara tribe of West Africa believe that gender is energetic and sexuality is spiritually based. Gay individuals have the ability to stand between the world of male and female. This allows them to be mediators between genders. They believe that gay individuals experience a state of vibrational consciousness which is higher than non–gay individuals and this allows them to stand between this world and the spirit world. This place between the worlds is called the gates and the gays are the guardians of the gates. The function of gatekeeping is decided prior to birth and becomes the life purpose of individuals who undertake it.[9 and 10]

Third Gender Identities Around the World[6]

Africa - Agule, Buyazi, Haja, Kitesha, Mzili, Wobo
Africa, South - Moffie Wor, Sitabane
Africa & Greece - Amazon
Albania - Posestra
Ancient Eastern Mediterranean - Tertium Genus Hominum
Arabia – Khaneeth, Khanith
Babylonia - Salzikrum
Borneo - Basir
Burma - Acault, Meinmasha
Dominican Republic - Guevedoche
Hawaii/Maori/Tahiti - Kanaka, Māhū Wahine (Vahine)
Hebrew - Aionolit, 'Almah
India - Chakka, Hijras, Jogappa, Khusra, Kliba, Kojja, Kothi, Nisarga, Sandha, Tritiya-prakrti
Indonesia - Waria
Islam - Mutarajjulat
Italy – Femmenielli, Femminielli, Femminiello
Japan - Newhalf, Shinjuku Boy, Wakashu
Malaysia - Maknyah
Māori – Akava'ine, 'Akava 'ine, Takatāpui
Māori, New Zealand – Wakawhahine
Mesopotamia – Kur.gar.ra, Ur.sal Dog
Mexico - Biza'ah, Machera, Muxe, Muxhe
Nepal - Metis
Nigeria - Dike-nwami
Norse – Ghoti
Old Israel - Aylonit, Saris, Tumtum
Oman - Xanith
Papua New Guinea - Kwol-aatmo
Peru (Inka) - Khawaja sara, Quariwarm
Philippines - Agi, Bading, Bakla, Bantut, Bayot, Binabae, Lakin-on, Transpinay
Roman - Bona, Galli/Gallae

(Continued next page)

Third Gender Identities Around the World[6]
(*Continued from previous page*)

Samoa – Fa'afafine
Siberia - Qa'cikicheca, Yirka'-la'ul
South America – Travesti
South Slavonic - Muskobanja
Thailand – Kathoey
Thailand/India Buddhist - Pandaka, Ubhatobyanjanaka
Tonga/Polynesia - Fakafefine, Fakaleiti, Leiti
Turkey/Persia - Bacchá, Bacha-baazi, Köçek
Zulu - Isangoma

QUEER AND ANDROGYNOUS FIGURES IN MYTHOLOGY

There are many mythological stories involving individuals with alternative gender and sexual identities. Many of them are creator stories.[11]

The Trickster exhibits gender–changing and same–sex practices. In Native American mythology, Coyote is the trickster god. S/he is sometimes male, sometimes female, and can be gay, straight, or a cross–dresser. Also from Native American mythology, the Changing One is a magical shape–shifter that appears in all sorts of sexual disguises. Bego–chidi is a Diné transgender creator trickster god. Loki is the Norse trickster, who has the ability to change genders and become pregnant.

Many creation myths begin with an androgynous primordial being, which contains all opposites. This being splits itself into male and female entities to begin the process of creation. In Hinduism, the primal man, Purusha divides into male and female. According to the Jewish Kabbalah, Adam Kadmon, the first human, was neither male nor female.

The Sacred Cosmic Egg has appeared in several myths of the androgynous Creator god as the vehicle to manifest his/her creation. Other creation myths that include bi–gender deities mention the Rainbow Serpent. The rainbow, originally a sign of hope and rebirth, is now also a symbol of gay liberation and represents the many colors of diversity.

Two Spirits play prominent parts in Diné creation stories. There are stories of *nadleehs* (Two Spirits) called Turquoise Boy and White Shell Girl. The Hopi have a transgender *kachina* (supernatural ancestor spirit) called "Kolhamana". Wiya Numpa is a Lakota hermaphrodite spirit, who appears to males and females, and requires them to begin cross–dressing. In the Mohave region, the Tipai, Ipai, and Yuma tribes believe that Wikami is a sacred mountain which is the source of the creator spirit that gave hermaphroditic spirit to the tribes.

The Sacred Twins are an archetype for gay men. The Twins rule relationships between equals especially between comrades, friends, lovers, and battle companions. The African creation story of the Dogon tells how humans possess two souls, one male and one female, so that they will not be unbalanced if born alone.

Plato, the Greek philosopher, believed that sexual attraction was the desire of incomplete humans attempting to fuse back together. He wrote a story about three kinds of beings: males, females, and hermaphrodites. They each had four legs and four arms however Zeus split each one in two because they became too powerful. The severed males became pederasts,[12] the severed females became lesbians, and the severed hermaphrodites became males who loved females and females who loved males.

QUEER AND ANDROGYNOUS DEITIES

Deities that had alternative gender and sexual identities are present in many different religions, cultures, and mythologies.[13]

In Polynesia, Ta'aroa is the androgynous creator god.

In the pre–Christian Philippines, there are two hermaphroditic gods, named "Bathala" ("Man and Woman in One") and "Malyari" ("Powerful One").

In Borneo, the Ngaju Dayak worship Mahatala–Jata, an androgynous god. The male part of this god (Mahatala) rules the Upperworld and the female part (Jata) rules the Underworld.

In Australia, Labarindja are mythological blue–skinned wild women. They are sometimes portrayed as having both a penis and a vagina. Ungud is an Aboriginal snake god who is sometimes male and sometimes female. He is associated with rainbows and the erections of the tribe's shamans. Angamunggi is a rainbow serpent who is father of men, the giver of life who was thought to have a womb.

In West Africa, Vondu is an androgynous god with both male and female traits.

In Ghana, the Akan have a pantheon of gods that manifest as androgynous and transgender deities. They are personifications of Jupiter (Abrao), Mercury (Aku), and Moon (Awo).

In Zimbadwe, the Shona are ruled by Mwari, an androgynous creator god who occasionally splits into separate male and female aspects.

In Haitian Vodou, some Lwa (intermediaries between humans and God) are associated with transgenderism or same–sex interactions. These include: Ghede Nibo, sometimes portrayed as a drag queen; Baron Lundy and Baron Limba, who are male lovers; Baron Oua Oua, who is closely linked to homosexuality; the Erzulie, who can manifest transgender or Amazonian traits; Erzulie Freda, who is a protector of gay men; and Erzulie Dantor who is associated with lesbians.

In Norse myth, Odin often disguised himself as a woman. He was very close to Loki, the trickster who could change gender at will.

In Phoenicia and Canaan, Astarte, the Great Mother, was sometimes depicted as a hermaphrodite. Her temples were served by the *kelabim*, a gay male priest caste.

In Aztec myth, Ometeotl (Two God) is a god of duality known as Ometecutli and Omecihuatl (also known as Tonacatecuhtli and Tonacacihuatl), who was both male and female. S/he was the first god and so created his/herself.

In Buddhism, Quan Yin is a bodhisattva. She was originally a male named Avalokiteshvara. She volunteered to forsake her divinity on the spiritual plane to spread compassion amongst humans. She is able to change gender at will.

In Hinduism, the Divine has both female and male qualities so deities were often depicted as Androgynes. Commonly male/female pairs: Shiva–Shakti, Sita–Rama, and Radha–Krishna. Ardhnarishwara is an androgynous deity, whose right side is male and left side female. Ardhanarishwar means the lord (*ishwar*) who is half (*ardha*) woman (*nari*). S/he is the union of Shiva and Shakti representing how the female and male principles of Spirit/Source/Creator are inseparable. Ganesha, the elephant–headed deity, is masculine in gender, but has breasts. Krishna transformed into a woman called Mohini and Vaikuntha Kamalaja is the androgynous form of Vishnu and his consort Lakshmi.

In Ancient Greece, Hermaphrodite is a bi–gender deity. Eros was a very lovely androgyne that became the patron and protector of homosexual love. Phanes was a beautiful golden–winged hermaphroditic deity wrapped in a serpent's coils. Zeus was known for his bisexual liaisons. It is not very common knowledge that he had a transgender form named Zeus Arrhenothelus, where he was considered both mother and father. Dionysus, the god of wine and love, was androgynous and became lovers with the gods Adonis and Hermaphrodite. Apollo and Hyacinth were male lovers and Hyacinth became a patron to same sex lovers. Tiresias was a blind prophet of Zeus, who transformed into a woman for seven years.

In Roman mythology, Janus was the god of gates, doors, or beginnings. Since he was often portrayed as two–faced, he became a symbol for Janus/Jana, an androgynous figure. Janus was used as a symbol for homosexuality for a period of time.

In Shintoism, Oyamakui is a transgender mountain spirit that protects industry and childbearing. Inari, is a multiple–gender spirit of agriculture and rice.

In Christianity, an early theologian, Tertullian (c. 160 – c. 225 CE), wrote that Jesus lived as a eunuch. Jakob Boehme, a 17th century mystic, also claimed that Christ was androgynous. He influenced many philosophers of his time to believe that humans would one day evolve into an androgynous state.

According to Leslie Feinberg in *Transgender Warriors*[6], and other authors, the following passages were included in the Torah to admonish transgender individuals who worshipped the Goddess in a time that patriarchal societies were replacing matrilineal societies.

"The woman shall not wear that which pertaineth unto a man, neither shall a man put on a woman's garment: for all that do so are abomination unto the Lord thy God." *–Deuteronomy 22:5 (Bible KJV, Public Domain)*

"He that is wounded in the stones, or hath his privy member cut off, shall not enter the congregation of the Lord." *–Deuteronomy 23:1 (Bible KJV, Public Domain)*

Queer and Androgynous Deities[13]

Adam Kadmon (*Jewish*) Androgynous form of Adam.

Adonis/Tammuz (*Phoenician/Greco-Roman/Mesopotamian*) Bisexual fertility god.

Apollo (*Greek*) Homosexual deity.

Ardhanari/Ardhanarishvara (*Hindu*) Androgynous deity of Shiva and Shakti.

Artemis/Diana (*Greco-Roman*) Her festivals included same-sex eroticism.

Astarte (*Phoenician/Canaanite*) Gender shapeshifter, sometimes a hermaphrodite.

Asushunamir (*Sumerian/Babylonian*) The first gay spirits called the Queer Ones.

Aten (*Egyptian*) Androgynous deity.

Athena/Minerva (*Greco-Roman*) Shapeshifts into a young man.

Bahuchara Mata (*Hindu*) Protector/patron goddess of transgender individuals.

Baphomet (*Europe*) Intersex deity.

Baron Samedi (*Vodoun*) Transgender deity.

Begochidiin (*Navajo*) Third gender deity.

Bona Dea (*Roman/Italian*) Lesbian deity.

Buddha (*Hindu*): Deity sometimes depicted as androgynous.

Chin (*Mayan*) Introduced homoerotic relationships to the Mayan nobles.

Damballah/Danbala/Oshumare (*Vodoun, Yoruba, Santeria, Candomble*) Androgynous bisexual Serpent Rainbow.

Dionysus/Bacchus (*Thracian/Greco-Roman*) Shapeshifted into a woman.

Erinlé Inle/Eyinle (*Yoruba*) Patron of gay individuals.

Eros (*Greek*) Androgynous patron and protector of homosexual love.

The Erzulie (*Vodoun*) Patron to gay men and lesbians.

Fro Ing/Ingwaz (*Norse*) Worshiped by cross-dressers.

(Continued next page)

Queer and Androgynous Deities[13]

(*Continued from previous page*)

Galaturra/Kurgarra (*Sumeria*) Sexless beings.

Ganesha (*Hindu*) Androgynous deity.

Ganymede (*Greek*) Gay lover of Zeus.

Gwydion (*Celtic*) Turned into an animal of the opposite gender.

Hapi (*Egyptian*) Androgynous deity.

Hatshepsut (*Egyptian*) Cross dressing pharaoh.

Hecate (*Greco-Roman*) Honored by gender-variant male priests called "*semnotatoi*".

Hermaphrodite (*Greek*) Intersexed deity.

Hermes/Mercury (*Greco-Roman*) Androgynous and bisexual deity.

Horus (*Egyptian*) Had homosexual intercourse with Set.

Hyacinth (*Greek*) Patron to gay individuals.

Hypnos (*Greek*) Bisexual deity.

Indra (*Hindu*) Bisexual and transgender deity.

Isis (*Egyptian*) Served by gay and transgender priests and priestesses.

Janus (*Roman*) Androgynous deity.

Joan of Arc (*French*) Cross dressing saint.

Kali Ma (*Hindu*) Male worshippers sometimes dress as Kali or ritually cut themselves as symbolic castration.

Ko'lhamana (*Zuni/Hopi*) Transgender kachina (supernatural ancestor spirit).

Loki (*Norse/Scandinavian/Germanic*) Gender shapeshifter.

Macha (*Celtic*) Male followers experience androgynous transformations.

Odin/Wotan (*Norse/German/Scandinavian*) Cross dressing deity.

Ometeotl (*Aztec*) Dual god Ometecutli (male) and Omecihuatl (female).

Pan/Faunus (*Greco-Roman*) Bisexual deity.

Quan Yin/Kuan Yin/Guan Yin (*Asian*) Avalokitesvara, a male Buddhist, renounced attaining nirvana to return as a female, Quan Yin, to spread compassion.

Queer and Androgynous Deities[13]

(Continued from previous page)

Sedna (*Inuit*) Gynandromorphous creation served by gay shamans.

Set/Seth (*Egyptian*) Pansexual deity.

Shai/Shait (*Egyptian*) Gender neutral deity.

Ta'aroa (*Polynesia*) Androgynous creator god.

Tem (*Egyptian*) The Great "He-She".

Tezcatlipoca (*Aztec*) Shapeshifts to female.

Tlazoteotl (*Aztec*) Transgender lesbian priestess.

Viracocha (*Inka*) Creator deity with both male and female attributes.

Vondu (*Africa*) Androgynous deity.

Wadj Wer (*Egyptian*) Androgynous deity.

Wiya Numpa (*Lakota*) Double woman, a hermaphrodite spirit which appears to males and females and requires them to begin cross-dressing.

Wu Tien Bao (*Chinese*) Manages love and sex between homosexual men.

Xochilpilli (*Aztec*) Patron of gay men, gender variance, and male prostitution.

Xochiquetzal (*Aztec*) Protector of lesbians, patron of non-reproducing sex.

Yemaya (*Yoruba, Santeria, Candomble*) Shapeshifts into a man, patron to gay, bisexual, and transgender men.

Zeus/Jupiter (*Greco-Roman*) Transgender form is Zeus Arrhenothelus, being both mother and father.

Note: A more comprehensive list of Queer and Androgynous Deities is available to download from my website: www.SoulSexAlchemy.com.

CONCLUSION

Androgynous, intersex, and third gender individuals have been present from ancient times to modern times throughout the world. They are present in mythological and creation stories from many cultures and religions. Why then is a binary system of gender still the mainstream model in most cultures?

It is interesting to observe that cultures that honor women and see them as equal to men, are the most accepting of third gender and Two Spirit individuals. Misogynistic cultures, on the other hand, believe it is derogatory and demeaning for a male–bodied individual to act with female characteristics. Being a masculine female–bodied individual is marginally accepted because it is perfectly understandable that a female would want to aspire to male–privilege and "superiority".

Indigenous cultural perspectives that are based on a circular concept of all things being connected and interrelated seem to embrace the three or more gender classification systems more easily than Western cultural perspectives that are based on the dualistic concept that all things have a polar opposite and act independently of one another. These dualistic–based belief systems perpetuate the binary sex system of only two legal gender statuses.

Today there are only two options, male or female, in binary gender systems. There is no place for individuals who have an identity that is *both* male and female or one that *alternates* between male and female. Yet the number of individuals who do not identify as either of the two legal choices is on the rise.

Cultures with three or more genders would work very well to accommodate trans* and intersex individuals. If third gender individuals were accepted, gone would be ostracism, shame, stigma, discrimination, and hate crimes perpetrated just because an individual is considered to be "different".

The cultures that have three or more gender identities were in existence for a long time before there was a possibility of medical intervention and surgical techniques to modify the Physical Body. Yet these cultures allowed for a wider acceptance of individuals that did not conform to the binary gender system.

Much of Western religious belief holds that sex is only to be used for procreation purposes. The indigenous view of sex is that it is natural and pleasurable. Sex was engaged in for two different purposes: 1) as reproductive sex is to create children and 2) as non–reproductive sex for pleasure. Therefore, the indigenous view of third gender sexuality is based on the fact that it is ok to have non–procreative sex.

Today transsexual individuals who live in a binary gender system are pressured to completely transit from one gender to the other. However, if there were a third gender option, how many might choose to remain at some identity between the two? How many individuals truly embody characteristics of both male and female? Would more individuals be asking for both male and female genitalia? After all, wouldn't that be the best of all worlds?

The Tale of Two Feathers: A Two Spirit Story

Once upon a time there was a Chameleon that had forgotten it could shapeshift into human form. Chameleon was quite sensitive and easily intimidated by the world so it spent its days being invisible by blending into its surroundings. It had a safe cave that it stayed in quite a lot.

One day, as Chameleon was peacefully dozing in its cave, a Spirit appears. Chameleon asks, "Who are you?" The Spirit replies, "I am The Reincarnationist." Chameleon asks, "Why are you here?" The Reincarnationist replies, "I am here to bestow the Power on you. You already have the gift of Sensitivity so that will balance with Power to keep your Ego in check. You will become the little Chameleon that could." Chameleon asks, "But why are you giving me the Power and the Gift?" The Reincarnationist replies, "It will soon be time for you to shapeshift into a human. You will be both male and female in one body. You will embody the masculine and feminine by blending both into one identity." Chameleon asks, "But how will this happen?"

The Reincarnationist then gives Chameleon the following directions: "Lie under the light of the next full moon to absorb her feminine energies and dream your body into being." Chameleon follows this direction and lies under the light of Grandmother Moon. Its body morphs into a human female body with fully developed female genitalia.

(Continued next page)

The Tale of Two Feathers: A Two Spirit Story

(Continued from previous page)

The next day in the cave, The Reincarnationist looks at Chameleon's body and nods with approval. Spirit says, "Tomorrow lie under Father Sun to balance Grandmother Moon's energies." So the next day, Chameleon once again follows the Reincarnationist's directions. Her female body begins another transformation, developing male genitalia alongside the female genitalia.

The next day back in the cave, The Reincarnationist nods approval again. Spirit tells Chameleon, "Tonight lie under the stars." And so, Chameleon does lie under the stars and as s/he does, Brother/Sister Star Dust falls on him/her and activates his/her Androgyny. Now his/her emotions, thoughts, and entire being is balanced perfectly with both masculine and feminine energies.

The next day The Reincarnationist is ecstatic; however, gives Chameleon one last set of instructions: "Lie under the sky today one last time." So as Chameleon lay beneath the sky, soaking up the healing energy of Mother Earth and the healing rays of Father Sun, a rainbow appears and shines its colors down upon him/her illuminating his/her body, chakras, and heart.

The next day The Reincarnationist says, "Your physical body is made of Mother Earth and your energy body is illuminated by Father Sun, Grandmother Moon, Brother/Sister Stars, and the Rainbow. It is now time to leave your cave and venture into the World. It will be a great journey that you travel as you share the Light that has energized your body with others. Now you no longer need to hide by blending into your surroundings. You will be visible so that you can guide others to the ways of the Light. Once in a while you may feel a need to return to the cave to rejuvenate but it will be a temporary respite and you will return to the World refreshed and ready to serve. I have one additional gift for you. That gift is your new name." And with that, The Reincarnationist blew the name "Two Feathers" into Chameleon's body.

NOTES:

[1] Comprehensive lists of Two Spirit terms, definitions, and tribal affiliations are available in the following texts:

Lang, Sabine. *Men as Women, Women as Men: Changing Gender in Native American Cultures.* University of Texas Press, 1998.

Roscoe, Will. *Changing Ones: Third and Fourth Genders in Native North America.* Palgrave Macmillan, 2000.

Roscoe, Will. *Living the Spirit: A Gay American Indian Anthology.* St. Martin's Griffin, 1988.

[2] Williams, Walter L. *The Spirit and the Flesh: Sexual Diversity in American Indian Culture.* Beacon Press, 1992.

[3] Naswood, Elton and Jim Mattee. "Mending the Rainbow: Working with Native LBGT/Two Spirit Community." Presentation at the National Indian Nations Conference. 2011. http://www.tribal-institute.org/2010/A3-EltonNaswoodPP.pdf

[4] Fire, John (Lame Deer) and Richard Erdoes. *Lame Deer, Seeker of Visions: The Life of a Sioux Medicine Man.* Touchstone, 1973.

[5] Roscoe, Will. *The Zuni Man–Woman.* University of New Mexico Press, 1992.

[6] Information on third gender cultures around the world was compiled from various sources on the internet as well as the following books:

Feinberg, Leslie. *Transgender Warriors: Making History from Joan of Arc to Dennis Rodman.* Beacon Press, 1997.

Herdt, Gilbert, Ed. *Third Sex, Third Gender: Beyond Sexual Dimorphism in Culture and History.* Zone Books, 1996.

Roscoe, Will. *Queer Spirits: A Gay Men's Myth Book.* Beacon Press, 1996.

Williams, Walter L. *The Spirit and the Flesh: Sexual Diversity in American Indian Culture.* Beacon Press, 1992.

[7] van Kampenhout, Daan. "Shaman Costumes." 1995. http://www.oocities.org/rainforest/vines/8366/shaman_costume.html

[8] Bhava, Sakhi. *Transgender Spirituality: Man into Goddess.* CreateSpace Independent Publishing Platform, 2012.

[9] Somé, Sobonfu. *The Spirit of Intimacy: Ancient African Teachings in the Ways of Relationships.* William Morrow Paperbacks, 2000.

[10] Hoff, Bert H. "Gays: Guardians of the Gates: An Interview with Malidoma Somé." *M.E.N. Magazine.* September, 1993.

[11] The following are excellent resources on creation myths:

Leeming, David Adams and Margaret Adams Leeming. *A Dictionary of Creation Myths.* Oxford University Press, 1996.

Roscoe, Will. *Queer Spirits.* Beacon Press, 1996.

Sproul, Barbara C. *Primal Myths: Creation Myths Around the World* Harper One, 1979.

[12] Pederasts are defined as men who have sexual relations, especially anal intercourse, with boys.

[13] Information on queer and androgynous deities was compiled from various sources on the internet as well as the following books:

Conner, Randy P. *Blossom of Bone–Reclaiming the Connections between Homoeroticism and the Sacred.* Harpercollins, 1993.

Conner, Randy P. and David Hatfield Sparks. *Cassell's Encyclopedia of Queer Myth, Symbol and Spirit: Gay, Lesbian, Bisexual and Transgendered Lore.* Cassell, 1997.

Kaldera, Raven. *Hermaphrodeities: The Transgender Spirituality Workbook.* Asphodel Press, 2009.

Penczak, Christopher. *Gay Witchcraft: Empowering the Tribe.* Red Wheel/Weiser, 2003.

CHAPTER 11

SELF–EMPOWERMENT SUPPORT SERVICES

Tools for Increasing Self–Knowledge and Self–Empowerment

Two Spirit &

TRANSGENDER SPIRITUAL SERVICES

***Trans*-form your *Trans*-ition because being *Trans*gender is a Life-long Journey**

Shine Your Light!
Own Your Power!

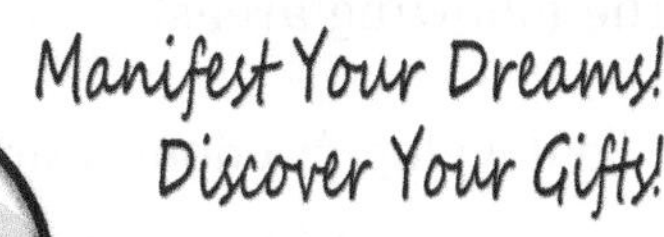
Manifest Your Dreams!
Discover Your Gifts!

TWO Spirit

Explore the spiritual aspects of living a self-empowered life.

- **Naming Ceremony** – Consecrate and celebrate your new name
- **Gratitude & Release Ceremony** – Release the old so the new can move in
- **Rites of Passage Ceremonies** – Consecrate and celebrate your new image and way of walking in the world
- **Body Retrieval** – Call in your new body parts and integrate them with your existing body

- **Soul Retrieval** – Retrieve soul parts lost or stolen in past experiences
- **Power Animal Retrieval** – Meet your personal animal spirit
- **Past Life Regression Journeys** – Includes journey to discover why you came into this life as a Two Spirit
- **Gender & Sexuality Workshops** -Includes Physical Body-Energy Body integration

CATALOGUE OF SUPPORT SERVICES

As a transpersonal hypnotherapist and a shamanic energy medicine practitioner I offer a series of spiritual services that assist individuals to discover who they are and to empower them to be healthy, holistic, and well–balanced. I have created ceremonies that support individuals with non–conforming gender and sexual identities.

The path to self–empowerment includes discovering who one is, honoring one's place in the world, identifying one's gifts, and sharing those gifts with the world. Many individuals have spent years in fear, shame, stigma, pain, isolation, and victimization. By tapping into one's soul purpose and finding one's spiritual path, the old painful skins can be shed and a new skin of hope, healing, and happiness can be stepped into.

These services and ceremonies are designed to aid individuals in the following areas:

1. To develop freedom from physical and emotional pain
2. To manifest financial security
3. To feel socially accepted
4. To increase spiritual awareness
5. To create self–empowerment

Following is a description of the various services I offer to support individuals' self-empowerment journeys:

NAMING CEREMONY

This ceremony can be used for anyone wishing to change a name or to sanctify a given name. A name is an energetic sign that identifies who an individual is. Each name carries a specific vibration.

A surname is the family name that you inherit at birth. A given name is the first name or familiar name that parent bestow upon an individual at birth. However, through identity growth or fluidity, these names may become obsolete.

Many people accept the names given at their birth as sacred and unchangeable. However, in some cultures, a name is fluid. For example, in some Native American tribes, a child would be named after something that was relevant at their birth. However, when they completed the rite of passage from childhood to adulthood, they were given a new name that represented who they had become.

In Australia, the Aborigine people do not celebrate birthdays but they celebrate naming ceremonies instead. As an individual grows into a new identity, they choose a new name associated to that identity. The entire tribe joins in celebrating the new name.

In pagan and magick traditions, individuals choose a secret name that they use in ceremony and ritual.

There are many ways to choose a new name. It can be done randomly by choosing a name that you like the sound of. It can be chosen based on its symbolic meaning. It can be found online by using a name generator. To be very meticulous about the energy of a new name, numerology can be used to choose a name with specific intent or meaning.

A modern name change is usually marked by applying for a new driver's license or identification card. Other legal documents including passports and social security cards also need to be changed. Quite often, the name is legally changed by a court order. However, the ceremony of taking on a new name is missing from our culture. Stepping into the energy of a new name should be honored with a ritual. This ritual can be performed in solitude or it can be a ceremony in which others are present as witnesses.

I have created a ceremony that involves everyone in the group blessing the new name as it is energetically integrated.

GRATITUDE AND RELEASE CEREMONY

I don't believe that anyone is truly stuck. We are usually exactly where we need to be at any given time. However, when we are in an unpleasant place in our lives, we begin to feel as if we are stuck there. Sometimes this stuck feeling is really a feeling of resistance. In order to move or shift, it becomes necessary to create a radical transformation in our perceptions.

In the Peruvian Andes there is a concept called "*ayni*", which means to be in right relationship. Ways to create right relationship are:

1. Be grateful for what you have. Formalize your gratitude through ceremony.
2. Radically forgive those that have wronged you. (I recommend reading *Radical Forgiveness*[1] by Colin Tipping.)
3. Remove resistance by accepting that your situation is an opportunity for growth. Its good medicine and a karmic healing.
4. Be grateful for blessings on their way.
5. Energetically release those situations and/or people that no longer serve you thereby making room for something new to flow in. Old contracts and vows may no longer be of service and can be broken through ritual. Formalize your releases through ceremony.

These steps help shift energy and get it flowing. Energy movement brings new and exciting prospects.

RITES OF PASSAGE CEREMONIES

A rite of passage is a ritual event that marks an individual's transition from one status to another. Ceremonies honor individuals and create a deeper bond to their community when others share in the celebration of rites of passage. Rites of passage are used to celebrate major milestones in an individual's life. The seven major transitions are identified as: birth, puberty, adulthood, marriage, parenthood, eldership, and ancestorship (death).

Transsexuals have some additional points of passage: second puberty (beginning of hormone therapy), transitioning (living 24/7 in a new gender role), and rebirth (being born again through completion of legal changes and/or genital reassignment surgery).

A rite of passage from womanhood to manhood might include a celebration of joining the adult male world. As a new man of the world, a transman calls in his masculine values to welcome his new self. He stands in self–empowerment and brings the gifts of his soul to harvest.

A rite of passage from manhood to womanhood might include a celebration of joining the adult female world. As a new woman of the world, a transwoman calls in her feminine values to welcome her new self into rebirth so that all the gifts of her soul can be nurtured.

A rite of passage for a gender fluid individual might include a celebration of releasing the old labels of a binary gender system and joining the world of gender fluidity.

POWER ANIMAL RETRIEVAL

A power animal is an animal spirit guide that watches over an individual from the spirit world. An individual can have multiple power animals that serve as guides and spirit helpers. Each animal has specific traits that can be used to support an individual as needed. Power animal retrievals help to restore an individual's personal power. A power animal can be retrieved a shaman journey.

SOUL RETRIEVAL

Soul retrieval is a process of bringing back soul parts that have been lost, stolen, or put away for safe keeping. An individual who has grown up with a non–conforming gender or sexual identity is very likely to have sent away soul pieces for safe keeping.

Soul parts may be lost in two fundamental ways:

- Parts of an individual's soul can be lost during traumatic events. Soul parts may be sent away for safe keeping as a means of defense and spiritual survival or they may have been left at the scene of a traumatic experience.

- Parts of an individual's soul may be stolen by others that are holding onto pieces for various reasons.

The symptoms of soul loss include: trauma; post–traumatic stress syndrome; shock; immune deficiency problems; chronic illness; coma; chronic depression; suicidal feelings; inability to heal; inability to move forward; long term grief; addictions; disassociation; lost memories; spaciness; inability to feel; feeling lost, incomplete, stuck, or dispirited; loss of control; feeling that something in life is missing; feeling that you want to return to a person/location for no good reason; or feeling that you lost something you can't get back.

The benefits of soul retrieval can be: feeling more present, grounded, whole and connected; moving forward by making decisions or changes easier; and making self–improvements.

BODY PART RETRIEVAL

The mechanics of body part retrieval are similar to those of soul retrieval; however, instead of bringing lost soul pieces back for integration, the energetic imprint of body parts are integrated with an individual. This ritual is a way to bring in a desired body part before genital reassignment surgery. For example, a male–to–female trans* individual may want to release a penis and "call in" a new vagina. Or a female–to–male trans* individual may want to release breasts and "call in" a new penis. The desired body parts are already imprinted on the Energy Body of a pre–op trans* individual. During a body part retrieval those energetic imprints are "pulled down into" the Physical Body, creating an energetic imprint in the Physical Body for the actual manifestation to occur through surgical procedure. In addition, an Energy Body tune–up should be completed before and after any surgical procedures.

CUSTOMIZED HYPNOSIS RECORDING

I create customized self–hypnosis recordings that include hypnotic scripts written specifically for each client's needs. These scripts provide positive affirmation statements and are written to communicate directly to the subconscious mind. The recording consists of the following parts:

1. ***Trance Induction*** – includes relaxation techniques and mental expectation creation through guided meditation.
2. ***Script Reading*** – includes post–hypnotic suggestions and affirmations.
3. ***Trance Return*** – includes the return to an alert, awakened state of consciousness.

Suggested specific areas of focus to include in the script for a trans* lifestyle are:

- ***Freedom from Physical Pain*** – Managing pain from surgery, electrolysis, or hormone injections.
- ***Freedom from Emotional Pain*** – Reducing depression and anxiety; reducing shame and stigma; increasing self–esteem and self–confidence; and improving relationships with family, friends, significant others and co–workers.
- ***Social Acceptance*** – Creating confidence in sexual attractiveness, finding comfort living in a new role, feeling safe in private and public situations, and taking pride in being a pioneer or role model for others.
- ***Financial Security*** – Manifesting money for medical bills and living expenses.
- ***Spiritual Assistance*** – Asking a higher power (based on your personal spiritual beliefs) for support and assistance, creating a foundation of spiritual guidance, and understanding your purpose in this life.

- ***Self–Empowerment*** – Creating goals for romance, relationships, family, prosperity, and health; and discovering what the Future Self looks like at one year and five years from now.

WORKSHOPS

The following energetic themes are common to individuals that grew up with non–conforming gender and sexual identities:

1. **The Physical Body is not grounded.** Many trans* individuals that do not like their Physical Body don't spend a lot of time in it. In other words, the Energy Body is only partially in the Physical Body. These individuals spend a lot of time in their head. If the Physical Body is not grounded, it is vulnerable to accidents and other physical problems.
2. **Energy boundaries may be weak or damaged.** If a trans* individual rejects the Physical Body because it doesn't match the Energy Body, the body becomes susceptible to invasion by foreign energy such as entities or imprints that can develop into disease. In addition, the Energy Body may have sustained rips, tears, and dents from life events that are in need of repair.
3. **Hyper–vigilance is strong.** The third eye, the home of intuition, of an individual with non–conforming gender and sexual identities is typically wide open due to hyper–vigilance and empathic skills.
4. **Holding shame creates low self–esteem.** Individuals with non–conforming gender and sexual identities are often shunned, stared at, and whispered about from early childhood on. A lifetime of being stigmatized creates feelings of worthlessness, paranoia, and not being loved.
5. **Preferred genitalia really are present.** Others may not see a trans* individual's true form but the kinesthetic feel is present for the individual. The body of a trans* individual does exist in an energetic state.

6. **There is no such thing as "being born in the wrong body".** There are no accidents or coincidences in the universe. Experiencing a trans* life is a part of the pre–birth contract that was created for this incarnation and may be related to karmic lessons.

To assist individuals in dealing with these concepts I offer classes and workshops. One example is my workshop called "Dreaming the Energetic Body: Bridging the Worlds between the Physical and the Energetic". This is an experiential workshop that focuses on aligning one's Physical Body image with one's mental picture of that body.

SOUL SCHOOL: A SHAMANIC MYSTERY SCHOOL

There are two rules of the road when you are traveling on a journey of personal transformation:

RULE #1: "Know Thyself." *–Ancient Greek Philosophy*

RULE #2: "To thine own self be true." *–Shakespeare*

"If I am not for myself who is for me? And being for my own self, what am I? And if not now, when?"

–Hillel

The only thing we can take with us out of this lifetime is the knowledge and wisdom that our soul acquires. So any gain we make in knowing ourselves will stay with us. These are the questions to ask in the quest for wisdom:

- Who am I?
- Where do I come from?
- Where am I going?
- What is my purpose?

- What are my gifts?

Each one of us is a prize from the Universe to our Self and from our Self to the Universe. Each one of us has a unique gift to give. Your personal prize is as precious as diamonds, more valuable than gold, and the most beautiful rainbow ever seen. By increasing self–love and improving self–respect, your energetic vibration increases to a level that allows you to manifest your heart's desires with ease. What we see when we look in the mirror is what the world reflects back to us. We get what we believe we deserve. When we believe we are not good enough or don't deserve what we want, we block the flow of abundance, prosperity, and love.

Soul School is a journey of personal transformation that clears past wounds to create the energy that will help you manifest the world you always desired. Soul School is your Wheel to Fortune because as you heal old wounds, cancel outdated vows and contracts, and create a luminous Energy Body, you are free to find the treasure you seek. You may think that it is peace, empowerment, energy, health, creativity, prosperity, spirituality, or love. But I guarantee that by the end of your journey, you will find that you are the treasure!

The curriculum of Soul School is based on the structure of the medicine wheel, which originated with the North American indigenous tribes. The medicine wheel is a powerful ceremonial tool and basis for teaching. Its circular concept supports the idea that all things are interrelated and move in cycles with no beginning and no end.

In Soul School we begin the journey around the wheel in the South where patterns of victimhood are released. Moving clockwise, the next direction is West where we step into self–empowerment and clear ancestral patterns. In the North we become self–referencing and reintegrate lost soul parts. In the East we become the creator as we dream our world into being. Lastly, we stand in the center where there is perfect balance.

Soul School is a smorgasbord of spiritual concepts offered for your sampling. Spiritual awareness is enhanced through learning enriching rituals and simple ceremonies. The curriculum is a combination of wisdom from energy medicine, transpersonal psychology, shamanism, indigenous spirituality, ceremonial crafts, and metaphysical principles. Students learn healing techniques that can be used on self, friends, family, and/or clients. Students become a community of like–minded souls and mentor each other through experiential exercises.

For more information about Soul School, A Shamanic Mystery School visit
www.DrakeInnerprizes.com/soulschool.htm.

NOTES:

[1] Tipping, Colin. *Radical Forgiveness: A Revolutionary Five–Stage Process to Heal Relationships, Let Go of Anger and Blame, Find Peace in Any Situation.* Sounds True, Incorporated, 2009.

EPILOGUE

CONCLUSION

Reviewing Our Journey through the Soul and the Secular

GENDER CHOICE

These symbols are representations of gender variance and therefore choice. They graphically portray the concept that gender identity is not linear but can have twists, turns, and even question marks.

(Two Symbols: Designers Unknown)

IDENTITY EMPOWERMENT

Viktor Frankl, a neurologist and psychiatrist, wrote *Man's Search for Meaning*[1], in 1946, which is about his experiences as a survivor of the death camps in World War II. Throughout his book, he maintains that life never ceases to have meaning even when faced with the grimmest of survival crises. An individual always has the freedom of choice at every moment. Survival is dependent on hope for the future, and if hope is lost, so is the individual. So in order to survive, an individual must be able to imagine the future.

Today many individuals with non–conforming gender and sexual identities may also be preoccupied with survival issues such as health, shelter, finances, and social interactions. Yet if an individual is to not only survive but thrive, there is a basic need to find self–empowerment. When I began writing, I thought the purpose of this book was to share the multi–dimensional concepts of gender and sexual identity. By the time I finished, I realized I wanted to emphasize identity empowerment.

As illustrated in the figure below, the umbrella that covers our identity shelters different dimensions of self–definition such as beliefs, perceptions, presentation, expression, social roles, desires, and attractions. These multiple facets are all independent but interconnected.

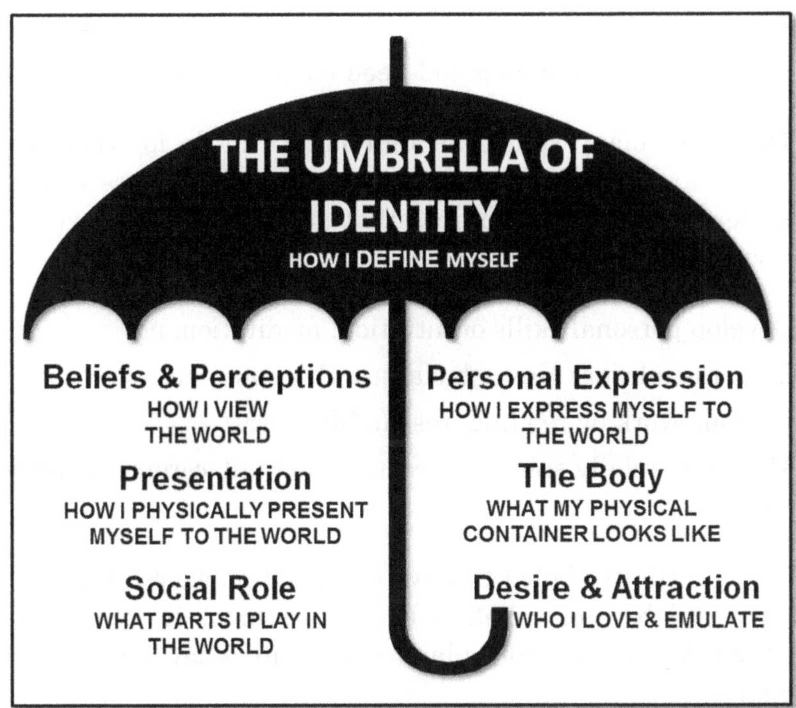

In the stages of development and coming out in Chapter 8, we saw that self–knowledge was the launch point for development of identity. I believe that an individual's self–esteem grows in proportion to their self–knowledge. Through identity development, an individual learns to love themselves.

Identity is a personal construct. An individual's identity should not be defined by others. Identity is a personal freedom. It is a basic human right to express our identity freely. Identity is the soul's path of evolution. The identity we develop in a lifetime is created for the specific purpose of learning and growing.

The following five "W" questions and one "H" question can be asked by those who are on a quest to solidify their identity:

1. ***Who*** am I?
2. ***Why*** am I here now?
3. ***Where*** am I going?
4. ***When*** do I step fully into my self–power?

5. ***What*** is my gift?
6. ***How*** much self–sourcing do I need for this journey?

There are many things an individual can do for themselves and there are many things that teachers and mentors will help with. Here is a list of resources that support self–empowerment development:

- Develop personal skills of intuition, meditation, etc.
- Do personal work through classes, therapies, etc.
- Do homework by reading, researching, etc.
- Maintain a daily spiritual practice of ritual, ceremony, prayer, etc.

If we scuttle the belief that we are a victim, we realize that we are powerful beyond belief. Self–empowerment is so important that I developed three formulas to illustrate what it is. The first formula is:

Self-Empowerment = Know Yourself + Love Yourself + Be Yourself + Share Yourself

- ***Know Yourself*** – Learn all you can about yourself. Travel your subconscious to reveal hidden memories.
- ***Love Yourself*** – Unconditionally. Constantly. Believe you deserve the best.
- ***Be Yourself*** – Serve yourself. Honor your boundaries. Be authentic by extracting the voices and influences of others.
- ***Share Yourself*** – Be of service to others. Share your gifts with the universe. Shine your light.

Self–security is created by striking a balance between being in a power position (*yang* energy) and being in a peaceful place (*yin* energy) so the second formula is:

Self-security (SS) = Power Position (PP) +
Peaceful Place (PP)

- ***A Power Place*** is the ownership of confidence, invulnerability, and assertiveness. It is the place self–actualized individuals source from. It is the boundary that separates "me" from "not me".
- ***A Peaceful Place*** is that space to go to when in need of respite, relaxation, rejuvenation, or reflection. If you do not yet have a peaceful place, visualize or feel yourself at your favorite natural location, such as a forest, beach, mountain, desert, or snow scene.

Now imagine that your soul is a whole pie with a filling of love and empowerment. The third formula is:

Peace = Identity + Empowerment
(P.I.E.)

Lastly, self–empowerment is opening your heart to yourself.

I wish you love and luck as you strive to see your own beauty and find your unique gifts. I hope that your journey of discovery ends in peace.

"The primary cause of unhappiness is never the situation but your thoughts about it."

–Eckhart Tolle

SUMMING IT ALL UP

We have journeyed around the universe to have a look at gender and sexual identity from as broad a perspective as possible. I have presented the following concepts of gender and sexual identity:

- Chapter 2 on Biological Origins of Gender and Sexual Identity has shown that there are many variations of gender and sex in the biological world, not just the two of male and female. These variations occur naturally not only in humans but also in the animal and plant world.
- Chapter 3 on Sociological and Psychological Origins of Gender and Sexual Identity has shown that non–conforming gender and sexual identities are gradually being eliminated from the books on mental disorders because these identities are natural and normal. Social awakening and subsequent law reform is in progress to reflect the birth of consciousness and personal identity freedom and expression.
- Chapter 4 on Spiritual Origins of Gender and Sexual Identity has presented information from channeled spiritual entities, past life therapists and researchers demonstrating that gender and sexual identities are chosen for the intentions of learning and expressing the soul's purpose.
- Chapter 10 on Two Spirits and Third Gender Cultures has shown that individuals with non–conforming gender and sexual identities have existed in virtually every creed and culture as well as many myths and creation stories.

I hope that you now have realized the following statements are fallacy:

- Gender identity is the same as sexual identity.
- There are only two genders, male and female.
- It is an individual's responsibility to judge what other individuals do with their body and how they express their identity.

Here is a list of healthy, self–empowered premises and beliefs:

- Self–identity is complex, multidimensional, and as unique to each individual as snowflakes are unique to one another.
- We are not victims of our gender and sexual identities. They were not "caused" but instead we "created" them to enhance our soul's experiences.
- The creation of self–identity is complex, multidimensional, and made up of seen and unseen forces, including: biological factors, sociological and psychological factors, and spiritual factors.
- Identity is the sacred right of every individual. It should not be imposed on an individual by others.
- There are various reasons for specific identities and those identities are created on an individual case basis by the soul and its personal guides.
- Living in different roles and identities while incarnated helps the soul to learn for the purpose of growth.
- Souls in the spirit world have no gender or sexuality designation. Their male and female qualities are perfectly balanced.
- Gender and sexuality are fluid and not permanently assigned at birth. All individuals are free to outside of the confines of a binary gender system.
- Past life experiences have a major effect on current gender and sexual identities.
- A soul may change gender and sexual identity from one lifetime to another.
- Sexual identity is a state of consciousness that drives the sexual activity of the Physical Body and the emotions of the heart.

- An individual's sexuality can best be identified by the target of their desire i.e. andro–loving, gyno–loving, pan–loving, etc. rather than on the basis of whether someone is "like" or "opposite" of themselves.
- Gender identity is state of consciousness and not based on the physical sex of the body.
- Gender and sexual identity are independent of each other however there is a strong interconnectedness.

The takeaway I hope you get from reading this book is that no matter who you are and how you identify, you are exactly who you are supposed to be at this given moment in time. Your mission, if you so choose to accept it, is to recognize your self–worth, amplify your self–love, and step into your personal power.

Fluidity is the new identity of the 21st century.
Acceptance is the new morality.
Self–empowerment is the new mantra.

> "Your enormous soul had so many choices of who it could show up as. It chose you."
>
> *–Jacob Nordby*

NOTES:

[1] Frankl, Viktor. *Man's Search for Meaning*. Pocket Books, 1997.

APPENDICES:

A: Passion Poems: The Authors Trans*ition Poetry

B: Inspirational Quotes

C: Days to Commemorate Gender Diversity and Alternative Sexual Orientation

D: International Bill of Gender Rights

E: Gender Diversity Etiquette

APPENDIX A:

PASSION POEMS: THE AUTHOR'S TRANS*ition POETRY

They say with age comes wisdom but for me self–esteem arrived with age. Or perhaps it grew with the distance I have traveled since my transition. I only know I feel completely different than I did in my earlier days. The following poems portray the pain, emotion, and confusion associated with my pre–transition and transition years (approximately 1970–1986). Thankfully I have kept them as a record because what I remember now are all the gifts of this lifetime.

WHY?

Rain rains...
Oranges are orange...
Bugs are buggy...
Then why am I a tomboy?

OUTCAST

You asked me
"Won't you stick out?"
I replied
"I never stick out
Because I never belonged."

NEW SCIENTIFIC DISCOVERY

I am the new discovery in Biology.
No more just feminine and masculine.
Now there is a neuter.
Proof?
me...

OPPOSITES

If opposites attract so strongly
Then why am I attracted
To the man I want to be?
Could it be I sense a deficit in me?
Completing myself must be the key.

ROUND FILED

Society has no place to put me
So they classified me,
And now I'm round filed.
I am individual,
You are society.
I am like no other one.
You are many of the same.
So we struggle.

MUTATION

Conflict of interest—
My masculine half responds to society's patriarchal attitudes,
Desires to be a man, supreme in the world.
Conflict of interest—
My feminine half responds to women's feminist attitudes,
Desires equality and privilege in a male world.
Conflict is anguish
Will I never be whole?
How does one balance opposing forces?
My soul is torn,
My brain is bruised,
Any my heart bleeds because of it.

METAMORPHOSIS

Will I always be a transsexual
Never be just a human?
Can't everyone see
What I want to be?
The scalpel is the afterthought.
The transition is already complete
I am now what I will be
After surgery.
I am now what
I have always been.

TRANSGENDERIZER

I once met a guy who was bi
He said "I want a mate to date.
Can't I find it all in one package of matter?"

So I introduced him to a man
Who once was a woman
But had the voice and demeanor of a tank commander.

Forever after my friend will enjoy
The head of a boy
With the jewels of a girl down under.

I've heard him to folks tell
And he made it clear as a bell
That variety is the spice of life for him thereafter.

THE LOST SELF–ESTEEM

Searching, searching for my lost self–esteem…
Could someone have beat it to death when I was a child?
Or perhaps it forgot to be born with me?
Perhaps I could still find it.
I looked under the bed, in the closet, under the couch
But I didn't find it.
Perhaps it was shot and bled to death
Or perhaps it died of loneliness and a broken heart.
Perhaps it fell from a great height and broke into a million pieces.
Perhaps it was crushed under a giant foot or
Perhaps it got too hot and blew up.
I looked deep into my soul but did not see it hiding there in some forgotten place.
Perhaps someone locked it up and threw away the key.
Perhaps it already passed away before I could use it.
It could have died from drugs and alcohol
Or malnutrition from lack of love and touch.
Perhaps I'll post a sign, "Self–Esteem Lost, Reward if Found"
Or maybe I could just buy a new one.
Maybe it ran away from home and couldn't find its way back.
Maybe it lives in another place under another name.
I just know that I've never felt balanced,
Never felt at home, never been relaxed,
Never had peace of mind, never felt at ease.
But wait, I think my self–esteem may have been blocked
From the weight of the secret I was carrying.
There was never any escape.
One's body follows one wherever one goes.
Yes, I know now that it was being trapped in the wrong body
That killed my self–esteem
And kept me locked in a prison of my own mind.

PERMANENCE

Is it true what they say?
        It's gay?
It's been a bi
        a dyke
        a het.
What's next?
It's been a girl
        a guy
        and sometimes a herm.
Can't it be anything perm—
        a–
        nent?
It's a Pandora's box.
Wish upon your magic wand.
It might be whoever
You want it to be.

WAR INJURY

I was born with a birth defect called transsexuality
And during the course of the change
I became everything I wanted to be
Except that I remain cockless.
I can't tell you how hard it's been
To be a man with no thing
So while you are with me, can't you pretend
That it's missing because of an old war injury?

MISMATCHED

I have never completed the sexual act, since my body parts aren't right.
My fingers stroke my beard even though others can't see it.
Shyness feels like a young boy about 14, all awkward and out of place.
The hair raises on the back of my neck and I cringe inside
Every time someone refers to me as a she, a her, or a woman.
The space that would have been my penis is always an empty spot in my pants.
I know I look funny since my movements don't match my body.
I can feel it inside, why can't others see it outside?

COMING CLEAN

I was once born in the body of a dame
So if you feel like fleeing, I won't place any blame.
My situation of physical maim
Has caused me among family and friends some fame.
Some may consider it a game
But they are the lucky ones born with brain and body the same.
Because I was cockless, for years I felt sexually lame.
But now that I've accepted it, I call your name.
So if you feel brave, take my reclusive heart to tame.
I'll come running to you as never before to anyone have I came.

CRYING OUT LOUD

Many times we go lonely just waiting
For the right one of them to come along
But where do we look?
People make us feel dangerous
When we walk into a restroom.
We want to take one of them into our arms
Because we could love them so well
But we wouldn't want one of them
To turn their face in horror.
We look at one of them
And think "I could give them everything".
But they aren't accepting
And we try our best
Not to let them know.
We must be hard and
Create a wall of steel
No one can penetrate,
"for the protection of society"
or "for the protection of ourselves".
The world needs love
But it won't accept ours.

CONVERSION

I am tired of people playing the games of God
That God wouldn't play.
People hurting people,
Calling a him "her" and a her "him",
Never caring what one another is.
People looking into other's bedrooms
Instead of their own,
Hypocritical people criticizing others.
They ask your name
Then call you something different.
Bigoted people doing in the name of God
Something God wouldn't do.

These people fear what they do not know
And make it impossible
For those who do.
But those who cast away the fear
And overcome the stigma,
These minor numbers do not suffer
For with the gift of knowledge
Comes strength.

LOVE AT FIRST SIGHT

You were everything
I thought you'd be.
The very first moment we met
I grabbed you tight.
This was it,
It was right.
You sent chills
Through my spine.
How my hips had hungered for you.
How my legs welcomed you home.
The prodigal son returns.
I feel balance within my body.
The symmetry is right.
I want you every day
By my side
Not just inside.
How surer I think,
How prouder I stand,
How taller I am.
With you, my new penis.

APPENDIX B:

INSPIRATIONAL QUOTES

GENDER

Class, race, sexuality, gender — and all other categories by which we categorize and dismiss each other — need to be excavated from the inside. – *Dorothy Allison*

We are all born naked. Everything else is drag, right? I am a gay man trapped in this body. – *Pamela Anderson*

Each of us helplessly and forever, contains the other, male in female, female in male, white in black, and black in white. We are part of each other. – *James Baldwin*

I wish people got as excited about all of the differences between each other as much as they get excited about all the different kinds of dogs in the park. – *Cooper Lee Bombardier*

Words like *masculine* and *feminine* have no definitions at all, since every ascribed characteristic is a stereotype. – *E. Tristan Booth*

There's only one gender: yours. – *Kate Bornstein*

If you really don't want to offend me, dear, just trash your assumptions and end the fear! I'm not he, I'm not she. There's more options, you see. I'm a blend. I transcend. I am. – *Kate Bornstein*

There's a real simple way to look at gender: Once upon a time, someone drew a line in the sands of a culture and proclaimed with great self–importance "On this side, you are a man; on the other side, you are a woman." It's time for the winds of change to blow that line away. Simple. – *Kate Bornstein*

If they see breasts and long hair coming they call it a woman. If beard and whiskers they call it a man. But, look, the Self that hovers in between is neither man nor woman. – *Devara Dasimayya*

I certainly didn't change my body because I thought I'd get special privilege. I changed my body because I wanted. It was the only way I could be seen as myself. – *Dominick*

Exclusive gender identity is not an expression of natural differences between the sexes but a suppression of natural similarities. – *Marilyn French*

As part of the female gender I was taught and learned self–sacrifice. As part of the male gender I was taught and learned self–importance. As part of the third gender I learned the importance of sacrificing everything I had been taught. – *Hap Hanchett*

We change neither gender nor sex. We just take steps to affirm what we have always known by hormonal and surgical means. – *Kaz*

We are diplomats. We are go–betweens for men and women. This is true whether we embrace or deny it. We are here to make peace with ourselves, our lovers, other transgender people, and to carve out a home in the cliffs that sprang up between the sexes. We belong to the holy order of the self–sacrificing diplomats. – *Tucker Lieberman*

Gender is in your head, sex is between your legs. – *S. Lewis*

Really advanced souls are androgynous because they reflect the complete and perfect balance of the *yin* and the *yang* in the soul itself. Most advanced spirit guides in heavenly place are androgynous. But even they are still learning so they will decide on a gender for the time being to learn from that. – *Shirley MacLaine*

There is no passion more powerful than transsexual desire.
– *Rachel Pollack*

We're trained to see only male or female and to plot people into those categories when they actually don't fit neatly at all. But if we pause, watch and listen closely we'll see the multiplicity of ways in which people are sexed and gendered. There exists a range of personal identifications around woman, man, in–between — we don't even have names or pronouns that reflect that in between place but people certainly live in it. – *Minnie Bruce Pratt*

The soul is both male and female or neither, whichever way you care to look at it. In fact, it is a lot more than both or neither. It is part of Divinity. – *John–Roger*

This paradigm of progression from female to male presents a view of gender that is like a river - flowing in one direction only. I propose that gender is much more like the ocean - large enough to contain many currents, channels, tides, and rhythms. – *Joe Samson*

As far as I'm concerned, being any gender is a drag. – *Patti Smith*

What is most beautiful in virile men is something feminine; what is most beautiful in feminine women is something masculine. – *Susan Sontag*

There are many gradations running from female to male; along that spectrum lie at least five sexes — perhaps even more. – *Anne Fausto–Sterling*

Within every man there is the reflection of a woman, and within every woman there is the reflection of a man. Within every man and woman there is also the reflection of an old man and an old woman, a little boy and a little girl. – *Hyemeyohsts Storm*

One who has a man's wings and a woman's also is in himself a womb of the world and, being a womb of the world, continuously, endlessly, gives birth. – *Lao Tzu*

The fact that the binary sex system is a fiction is written in the bodies of intersex people. – *Unknown*

All gender is drag. – *Riki Wilchins*

It is fatal to be a man or woman pure and simple: one must be a woman manly, or a man womanly. – *Virginia Woolf*

SEXUALITY

Bisexuality does double your chances for a date on Saturday night. – *Woody Allen*

Sensuality wanting a religion, invented Love. – *Natalie Barney*

Sexuality is completely natural however mainstream culture and society have falsely turned it into something considered to be controversial and perverse. We should not ever condemn, fear, or distort any of the beautiful and sacred properties of Nature. – *Damien Carrion*

Every desire of your body is holy. – *Hafiz*

Bisexuality means I am free and I am as likely to want to love a woman as I am likely to want to love a man, and what about that? Isn't that what freedom implies? – *June Jordan*

Making love is the interface of the physical and the spiritual, the mortal and the immortal. Making love is the balm and the bond, the giving and the gift. – *Daphne Rose Kingman*

Males do not represent two discrete populations, heterosexual and homosexual. The world is not to be divided into sheep and goats. Not all things are black nor all things white. It is a fundamental of taxonomy that nature rarely deals with discrete categories. Only the human mind invents categories and tries to force facts into separated pigeon–holes. The living world is a continuum in each and every one of its aspects. The sooner we learn this concerning human sexual behavior, the sooner we shall reach a sound understanding of the realities of sex. – *Alfred Kinsey*

Homosexuality was invented by a straight world dealing with its own bisexuality. – *Kate Millett*

Sexual activity feeds the spirit. – *Diana Richardson*

Now that our sexual experience is increasingly available to us as a subject for contemplation, we have to extend our language to express our new consciousness until we have as many words for sexuality as the Eskimo has for snow, that pervasive, beautiful, and mortal climate in which we all live. – *Jane Rule*

When two people come together in a safe place of connection, truthfulness, and openness, tremendous healing and growth is possible. Add to this a willingness to explore any wounds and desires, connect erotically, and be utterly shameless. – *Allen Siewart*

I want an incisive, inquisitive, insightful, irreverent mind. I want someone for whom philosophical discussion is foreplay. I want someone who sometimes makes me go ouch due to their wit and evil sense of humor. I want someone that I can reach out and touch randomly. I want someone I can cuddle with. I decided all that means that I am sapiosexual. – *Urban Dictionary*

He has told me he likes men as well as he likes women, which seems only natural, he says, since he is the offspring of two sexes as well as two races. No one is surprised he is biracial; why should they be surprised he is bisexual? – *Alice Walker*

ENERGY BODY AND ENERGY MEDICINE

Vibration Activation: Everything is vibrating energy. Vibration + Activation = Manifestation. – *Andydooley.com*

The energy of the mind is the essence of life. – *Aristotle*

Our feelings are energy, so when you find the energy you want you can attach it to a desire. – *Linda Armstrong*

Thoughts and words are energy. They do have a physical power. – *The Attraction Signal*

Life will manifest for you in direct proportion of what you are vibrating at energetically. – *BakertheBrand.com*

Everything that happens in all material, living, mental, or even spiritual processes involves the transformation of energy. Every thought, every sensation, every emotion is produced by energy exchanges. – *J. G. Bennett*

A higher vibrational level will increase your skills, abilities, and passions. It increases awareness, psychic abilities, level of happiness, and quality of life. – *Inelia Benz*

Life begets life. Energy creates energy. It is by spending oneself that one becomes rich. – *Sarah Bernhardt*

What you vibrate you become. – *Yogi Bhajan*

Love is the immortal flow of energy that nourishes, extends and preserves. Its eternal goal is life. – *Smiley Blanton*

The human body is made up of over 75 trillion cells, all of which vibrate. The higher the vibration, the healthier the cells. Disease, sickness, depression, anger, jealousy (negative things) make our cells vibrate at a lower rate. Love, happiness, laughter, compassion, and other positive things make our cells vibrate at a higher frequency. When we are happy and positive, we feel good mentally and physically; when we are sad or angry, we feel negative mentally and drained physically. – *Sheila M. Burke*

Visualization is the steering wheel of magic. It insures that the energy goes to the proper place. – *Scott Cunningham*

Every situation no matter how challenging is conspiring to bring you into greater vibrational energy. Will you receive it? – *Panache Desal*

Energy is all there is. You are a latticework of energies. – *Donna Eden*

Everything is energy and that's all there is to it. Match the frequency of the reality you want and you cannot help but get that reality. It can be no other way. This is not philosophy. This is physics. – *attributed to Albert Einstein, Darryl Anka, and Bashar*

Energy cannot be created or destroyed, it can only be changed from one form to another. – *Albert Einstein*

Everything is energy. Your thought begins it. Your emotion amplifies it, and your action increases the momentum. – *www.facebook.com/IndigoChildSurvivalGuide*

The medicine of the future will be energy medicine, and chemical medicine will be a subset of medicine as a whole. Probably 80 percent of medicine will be energy medicine, and 20 percent chemical medicine. – *Robert Jacobs*

Love the moment and the energy of that moment will spread beyond all boundaries. – *Corita Kent*

We consist of two parts: a spirit of fire and a fort of flesh.
– *Morgan Llywelyn*

The next big frontier in medicine is energy medicine. – *Mehmet Oz*

Everything is made of light and the space between isn't empty. – *Don Miguel Ruiz*

In truth, I am not my body, my race, religion, or other beliefs, and neither is anyone else. The real self is infinite and much more powerful — a complete and whole entity that isn't broken or damaged in any way. The infinite me already contains all the resources I need to navigate through life, because I'm One with Universal energy. In fact, I am Universal energy. – *Anita Moorjani*

Like Attracts Like. You are pure energy. Everything you think, say, feel, and do sends ripples out to the Universe. Whatever you put out there you will attract the same in turn. It's not karma nor some judgment, but neutral. It's the Universal Law of Same Vibrational Frequency and Wavelengths for both in the natural physical world and other dimensions. – *Lady Michelle–Jennifer Santos*

If you want to find the secrets of the universe, think in terms of energy, frequency and vibration. – *Nikola Tesla*

It is the mind that makes the body. – *Sojourner Truth*

We come from energy and turn back into energy. We are all matter for only a very short time. Make sure that when you are matter you matter. – *Unknown*

You are the alchemist. Energy goes where intent flows. – *Unknown*

Where attention goes energy flows. – *Unknown*

The fact that there is a Beginning or an End is just a concept seeded into your mind by society. You are Constant, Continuous, Infinite Energy and energy never ends, it transforms. – *Unknown*

The Physical Body is but an extension of the spirit. When it is time for the calling up of those upon your plane to higher frequencies, your body is going to be a part of the past, and your Energy Body a part of the future. – *Ra via David Wilcock*

Passion is energy. Feel the power that comes from focusing on what excites you. – *Oprah Winfrey*

SELF EMPOWERMENT

Resolve to be thyself and know, that he who finds himself, loses his misery. – *Matthew Arnold*

I am not a human being, I am a human becoming. – *Samuel Avital*

Be your own guru, your own teacher. You have the lamp within you. Light it and march on without fear. – *Sai Baba*

Not everything that is faced can be changed but nothing can be changed until it is faced. – *James Baldwin*

One will never reach distant shores, if he chooses to remain upon the dock, in fear his little ship of dreams may be dashed against the rocks. – *F. Bolen*

Alas the fearful unbelief is unbelief in yourself. – *Thomas Carlyle*

Beauty begins the moment you decide to be yourself. – *Coco Chanel*

Everything will change when your desire to move on exceeds your desire to hold on. – *Alan H. Cohen*

It takes courage to grow up and become who you really are. – *e.e. cummings*

Nothing in life is to be feared. It is only to be understood. – *Maria Curie*

Be thine own palace or the world's thy jail. – *John Donne*

It is the chiefest point of happiness that a man is willing to be what he is. – *Erasmus*

It is better to be hated for what you are than to be loved for what you are not. – *Andre Gide*

If you bring forth that which is within you, then that which is within you will be your salvation. If you do not bring forth that which is within you, then that which is within you will destroy you. – *Gnostic Gospels*

All adversity is really an opportunity for our souls to grow. – *John Gray*

The place where you are right now Spirit circled on a map for you. – *Hafiz*

You can't change the music of your soul. – *Katherine Hepburn*

Appreciate your uniqueness. – *Captain Kangaroo*

The best way to predict the future is to invent it. – *Alan Kay*

Your fears are just guideposts to growth. Surpass them and embrace your inner light. – *Joe Keane*

The most common form of despair is not being who you are. – *Soren Keirkegaard*

Conformity is the jailer of freedom and the enemy of growth. – *John F. Kennedy*

As long as you are trying to be something other than what you actually are, your mind wears itself out. – *J Krishnamurti*

The truth of a thing is the feel of it, not the think of it. – *Stanley Kubrick*

We cannot know the truth by what seems to be true from a single point of view. – *Christian Larson*

To grow beyond the expectations we're raised with is a radical act necessary to the claiming of one's full self. – *Ann Linnea*

You will either step forward into growth or you will step back into safety. – *Abraham Maslow*

There is only one success — to spend your life in your own way. – C*hristopher Morley*

Always and above all else, follow your own heart, for only then can you truly live the gift that is your life. – *Sally Morningstar*

How glorious it is and also how painful to be an exception. – *Alfred de Musset*

Live free or die. – *New Hampshire License Plate*

Growth is the only evidence of life. – *John Henry Newman*

The more you know who you are and what you want, the less you let things upset you. – *Stephanie Perkins*

Learn what you are and be such. – *Pindar*

I am what I am. – *Popeye*

Only as high as I reach can I grow, / Only as far as I seek can I go, / Only as deep as I look can I see, / Only as much as I dream can I be. – *Karen Ravn*

The curious paradox is that when I accept myself then I can change. – *Carl Rogers*

Anyone who sets out on a journey of self–development will be aided. There will be guides and teachers who will appear, and spiritual protectors to watch over the traveler. No test will be given that the traveler does not already have the strength to meet. – *The Sacred Tree*

By endurance we conquer. – *Ernest Shackleton*

To know what you prefer, instead of humbly saying "Amen" to

what the world tells you ought to prefer, is to have kept your soul alive. – *Robert Louis Stevenson*

Some great loss or disability on the level of form has become an opening to the spirit. – *Eckhardt Tolle*

Let everything be allowed to do what it naturally does so that its nature is satisfied. – *Chuang Tzu*

I am. These are two of the most powerful words in the universe because what you put behind them defines you. – *Unknown*

What you possess in the world will be found at the day of your death to belong to someone else. But what you are will be yours forever. – *Henry Van Dyke*

It's the soul's duty to be loyal to its own desires. It must abandon itself to its master passion. – *Rebecca West*

One's real life is often the life one does not lead. – *Oscar Wilde*

Selfishness is not living as one wishes to live. It is asking others to live as one wishes to live. – *Oscar Wilde*

Our deepest fear is not that we are inadequate. Our deepest fear is that we are powerful beyond measure. It is our light, not our darkness, that most frightens us. We ask ourselves who am I to be brilliant, gorgeous, talented, fabulous? Actually who are you not to be? You're playing small does not serve the world. There is nothing enlightening about shrinking so that other people won't feel unsure around you. We were born to make manifest of the glory of Spirit that is within us. It is not just in some of us; it is in everyone. As we let our light shine we unconsciously give other people permission to do the same. As we are liberated from our own fear our presence automatically liberates others. – *Marianne Williamson*

REINCARNATION

Do you have any idea how many lives we must have gone through before we even got the first idea that there is more to life than eating, or fighting, or power in the Flock? A thousand lives, ten thousand! We choose our next world through what we learn in this one. – *Richard Bach, Jonathan Livingston Seagull*

The soul is not the body and it may be in one body or in another, and pass from body to body. – *Giordano Bruno, Italian philosopher burned at the stake by the Inquisition for his teachings about reincarnation.*

You've inherited most from yourself, not from your family. – *Edgar Cayce*

Reincarnation makes life what it is intended to be — a glorious adventure in which victory is absolutely sure to be ours if we persist. It proves that man is master of his fate on his road to the stars. – *Shaw Desmond*

The soul is not born; it does not die; it was not produced from anyone. Unborn, eternal, it is not slain, though the body is slain. – *Ralph Waldo Emerson quoting Katha Upanisad*

As a man, casting off worn out garments taketh new ones, so the dweller in the body, entereth into ones that are new. – *Epictetus*

I believe we are reincarnated. You, I, we reincarnate over and over. We live many lives, and store up much experience. Some are older souls than others and so they know more. It seems to be an intuitive gift. It is really hard–won experience. – *Henry Ford*

When the physical organism breaks up, the soul survives. It then takes on another body. – *Paul Gauguin*

Forget not that I shall come back to you. A little while, a moment of rest upon the wind, and another woman shall bear me. – *Khalil Gibran*

It's not a simple hierarchy where past affects present and present affects future; instead, each affects the other to form an interwoven network of events. The comic strip *B.C.* had a cartoon about this in which a palmist, while looking at a client's palm, exclaimed "This is amazing! I have never seen a lifeline that formed a complete circle." To which the client replies "I'm into reincarnation." – *Amit Goswami*

Reincarnation is essential to enable the soul to evolve to its Divine right. – *R.F. Goudey*

The extent of the logical evidence for reincarnation is amazing. It is found to explain justly many of the problems of daily life. It reasonably accounts for such psychological problems as sudden friendships, awakening memories of past associations, certain strange actions of children, the nature of genius, obsession, and dual personality. By this doctrine the world becomes a huge training school, guided by law, and ruled by Divine Justice, instead of being a bewildering maze of chaotic and chance accidents. – *R.F. Goudey*

I am certain that I have been here as I am now a thousand times before, and I hope to return a thousand times. – *Johann Wolfgang von Goethe*

Souls are poured from one into another of different kinds of bodies of the world. – *Jesus Christ in Gnostic Gospels*

God generates beings, and sends them back over and over again, till they return to Him. – *Koran*

I did not begin when I was born, nor when I was conceived. I have been growing, developing, through incalculable myriads of millenniums... All my previous selves have their voices, echoes, promptings in me...Oh, incalculable times again shall I be born. – *Jack London*

I hold that when a person dies / His soul returns again to earth; / Arrayed in some new flesh disguise / Another mother gives him birth / With sturdier limbs and brighter brain. – *John Masefield*

Live so that thou mayest desire to live again. That is thy duty for in any case thou wilt live again! – *Freidrich Nietzsche*

There is one and the same soul in many bodies. – *Plotinus*

This life is but a brief tenure, one of many perspectives a spirit must experience in the quest for eternity. – *Brian Rathbone*

I feel as though I have lived many lives, experienced the heights and depths of each and like the waves of the ocean, never known rest. Throughout the years, I looked always for the unusual, for the wonderful, for the mysteries at the heart of life. – *Leni Riefenstahl*

It's so silly. All you do is get the heck out of your body when you die. My gosh, everybody's done it thousands of times. Just because they don't remember, it doesn't mean they haven't done it. – *J.D. Salinger*

I am confident that there truly is such a thing as living again, that the living spring from the dead, and that the souls of the dead are in existence. – *Socrates*

As we live through thousands of dreams in our present life, so is our present life only one of many thousands of such lives which we enter from the other more real life and then return after death. Our life is but one of the dreams of that more real life, and so it is endlessly, until the very last one, the very real, the life of God. – *Leo Tolstoy*

What if when we die the light at the end of the tunnel we see is just us being pushed out of another vagina? – *Unknown*

Reincarnation is making a comeback. – *Unknown*

It is not more surprising to be born twice than once; everything in nature is resurrection. – *Voltaire*

No doubt I have died myself ten thousand times before. I laugh at what you call dissolution, and I know the amplitude of time. – *Walt Whitman*

APPENDIX C:

DAYS TO COMMEMORATE GENDER AND SEXUAL IDENTITY DIVERSITY

On these memorial days set aside to honor gender non–conforming individuals and individuals with diverse sexual identities, let us grieve for all those who have died at the violent hands of the fearful and ignorant and let us honor those who have the courage to walk their personal and unique path.

LGBT* Health Awareness Week	Mar 14–20
International Day of Transgender Visibility	Mar 31
Day of Silence to Protest Bullying	Apr 19
International Day against Homophobia and Transphobia	May 17
Harvey Milk Day	May 22
Pride Month and LGBT* History Month	June
Stonewall Riots Anniversary	Jun 27
International Drag Day	Jul 16
Celebrate Bisexuality Day	Sep 23
National Coming Out Day	Oct 11
Ally Week	Oct 13–17
Spirit Day (Day against Bullying)	Oct 17
Intersex Awareness Day	Oct 26
Intersex Solidarity Day	Nov 8
Transgender Day of Remembrance	Nov 20

APPENDIX D:

INTERNATIONAL BILL OF GENDER RIGHTS

Following is the International Bill of Gender Rights (IBGR) [1] that was adopted by the International Conference on Transgender Law and Employment Policy (ICTLEP) in 1993.

The Right to Define Gender Identity

All human beings carry within themselves an ever–unfolding idea of who they are and what they are capable of achieving. The individual's sense of self is not determined by chromosomal sex, genitalia, assigned birth sex, or initial gender role. Thus, the individual's identity and capabilities cannot be circumscribed by what society deems to be masculine or feminine behavior. It is fundamental that individuals have the right to define, and to redefine as their lives unfold, their own gender identities, without regard to chromosomal sex, genitalia, assigned birth sex, or initial gender role.

Therefore, all human beings have the right to define their own gender identity regardless of chromosomal sex, genitalia, assigned birth sex, or initial gender role; and further, no individual shall be denied Human or Civil Rights by virtue of a self–defined gender identity which is not in accord with chromosomal sex, genitalia, assigned birth sex, or initial gender role.

The Right to Free Expression of Gender Identity

Given the right to define one's own gender identity, all human beings have the corresponding right to free expression of their self–defined gender identity. Therefore, all human beings have the right to free expression of their self–defined gender identity; and further, no individual shall be denied Human or Civil Rights by virtue of the expression of a self–defined gender identity.

The Right to Secure and Retain Employment and to Receive Just Compensation

Given the economic structure of modem society, all human beings have a right to train for and to pursue an occupation or profession as a means of providing shelter, sustenance, and the necessities and bounty of life, for themselves and for those dependent upon them, to secure and retain employment, and to receive just compensation for their labor regardless of gender identity, chromosomal sex, genitalia, assigned birth sex, or initial gender role.

Therefore, individuals shall not be denied the right to train for and to pursue an occupation or profession, nor be denied the right to secure and retain employment, nor be denied just compensation for their labor, by virtue of their chromosomal sex, genitalia, assigned birth sex, or initial gender role, or on the basis of a self–defined gender identity or the expression thereof.

The Right of Access to Gendered Space and Participation in Gendered Activity

Given the right to define one's own gender identity and the corresponding right to free expression of a self–defined gender identity, no individual should be denied access to a space or denied participation in an activity by virtue of a self–defined gender identity which is not in accord with chromosomal sex, genitalia, assigned birth sex, or initial gender role.

Therefore, no individual shall be denied access to a space or denied participation in an activity by virtue of a self–defined gender identity which is not in accord with chromosomal sex, genitalia, assigned birth sex, or initial gender role.

The Right to Control and Change One's Own Body

All human beings have the right to control their bodies, which includes the right to change their bodies cosmetically, chemically, or surgically, so as to express a self–defined gender identity.

Therefore, individuals shall not be denied the right to change their bodies as a means of expressing a self–defined gender identity; and further, individuals shall not be denied Human or Civil Rights on the basis that they have changed their bodies cosmetically, chemically, or surgically, or desire to do so as a means of expressing a self–defined gender identity.

The Right to Competent Medical and Professional Care

Given the individual's right to define one's own gender identity, and the right to change one's own body as a means of expressing a self–defined gender identity, no individual should be denied access to competent medical or other professional care on the basis of the individual's chromosomal sex, genitalia, assigned birth sex, or initial gender role.

Therefore, individuals shall not be denied the right to competent medical or other professional care when changing their bodies cosmetically, chemically, or surgically, on the basis of chromosomal sex, genitalia, assigned birth sex, or initial gender role.

The Right to Freedom from Psychiatric Diagnosis or Treatment

Given the right to define one's own gender identity, individuals should not be subject to psychiatric diagnosis or treatment solely on the basis of their gender identity or role.

Therefore, individuals shall not be subject to psychiatric diagnosis or treatment as mentally disordered or diseased solely on the basis of a self–defined gender identity or the expression thereof.

The Right to Sexual Expression

Given the right to a self–defined gender identity, every consenting adult has a corresponding right to free sexual expression.

Therefore, no individual's Human or Civil Rights shall be denied on the basis of sexual orientation; and further, no individual shall be denied Human or Civil Rights for expression of a self–defined gender identity through sexual acts between consenting adults.

The Right to Form Committed, Loving Relationships and Enter into Marital Contracts

Given that all human beings have the right to free expression of self–defined gender identities, and the right to sexual expression as a form of gender expression, all human beings have a corresponding right to form committed, loving relationships with one another, and to enter into marital contracts, regardless of their own or their partner's chromosomal sex, genitalia, assigned birth sex, or initial gender role.

Therefore, individuals shall not be denied the right to form committed, loving relationships with one another or to enter into marital contracts by virtue of their own or their partner's chromosomal sex, genitalia, assigned birth sex, or initial gender role, or on the basis of their expression of a self–defined gender identity.

The Right to Conceive, Bear, or Adopt Children; The Right to Nurture and Have Custody of Children and to Exercise Parental Capacity

Given the right to form a committed, loving relationship with another, and to enter into marital contracts, together with the right to express a self–defined gender identity and the right to sexual expression, individuals have a corresponding right to conceive and bear children, to adopt children, to nurture children, to have custody of children, and to exercise parental capacity with respect to children, natural or adopted, without regard to chromosomal sex, genitalia, assigned birth sex, or initial gender role, or by virtue of a self–defined gender identity or the expression thereof.

Therefore, individuals shall not be denied the right to conceive, bear, or adopt children, nor to nurture and have custody of children, nor to exercise parental capacity with respect to children, natural or adopted, on the basis of their own, their partner's, or their children's chromosomal sex, genitalia, assigned birth sex, initial gender role, or by virtue of a self–defined gender identity or the expression thereof.

[1] International Conference on Transgender Law and Employment Policy (ICTLEP). "International Bill of Gender Rights (IBGR)." Last modified June, 1995.
http://my.execpc.com/~dmmunson/billrights.htm

APPENDIX E:

GENDER DIVERSITY ETIQUETTE

Here is a list of guidelines for gender diversity etiquette. This is the time in our social consciousness progression to accept, honor, and understand variations in gender identity.

DO (How to Treat Everyone):

Stand up for gender diversity.
Respect other individual's gender identity.
Address individuals by their preferred name.
Address individuals by the pronouns they prefer.
Respect other individual's privacy and confidentiality.
If you make a mistake with a pronoun or name, move on.
Educate yourself and be familiar with the vocabulary of gender.
Be patient and supportive of individuals with non–conforming genders.
Phrase your questions in a way that affirms an individual's gender identity.
Avoid asking private and personal questions or ask permission to ask questions.
Treat other individuals with honor and respect just as you would like to be treated.
Allow individuals of all gender identities to use public restrooms in peace and trust that each individual knows which restroom matches their identity.

DON'T (How to Treat Individuals with Alternative Gender Identities):

Don't "out" anyone.
Don't ask to see old photos.
Don't make jokes at anyone's expense
Don't ever use the word "real" or "normal".
Don't ask about genitalia or surgical status.

Don’t ask others what their birth name was.
Don't assume gender or sexual identity is a choice.
Don’t use slang words that are very likely derogatory.
Don’t assume that all women have vaginas and all men have penises.
Don’t assume that individuals with non–conforming gender are kinky.
Do not categorize or stereotype individuals with non–conforming gender.
Don’t make assumptions about other’s sexual orientation or gender identity.
Don’t assume that individuals with non–conforming gender are mentally ill.
Never use violence, abuse, bashing, bullying, or exploitation against any individual.
Don’t assume every individual with non–conforming gender is an expert on gender issues.
Don’t use wrong pronouns or make assumptions about other individual’s gender identities.
Don’t discriminate against, ostracize, or stigmatize individuals because they are different than you.

Don’t judge individuals with non–conforming gender based upon your personal religious beliefs.

DON’T SAY (What Not to Say to Individuals with Alternative Gender Identities):

“Are you done?”
“You pass really well.”
“What are you really?”
“How do you have sex?”
“Are you pre–op or post–op?”
“Have you had the surgery?”
“Which restroom do you use?”
“You are so brave/courageous.”
“You are in the wrong restroom.”

"How do you go to the restroom?"
"You don't look like a man/woman."
"I can still see the man/woman in you."
"I'll never get that pronoun/name right."
"You will always be a man/woman to me."
"Why would you transition if you're going to be gay?"
"When did you decide to become trans*/gender fluid, etc.?"
"Are you afraid that people will hate you or want to hurt you?"
"What is your real name?" (implying the one you were given at birth)
"If you [*did something*] a certain way, you would be more masculine/feminine."

GLOSSARY OF GENDER AND SEXUALITY TERMS

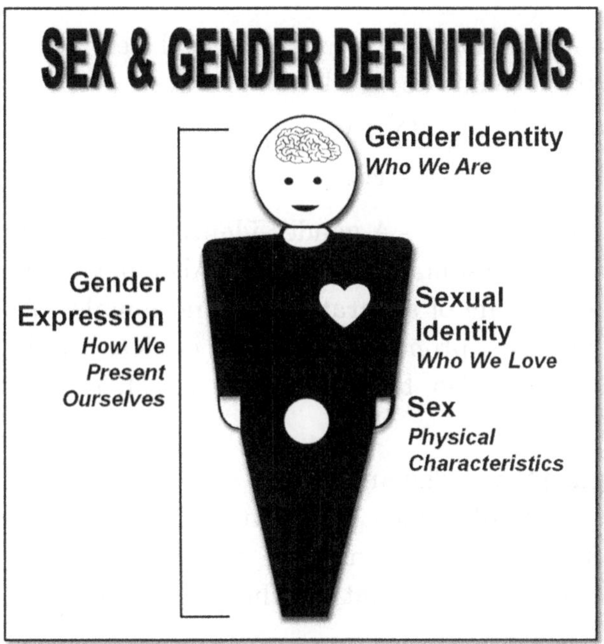

Many new gender and sexual identity terms have been created in recent years. Similar terms seem to have little to no differentiation between them. The option of having an alternative identity wasn't even available until the late twentieth century. I believe that the new influx of terms is a result of individuals trying to describe their alternative identity. I suspect as individuals become more comfortable in gender fluidity, many of these labels will disappear and we will all simply assume our own unique identity that does not require a label. Perhaps eventually the various labels can be brought together under one acronym that represents the state of infinite choice that multiple identities provide – AGASI, Alternative Gender and Sexual Identity.

Many of the identity terms below also have pride flags associated with them. A color version of the pride flags can be downloaded at www.soulsexalchemy.com.

GENDER IDENTITY TERMS

AGASI – Acronym for Alternative Gender and Sexual Identity

Agender – An individual of any physical sex but with a null gender identity. (Same as Gender Neutral).

Androgynous (Androgyne) – An individual that has both male and female gender characteristics.

Bigender (Ambigender) – A gender identity structure that allows for only two genders: male and female. Also may be an individual that lives a dual life of separate male and female roles including separate names, pronouns, social circles, and identities. Ambigender may also be interpreted as short for ambiguous gender.

Birth Assigned Sex – The anatomical sex as determined by biology or genetics. Not all babies are born with genitalia that can be clearly defined as either male or female. And not all babies develop a gender identity that matches their birth assigned sex.

Boi (Boy) – A lesbian or gender–queer individual who identifies mostly with their male energy and presents as male in their appearance.

Cisgender – An individual whose gender identity and gender role matches their birth assigned sex. They fit well into the binary gender system. *Cis* is Latin for "on the same side" or "on this side of".

Demiboy – An individual who partially identifies as a boy or man, no matter what their assigned gender at birth is.

Demigirl – An individual who partially identifies as a girl or woman, no matter what their birth assigned sex is.

Drag (Crossdresser) – An individual that dresses in clothing opposite their birth assigned sex.

Eunuch – A male who has been castrated.

Female (Woman, Cis Woman) – An individual whose gender identity of female matches her birth assigned sex of female.

Femme – An individual, usually gay or lesbian, who exhibits stereotypical feminine traits, often in an exaggerated way.

Gender Binary – A gender identity structure that allows for only two genders: male and female.

Gender Diversity – Individuals that do not identify as being either male or female but as a mix of both. A person may feel more male some days and more female other days or these individuals do not want to be classified as male or female. Other terms used are: ambigender, androgynous, creatively gendered, gender bender, gender blender, gender breaker, gender diverse, gender dysphoric, gender fairy, gender fluid, gender fuck, genderfree, gender chameleon, gender nonconformist, gender outlaw, gender queer, gender revolutionary, gender shapeshifter, gender transgressor, gender trickster, gender variant, gynandrous, human–gender, intergender, metagender, multigender, nongender, omnigender, pan–gender, per, polygender, third–gender, trans–androgynous, trans–variant, tweener, and variant expressive.

Gender Free – An individual that does not identify with the accepted definitions and standards of binary gender structures.

Gender Fluid – An individual whose identity changes between male, female, and neutral.

Gender Identity – The way in which an individual expresses their gender. Sex is the biological classification of male or female. Gender is associated with the mental body and sex is associated with the physical body.

Gender Neutral – An individual of any physical sex with a null (no) gender identity.

Gender Nonbinary – A gender identity structure that embraces a rainbow of genders rather than just male and female.

Gender Queer – An individual whose gender identity is different than that assigned at birth. These individuals may identify as both male and female, or as neither male nor female (genderless or agender).

Gender Questioning – An individual who is questioning their current gender identity, role, and/or expression.

Gender Variant (Gender Nonconforming) – An individual's behavior or gender expression does not match the gender roles set by society for males and females.

Hermaphrodite – Obsolete term for intersexual.

Human–gender – An individual whose gender identity is not based on masculine or feminine characteristics but on the entire range of human characteristics.

Intergender – An individual who identifies across or beyond male/female gender ideals.

Intersexual – An individual displaying ambiguous sexual characteristics of both male and female at birth. It is not proper to use this term as a noun or verb i.e. "intersexed".

LGBT* – LGBT* is commonly used as an acronym for the Lesbian, Gay, Bisexual, and Transgender community. Other letters that are frequently added are: "G" for Genderqueer, "T*" for Transgender, Transsexual, and Third Gender, "Q" for Queer and Questioning, "I" for Intersex, "A" for Ally, Asexual, Androgynous, and Autosexual, "P" for Pansexual, and "H" for Heterosexual, Hetero–flexible, and Homo–flexible.

Male (Man, Cis Man) – An individual whose gender identity of male matches his birth assigned sex of male.

Metagender – An individual who has a tenuous connection to the concept of gender. Meta usually means "after" or "beyond".

Multigender – Individuals with multiple gender identities such as nonbinary or trans*.

Metrosexual – A heterosexual male who is focused on his personal grooming, wardrobe, and appearance.

Neutrois – An individual that does not identify with gender and often feels that they fall neutrally between male and female. This non–gendered class includes agender, gender neutral, genderless, or having a null gender.

Neuter – An individual who has no sex or gender identification.

Nongender – An individual who has no gender identification.

Pangender (Polygendered, Omnigender) – An individual that possesses all genders. The term emphasizes there are more than only two genders.

PoMogendered – Short for "postmodernly gendered", which means an individual has a non–orientation. They disregard gender and sexual labels altogether. From the book *PoMoSexuals: Challenging Assumptions about Gender and Sexuality* edited by Carol Queen and Lawrence Schimel.

Postgenderist – An individual whose social and political viewpoint supports the elimination of human gender identity and includes the advocacy of assistive reproductive technology.

Queen – A feminine gay man. May also be short for Drag Queen.

Third Gender – An individual that identifies as neither male nor female or as both male and female.

Tomboy – A girl who exhibits characteristics or behaviors considered typical of a boy.

Trans* – Trans with an asterisk is a relatively new label that represents an umbrella under which any variation that is not cisgender is represented. Identities that may be included are: agender, androgynous, bigender, gender fluid, genderqueer, intergender, multigender, nongender, transgender, transsexual, transwoman, transman, transvestite, third gender, and two spirit. There is some disagreement about whether the following identities are under the trans* umbrella: crossdresser, drag performer, drag queen, drag king, intersex, and transvestite fetishists. *Trans* is Latin for "on the other side" or "across".

Trans Ally – Cis individuals that support the Trans* community and activities.

Trans–androgynous – An individual who identifies as trans* as well as exhibits neither or both masculine and feminine characteristics.

Transfeminine – An individual who was assigned male at birth but whose gender identity is more female than male. They often identify as feminine of center (more feminine than masculine).

Transgender – An individual whose gender identity is different than the birth assigned sex. These individuals may or may not have taken steps to change their birth assigned sex. It is not proper to use this term as a noun or verb i.e. "transgendered".

Transgenderist – An individual living or preferring to live in a gender role opposite their birth assigned sex. Usually refers to a transsexual who does not intend to have genital reassignment surgery or hormone therapy.

Transmasculine – An individual who was assigned female at birth but whose gender identity is more male than female. They often identify as masculine of center (more masculine than feminine).

Transsexual – An individual that emotionally and psychologically feel that they belong to the opposite gender of their birth assigned gender. These individuals usually take steps to change their birth assigned sex through Hormone Replacement Therapy (HRT) and Genital Reassignment Surgeries (GRS). Sex Reassignment Surgery (SRS) and Gender Reassignment Surgery (GRS) are now considered obsolete terms by many. The correct terms are Gender Confirmation Surgery (GCS), Genital Reconstruction Surgery (GRS), or Genital Reassignment Surgery (GRS).

Transman (FTM, F2M) – A female–to–male trans* individual.

Transvestite – An individual that likes to dress and spend part time in the gender role that is opposite the birth assigned sex. These individuals do not desire to change their birth assigned sex.

This term is considered obsolete and has been replaced by the term "Cross Dresser".

Transwoman (MTR, M2F) – A male–to–female trans* individual.

Trigender – An individual whose gender identity changes between male, female, and third gender.

Twink – Boyish–looking, young gay man, typically aged 18–22, that may have some effeminate characteristics.

Two Spirit – Gender queer individuals that fulfill mixed gender roles in Native American and Canadian First Nations groups.

SEXUAL IDENTITIES

AGASI – Acronym for Alternative Gender and Sexual Identity

Ambiphilia (Biphilia) – An individual that is sexually, romantically, or emotionally attracted to both masculinity (men) and femininity (women).

Androphilia – An individual that is sexually, romantically, or emotionally attracted to men and masculinity.

Androgynephile – An individual that is sexually, romantically, or emotionally attracted to males and females.

Asexual – An individual that feels little or no sexual attraction to anyone.

Autochorissexual – An asexual individual that is disconnected from targets of arousal. They may experience sexual fantasies but lack the desire to be a participant in the sexual activities.

Autosexual – An individual that prefers masturbation over other forms of sexual attraction.

Banjee – A young Latino, Black, or multiracial man, dressing in masculine urban fashion, who has sex with men.

Bicurious – An individual that is considering experimenting sexually with individuals of the same sex.

Bisexual – An individual sexually, romantically, or emotionally attracted to both males and females.

Celibate – An individual who abstains from all sexual activity. These individuals can have any sexual orientation but do not act on it.

Chameleosexual – An individual whose sexual role is dependent on what the gender orientation of their partner is. In other words, an individual that is sexually versatile depending on the gender of their partner.

Demisexual – An individual that does not feel sexual attraction until a strong emotional bond has formed.

Ex–gay – An individual who changed their sexual orientation to heterosexual as a result of participating in ex–gay therapy.

Gynephilia – An individual that is sexually attracted to women and femininity.

Heterosexual (Straight) – Male–identified individuals who are sexually, romantically, or emotionally attracted to females and female–identified individuals who are sexually, romantically, or emotionally attracted to males.

Hetero–Flexible – A heterosexual individual that is open to the possibilities of having a romantic, emotional, or sexual homosexual relationship.

Homosexual (Gay) – A male–identified individual who is sexually, romantically, or emotionally attracted to other males.

Homo–Flexible – A homosexual individual that is open to the possibilities of having a romantic, emotional, or sexual heterosexual relationship.

Lesbian – A female–identified individual who is sexually, romantically, or emotionally attracted to other females.

Lipstick Lesbian – Lesbians that are within the feminine gender spectrum.

Lithsexual – An individual that feels attraction but does not want the feeling returned in any way.

Monosexual – An individual that is sexually and romantically attracted to individuals that identify as one gender i.e. loving males (androphilia) or loving females (gynephilia).

Panphilia – An individual that is sexually, romantically, or emotionally attracted to individuals of all genders.

Pansexual (Omnisexual, Multisexual) – An individual that is sexually, romantically, or emotionally attracted to individuals of all genders.

Polyamorous – Individuals who desire or practice having more than one intimate partner at a time with the consent of all individuals involved.

Polysexual – An individual whose gender identity is non–binary and who is sexually, romantically, or emotionally attracted to individuals of all genders.

PoMosexual – Short for "postmodernly sexual", which means an individual has a non–orientation. They disregard gender and sexual labels altogether. From the book *PoMoSexuals: Challenging Assumptions about Gender and Sexuality* edited by Carol Queen and Lawrence Schimel.

Queer – A reclaimed term that now refers to the sexual minority community or for marginalized groups of individuals.

Questioning – An individual who questions or is uncertain of their gender or sexual identity.

Sapiosexual – An individual who is romantically or sexually attracted to intelligence finding intellectual stimulation sexually arousing.

Sexual Identity (Sexual Orientation) – The way in which an individual expresses their sexual and romantic interests. The term "sexual preference" is avoided as it infers identity is a choice.

Skoliosexual – An individual that is sexually or romantically attracted to individuals with non–binary gender identities.

Straight Ally – A heterosexual individual that supports the LGBT* community and activities.

Versatile – An individual who considers themselves to be sexually both a top (the giver) and a bottom (the receiver).

ROMANTIC IDENTITIES

Akoiromantic – An individual who has a romantic attraction which does not need to be reciprocated.

Androgynoromantic (Androgyneromantic) – An individual who is romantically attracted to individuals expressing femininity and masculinity without implying the gender of the individual experiencing the attraction.

Androromantic – An individual who is romantically attracted to individuals expressing masculinity.

Aromantic (Antiromantic) – An individual that does not experience romantic attraction towards anyone.

Biromantic – An individual who is romantically attracted to both males and females.

Cupioromantic – An individual who has desire for a romantic relationship despite not experiencing romantic attraction.

Demiromantic – An individual that feels sexual attraction only after a strong emotional bond has been formed.

Greyromantic – Greyromantic can be a blanket term for an individual who falls anywhere between Romantic and Aromantic. It is also an umbrella term that includes Lithromantics and Demiromantics.

Gynoromantic (Gyneromantic) – An individual who is romantically attracted to individuals expressing femininity.

Heteroromantic – An individual who is romantically attracted to individuals with a gender other than their own.

Homoromantic – An individual who is romantically attracted to individuals of the same gender.

Idemromantic – An individual who experiences romantic and platonic feelings in the same way.

Lithromantic – An individual that feels attraction but does not want this feeling returned in any way.

Monoromantic – An individual who is romantically attracted to individuals of only one gender identity.

Neutroisromantic – An individual who is romantically attracted to individuals of null, non–gendered, or non–binary gender identity.

Panromantic (Omniromantic, Ambiromantic) – An individual who is romantically attracted to individuals with any gender including those expressing masculine, feminine, and intersex/third gender–mixing.

Polyromantic – An individual who is romantically attracted to multiple, but not all, genders.

Quoiromantic – An individual who is unable to distinguish the difference between romantic and platonic feelings, or cannot define romantic attraction, therefore does not know whether or not they have experienced it.

Recipromantic – An individual who has a romantic attraction only after another individual is romantically attracted.

Requiesromantic – An individual who has little to no romantic attraction because of some mental or emotional exhaustion, likely due to bad experiences of romance in the past.

Transromantic (Skolioromantic) – An individual who is romantically attracted to individuals of variant or ambiguous gender or to transgender or intersex individuals.

Wtfromantic – An individual who does not experience romanticism in the traditional manner but who cannot say they are fully aromantic or greyaromantic. The specific meanings of the identity is up to each individual. Wtfromantic is generally used as a catch–all term for individuals who fall in the category of semiromantic or alternatively romantic, but do not better fit into any other label.

BIBLIOGRAPHY

BOOKS ON GENDER

Bornstein, Kate. *My New Gender Workbook: A Step–by–Step Guide to Achieving World Peace Through Gender Anarchy and Sex Positivity*. Routledge, 2013.

Erickson–Schroth, Laura. *Trans Bodies, Trans Selves: A Resource for the Transgender Community*. Oxford University Press, 2014.

Fausto–Sterling, Anne. *Sexing the Body: Gender Politics and the Construction of Sexuality*. Basic Books, 2000.

Garbacik, Jaimee. *Gender and Sexuality for Beginners*. For Beginners, 2013.

Heilbrun, Carolyn G. *Toward A Recognition of Androgyny*. W. W. Norton & Company, 1982.

Killermann, Sam. *The Social Justice Advocate's Handbook: A Guide to Gender*. Impetus Books, 2013.

Lev Arlene Istar. *Transgender Emergence: Therapeutic Guidelines for Working with Gender–Variant People and Their Families*. Routledge, 2004.

Meyerowitz, Joanne. *How Sex Changed: A History of Transsexuality in the United States*. Harvard University Press, 2004.

Roughgarden, Joan. *Evolution's Rainbow: Diversity, Gender, and Sexuality in Nature and People*. University of California Press, 2004, 2013.

Serano, Julia. *Whipping Girl: A Transsexual Woman on Sexism and the Scapegoating of Femininity*. Seal Press, 2007.

Singer, June. *Androgyny: Toward a Theory of Sexuality*. Doubleday, 1976.

Stryker, Susan. *Transgender History*. Seal Press, 2008.Zolla, Elemire. *The Androgyne: Reconciliation of Male and Female*. Crossroad Pub Co, 1981.

BOOKS ON SEXUALITY

Bishop, Clifford. *Sex and Spirit.* Little Brown Company, 1997.

Camphausen, Rufus C. *The Encyclopedia of Sacred Sexuality.* Inner Traditions, 1999.

Conner, Randy P., David Sparks, and Mariya Sparks. *Cassell's Encyclopedia of Queer Myth, Symbol and Spirit: Gay, Lesbian, Bisexual and Transgender Lore.* Cassell, 1998.

Feuerstein, Georg. *Sacred Sexuality: The Erotic Spirit in the World's Great Religions.* Inner Traditions, 2003.

Huerta, Christian de la. *Coming Out Spiritually: The Next Step.* Tarcher, 1999.

Johnson, Toby. *Gay Spirituality: Gay Identity and the Transformation of Human Consciousness.* White Crane Books, 2004.

Kear, Lynn. *We're Here: An Investigation into Gay Reincarnation.* Retropolitan, 1999.

Kraig, Donald Michael. *Modern Sex Magick: Secrets of Erotic Spirituality.* Llewellyn Publications, 2002.

Lorius, Cassandra. *The Sacred Sex Bible: A Guide to Sex and Spirit in the East and West.* Firefly Books, 2011.

Mann, A.T. and Jane Lyle. *Sacred Sexuality.* Element Books Ltd, 1995.

Prine, Kirk. *Erotic Body Prayer: Pathways to Pray Through the Body and Build Ecstatic Community.* Lulu.com, 2006.

Ramer, Andrew. *Two Flutes Playing: A Spiritual Journeybook for Gay Men.* White Crane Books, 2005.

Ritter, Kathleen Y. and Anthony I. Terndrup. *Handbook of Affirmative Psychotherapy with Lesbians and Gay Men.* The Guilford Press, 2002.

Roscoe, Will. *Queer Spirits.* Beacon Press, 1996.

Thompson, Mark. *Gay Spirit: Myth and Meaning.* St. Martin's Griffin, 1988.

BOOKS ON INTERSEXUALITY

Callahan, Gerald N. *Between XX and XY: Intersexuality and the Myth of Two Sexes.* Chicago Review Press, 2009.

Preves, Sharon E. *Intersex and Identity: The Contested Self.* Rutgers University Press, 2003.

BOOKS ON TWO SPIRITS AND THIRD GENDER

Conner, Randy P. *Blossom of Bone–Reclaiming the Connections between Homoeroticism and the Sacred.* Harpercollins, 1993.

Feinberg, Leslie. *Transgender Warriors: Making History from Joan of Arc to Dennis Rodman.* Beacon Press, 1997.

Herdt, Gilbert, ed. *Third Sex, Third Gender: Beyond Sexual Dimorphism in Culture and History.* Zone Books, 1996.

Jacobs, Sue–Ellen, Wesley Thomas, and Sabine Lang, eds. *Two–Spirit People: Native American Gender Identity, Sexuality, and Spirituality.* University of Illinois Press, 1997.

Lang, Sabine. *Men as Women, Women as Men: Changing Gender in Native American Cultures.* University of Texas Press, 1998.

Nanda, Serena. *Gender Diversity: Crosscultural Variations.* Waveland Press, 2014.

Roscoe, Will. *Changing Ones: Third and Fourth Genders in Native North America.* Palgrave Macmillan, 2000.

Roscoe, Will. *Living the Spirit: A Gay American Indian Anthology.* St. Martin's Griffin, 1988.

Roscoe, Will and Stephen O. Murray. *Boy–Wives and Female Husbands: Studies of African Homosexualities.* Palgrave Macmillan, 2001.

Williams, Walter L. *Spirit and the Flesh: Sexual Diversity in American Indian Culture.* Beacon Press, 1992.

BOOKS ON NON-CONFORMING GENDER AND SEXUAL IDENTITIES FROM DIFFERENT SPIRITUAL VIEWPOINTS

Alford–Harkey, Marie and Debra W. Haffner. *Bisexuality: Making the Invisible Visible in Faith Communities*. Religious Institute, 2014.

Bhava, Sakhi. *Transgender Spirituality: Man into Goddess.* CreateSpace Independent Publishing Platform, 2012.

Cheng, Patrick S. *Radical Love: An Introduction to Queer Theology.* Seabury Books, 2011.

Cornwall, Susannah. *Sex and Uncertainty in the Body of Christ: Intersex Conditions and Christian Theology.* Equinox Publishing, 2010.

Dzmura, Noach. *Balancing on the Mechitza: Transgender in Jewish Community.* North Atlantic Books, 2010.

Ford, Michael Thomas. *The Path of the Green Man: Gay Men, Wicca and Living a Magical Life.* Citadel, 2005.

Habib, Samar, ed. *Islam and Homosexuality (2 Volumes).* Praeger, 2009.

Kaldera, Raven. *Hermaphrodeities: The Transgender Spirituality Workbook.* Asphodel Press, 2009.

Kugle, Scott Siraj al–Haqq. *Homosexuality in Islam: Critical Reflection on Gay, Lesbian, and Transgender Muslims.* Oneworld Publications, 2010.

Leone, Katie. *The Transsexual and the Cross: Disproving the Myth that Transsexuality is a Sin.* CreateSpace Independent Publishing Platform, 2013.

Leyland, Winston, ed. *Queer Dharma: Voices of Gay Buddhists Vol. 1 and Vol. 2.* Gay Sunshine Press, 1997 and 1999.

Michaelson, Jay. *God vs. Gay? The Religious Case for Equality.* Beacon Press, 2012.

Mollenkott, Virginia Ramey. *Omnigender: A Trans–Religious Approach.* Pilgrim Press, 2007.

Nyland, A. *Study New Testament for Lesbians, Gays, Bi, and Transgender: With Extensive Notes on Greek Word Meaning and Context.* Smith & Stirling Publishing, 2007.

Penczak, Christopher. *Gay Witchcraft: Empowering the Tribe.* Red Wheel/Weiser, 2003.

Roscoe, Will, and Stephen O. Murray, eds. *Islamic Homosexualities: Culture, History, and Literature.* NYU Press, 1997.

Roscoe, Will. *Jesus and the Shamanic Tradition of Same Sex Love.* Lethe Press, 2013.

Sheridan, Vanessa. *Crossing Over: Liberating the Transgendered Christian.* Pilgrim Press, 2001.

Thumma, Scott and Edward R. Gray. *Gay Religion.* AltaMira Press, 2004.

Tanis, Justin Edward. *Trans–Gendered: Theology, Ministry, and Communities of Faith.* Pilgrim Press, 2003.

Tigert, Leanne McCall and Maren C. Tirabassi. *Transgendering Faith: Identity, Sexuality, and Spirituality.* Pilgrim Press, 2004.

BOOKS ON THE ENERGY BODY

Dale, Cyndi. *The Subtle Body: Encyclopedia of Your Energetic Anatomy.* Sounds True, 2009.

Dale, Cyndi. *The Subtle Body Practice Manual: A Comprehensive Guide to Energy Healing.* Sounds True, 2013.

Eden, Donna. *Energy Medicine: Balancing Your Body's Energies for Optimal Health, Joy, and Vitality.* Jeremy P. Tarcher, 2008.

Eden, Donna. *The Energy Medicine Kit.* Sounds True, 2005.

BOOKS ON REINCARNATION AND NDE (Near Death Experience)

Backman, Linda. *Bringing Your Soul to Light: Healing Through Past Lives and the Time Between.* Llewellyn Publications, 2009.

Cannon, Georgina. *Return Again: How to Find Meaning in Your Past Lives and Your Interlives.* Weiser Books, 2012.

Dale, Liz. *Crossing Over & Coming Home: 21 Authors Discuss the Gay Near–Death Experience as Spiritual Transformation.* Emerald Ink Publishing, 2008.

Linn, Denise. *Past Lives, Present Miracles: The Most Empowering Book on Reincarnation You'll Ever Read in this Lifetime!* Hay House, 2008.

Newton, Michael. *Destiny of Souls: New Case Studies of Life Between Lives.* Llewellyn Publications, 2000.

Newton, Michael. *Journey of Souls: Case Studies of Life Between Lives.* Llewellyn Publications, 1994.

Taylor, Sandra Anne. *The Hidden Power of Your Past Lives: Revealing Your Encoded Consciousness.* Hay House, 2011.

INDEX

ACKNOWLEDGEMENTS

I traveled quite a long journey to birth this book. First, I had to live most of my life to gather enough experience and wisdom to provide the foundation of understanding required to share these expansive concepts of gender and sexual identity. Second, I had to research the material thoroughly. Then I had to write it all down and create the illustrations. Next, I relied on others to edit my work. And lastly, I revised and rewrote extensively.

I could not have completed this journey to publication without the assistance of some individuals I would like to express my deepest gratitude for. I am thankful to my beta readers, especially Chichi Rivera and Moria Feighery–Ross, and to my editors:

- Dawn Bielawski, my technical editor, who specializes in scientific and medical writing. She also has a spiritual background in shamanism so she was a perfect fit for editing this book. Her web page is www.theeditingandwritingalchemist.com.

- Alexandra Folts, my content editor, is a transpersonal life coach and astrologer. She has previous experience in editing other manuscripts. Her web page is www.astrologywithalexandra.com.

- Kimberly Martin, of Jera Publishing, who did my book design review. Her company has many services that support self-publishing authors. Her web page is www.self-pub.net.

I would like to thank my photographer, Karen Bates, for the wonderful work she did on providing professional photos of me. Her web page is www.karenbatesphoto.com.

I thank all the people, including family, friends, colleagues, co–workers, teachers, medical providers, therapists, and past life clients that have aided me in making my journey possible. Your names are too numerous to list but my appreciation is overflowing for you.

I am deeply grateful for the Internet, which has become the world's largest library. Without it, much of the research for this book would not have been possible. Not only is the internet a vast repository of information but it is also bringing geographically isolated individuals with alternative gender and sexual identities together into community.

Lastly, I gratefully acknowledge my spirit guides for whispering wisdom in my ears and sharing with me what they wanted presented in this book. I know that I could not have accomplished all that I have in this lifetime without their guidance. Aho!

ABOUT THE AUTHOR

Drake Bear Stephen BA, CHT

Web: www.DrakeInnerprizes.com

www.SoulSexAlchemy.com

Email: drakebearstephen@pacbell.net

Drake is a Transpersonal Hypnotherapist, Shamanic Energy Medicine Practitioner, and a Reiki Master. He specializes in Past Life Therapy. Drake has a variety of background experience that includes a 37 year career in telecommunications. He has a B.A. in art and psychology and is certified as a hypnotherapist, energy medicine practitioner, shamanic practitioner, NLP practitioner, and Reiki practitioner. He has studied metaphysics and spirituality for the past thirteen years. He currently lives east of San Francisco in California. He offers a **SOUL SERIES**, which consists of the following:

- **SOUL SESSIONS**: He uses energy medicine and shamanic healing to work with clients. He offers a soup to nuts, holistic approach to healing body, mind, heart, and spirit. He works with the Physical Body and the Energy Body in the present life, past lives, and between lives.

- **SOUL CEREMONIES**: He performs ceremonies for different occasions such as birth, death, marriage, anniversaries, birthdays, holidays, and other rites of passage. He also does clearing ceremonies for homes and businesses.

- **SOUL SCHOOLS**: He teaches workshops on various subjects as well as Attunement to Reiki and Soul School: A Shamanic Mystery School. He also appears on radio and TV. He is available for speaking engagements on the subjects of Reincarnation and Past Life Therapy, Shamanic Energy Medicine, and Soul Sex: The Alchemy of Gender and Sexuality.

Please visit www.SoulSexAlchemy.com for free downloads associated with *Soul Sex: The Alchemy of Gender and Sexuality.*

081615

Lightning Source UK Ltd.
Milton Keynes UK
UKOW06f2205061115

262259UK00006B/167/P